KW-328-553

Planned to death

Other books by J. Douglas Porteous

The Company Town of Goole: an essay in urban genesis (1969)
Canal Ports: the urban achievement of the Canal Age (1977)
Environment & Behavior: planning and everyday urban life (1977)
The Modernization of Easter Island (1981)
Degrees of Freedom (1988)
The Mells (1988)

Planned to death
The annihilation
of a place called Howdendyke

J. Douglas Porteous

LIVERPOOL INSTITUTE
OF HIGHER EDUCATION
LIBRARY
WOOLTON
LIVERPOOL,

Manchester University Press

Copyright © J. Douglas Porteous 1989

Published by Manchester University Press
Oxford Road, Manchester M13 9PL, UK

British Library cataloguing in publication data
Porteous, J. Douglas
    Planned to death: the annihilation
    of a place called Howdendyke
    1. Humberside. Howden, history   I. Title
    942.8′35

ISBN 0 7190 2831 0 *hardback*

LIVERPOOL INSTITUTE
OF HIGHER EDUCATION

Order No.
    ∠535

No.
138431

914.274

Control No.

Catal.
    8 JAN 1992

Printed and bound in Great Britain by
Courier International Ltd, Tiptree, Essex

For the people of Howdendyke:
neighbours, friends, kin

Going, Going

I thought it would last my time—
The sense that, beyond the town,
There would always be fields and farms,
Where the village louts could climb
Such trees as were not cut down ...

On the Business Page, a score
Of spectacled grins approve
Some takeover bid that entails
Five per cent profit (and ten
Per cent more in the estuaries) ...

It seems, just now,
To be happening so very fast;
Despite all the land left free
For the first time I feel somehow
That it isn't going to last,
That before I snuff it, the whole
Boiling will be bricked in ...

And that will be England gone,
The shadows, the meadows, the lanes ...
There'll be books; it will linger on
In galleries; but all that remains
For us will be concrete and tyres.

Most things are never meant.
This won't be, most likely: but greeds
And garbage are too thick-strewn
To be swept up now, or invent
Excuses that make them all needs.
I just think it will happen, soon.

Philip Larkin

Contents

Figures

Plates

Preface

... I by the tide
Of Humber would complain.
Andrew Marvell

Scenario: Howdendyke, North Humberside, England, 1 April 1991. Mavis Westoby, an elderly widow, watches the immense yellow bulldozer press forward, strain, and heave her cottage to the ground. With a rending cry the shapely, once lived-in dwelling becomes a shapeless, unbearable heap of brick rubble. Dust settles. Mavis is too grieved to weep, even when she reaches her nice new council flat in the nearby town. The professor watches the same bulldozer move on to the house in which he spent his childhood. The Post Office has been embedded in the bank of the River Ouse for over two centuries. It is a strong building; the machine has to torture it to death bit by bit. Beams creak. Bricks find their angle of repose. The professor flies sadly back to Canada. He wrote this book.

Since the late 1960s the village of Howdendyke has been slowly planned to death. This book attempts to answer three simple questions which any observer of the above scenario might ask. Why, and by what process, is the village being destroyed? What was it like to live there before the process of annihilation began? And how did it grow to be like that? These questions are answered, in reverse order, in the three parts of this volume.

The history of Howdendyke falls rather neatly into three periods. The village began as a small river port, serving the town of Howden from medieval times to the mid-nineteenth century (Part I: chapters 2, 3). The succeeding era (1857–1960) was dominated by the Anderton family whose agricultural fertilizer factory sustained the village despite loss of the port function (Part I, chapters 4, 5; Part II). The revival of Howdendyke as a port, from the 1960s, is analyzed in Part III, which relates the process of community destruction consequent upon this renewal of an old function.

Intellectuals and mystics like to trichotomize experience. The three parts of this book can be seen, in substantive terms, as local history, biography and autobiography, and planning critique. They are necessarily written in somewhat differing styles, the first solidly academic, the second lyrical and celebratory, the third in the more open prose of the urban planning critic. Links between the three parts are sustained by the webs of family history and place biography. In more abstract terms, using Gosling's (1980) arresting trichotomization of situations (abortions, orgies, and crucifixions), Part I builds slowly up to the orgy of Part II, followed rapidly by crucifixion. Following Blake, Part II's Song of Innocence gives way to Part III's Songs of Experience.

Alternatively, the book may be read in biblical and symphonic form. The overture, chapter one, is a brief recitative which encapsulates the whole. Genesis, the second movement (*Andante con moto*), dispassionately delineates major themes, some of which prove to be foreshadowings of a troubled future. Chronicles, a lively scherzo (*Allegro con brio*) intervenes, but there is an underlying tone of apprehension. Revelations, the tragic fourth and final movement (*Adagio assai*), is an inverted reprise of earlier themes, presaging destruction. As, at the time of writing (1986) the village is only a little more than half-destroyed, the symphony is unfinished.

The theme, then, is *topocide* – the deliberate killing of a place. This issue is approached from the standpoints of history, geography, rural planning, planning critique, and personal geoautobiography. The philosophic under-pinnings are both humanist and activist. Methods are eclectic, ranging from archival search, through computer analysis of census data, to depth interviews and personal recollection. These substantive, philosophical, and methodological issues are dealt with in the Appendix (Chapter 12: 'A much longer, more general introduction') which thus permits the reader to plunge straight into the story at Chapter 1 ('A brief, specific introduction').

Acknowledgements

I have spent over five years accumulating material for this book, and during that time have received assistance from many people. If any are omitted from this acknowledgement, I apologize in advance, being able to blame only a bad memory and a surfeit of material from a multitude of sources.

Personnel at the following record repositories provided able assistance: Boothferry Borough Council Planning Department, in particular Mr Learoyd, Mr Bruins and Mr Rowbotham; the Borthwick Institute of Historical Research, University of York; the British Library; the Church Commissioners' archives, London; the Church of Jesus Christ of Latter-Day Saints, Huddersfield archives; the County Library at Beverley, in particular Mr Philip Brown; County Record Offices in Doncaster, Durham, Lincoln, and Nottingham; the Department of Paleography and Diplomatic, University of Durham; the General Record Office, St Catherine's House, London; Goole Local History Library; HM Customs and Excise Records, Kings Beam House, London, and local offices at Goole and Hull; Hull University archives; Kilpin Parish Council; the Post Office Archives, London; and the Public Record Office, Kew. I spent most time, however, in the Humberside County Record Office at Beverley, and wish to thank Mr Holt, Mrs Boddington, Mr Snowden, and Mr Powell for their unfailing assistance.

Access to private archives was kindly provided by: Mr Charles Anderton of George Anderton & Sons Ltd. of Cleckheaton; Mr M. Scott, Mr B. Naylor, and Mrs J. Copson of Hargreaves Fertilisers Ltd. (now BritAg) of York; Father Barry Keaton, Rector of Howden; Mrs B. Martinson; Mr A. H. Moody; and Mr A. Ransome. Mrs G. A. Brown, Mr Peter Butler (former Editor, Goole Times Newspapers), Mr P. T. Cassidy, Dr G. D. Gaunt, Mrs Peggy Grogan, Dr Alan Harris, Mrs J. B. Horsley, and Mrs J. Myers ably responded by mail to a variety of questions.

Property deeds were graciously provided for my perusal by Hargreaves Fertilisers Ltd. (now BritAg), Howden Glucose Ltd. (Tate & Lyle plc), Mrs B. Jarred, Mrs M. Lawton, Mrs B. Martinson, and Wykeland Ltd. These were invaluable for a reconstruction of the growth of Howdendyke in the eighteenth and nineteenth centuries. Almost the whole village was covered by these deeds. The only deeds to which I was unable to gain access were those of Humberside Sea & Land Ltd. and J. Wharton and Sons (owners of Ferry House).

Interviews with company officials were granted by Mr M. Scott and Mr B. Naylor of Hargreaves Fertilisers Ltd. (now BritAg), Mr D. Scarr of D. E. Scarr (Shipbuilders) Ltd., and Mr R. Leitch of Humberside Sea & Land Ltd. Other interviews were given by Mr D. Learoyd, Chief Planning Officer, and Mr Hibbert, Chief Housing and Environmental Services Officer, Boothferry Borough, and Mr Bob Park, Mayor of Boothferry Borough. Most of all, of course, I am grateful for the many personal interviews I had with a large number of Howdendyke's past and present residents.

Acknowledgements

Their hospitality and forbearance are much appreciated. Research ethics, however, prevent me from naming these friends and former neighbours.

Assistance with the research came from a number of quarters. It could not have been undertaken without the generous support of grants from the Social Sciences and Humanities Research Council of Canada and the University of Victoria. Dorian Bingham painstakingly perused local newspapers, Colin Laverick worked for me in a number of archives, Ken and Annie Beaumont and Betty Jarred helped with my retrospective Howdendyke 'census' of 1951–81, Jane Mastin and Carol Porteous computer analyzed masses of census data. Carol Porteous and Susan Bannerman transcribed interview tapes with patience and good humour. To all these my thanks.

The manuscript was physically produced through the good offices of the Department of Geography of the University of Victoria. Vicky Barath, Stella Chan and Lynn Goodacre cheerfully fed my hand-written drafts into the word-processor, and Ole Heggen, Ken Josephson, Diane Macdonald and Ian Norie dealt with the cartographic and photographic work with their usual competence.

The poem 'Going, Going' is reprinted by permission of the Controller of Her Majesty's Stationery Office. A version originally appeared in *How do you want to live?* (HMSO 1972). Words from 'Palaces of Gold' by Leon Rosselson are used by permission of Harmony Music Ltd., 19/20 Poland Street, London WIV 3DD (© 1967, International Copyright Secured, All Rights Reserved).

Finally, I am indebted to Gavin for inspiration, to Carol for her encouragement, to many students for listening, to Susan Bannerman, Bruce McDougall, and Sandra Smith for their enthusiasm and searching comment, and to the Saturna Island Think Tank, for being there.

J. Douglas Porteous   *Saturna Island, June 1986*

1

A brief, specific introduction

Never before have so many people been uprooted.
Industrialization ... require[s] ... a new kind of violence.
John Berger

As I write this, in summer 1986, a village is being destroyed. As you read it, the processes of bulldozing and levelling may still be going on, or destruction may be complete. With luck, or a compassionate change of mind on the part of local elites, some part of the village may yet remain. But much less than half, for of the more than seventy dwellings there in 1965 only a little over thirty were occupied twenty years later.

I begin this introduction with what writers of yore called 'the argument', and which academics, secure in their unassailable detachment, now call a synopsis. In early modern times the village of Howdendyke was merely the landing for a ferry across the Yorkshire Ouse, ten miles downstream from Selby and close to the minster town of Howden, East Yorkshire. Only in the late eighteenth and early nineteenth centuries did the efforts of a number of small entrepreneurs result in the growth of a small river port with associated, very small scale, industries. The area remained largely agricultural, even when in 1857 one George Anderton arrived from the West Riding of Yorkshire to set up a chemical fertilizer manufactory.

Industries were rare in this agricultural landscape and people streamed into the settlement, which grew into a village. The former 'open' village, of many independent entrepreneurs and house-owners, was gradually transformed, over the next century, into a 'closed' village almost wholly owned by a family firm which eventually became G. H. Anderton Fertilizers Ltd. The Anderton regime, however, did not solely concern itself with its Ouse Chemical Works' profitability. Three generations of Andertons, dying out only in 1959, acted, whether positively or negatively, as squires of the village and beneficent custodians of its social life.

This style of control, often erroneously termed 'feudal', was abruptly replaced in the 1960s by new management in the form of a corporation known as Hargreaves Fertilizers Ltd. Simultaneously, a zone of agricultural land twice as big as the village was developed after 1968, ostensibly for riverside industry, but actually as a mere cargo-handling facility in probable competition with

1

existing Humber ports and in apparent contravention of county planning guidelines.

Private enterprise, planners, and politicians were all responsible for this radical transformation, although by no means equally responsible. The net result was a three-fold expansion of industrial land, which increased job opportunities in the area. By-products of this possibly laudable development, however, were the growth of pollution and environmental degradation, and the slow but inexorable reduction of the residential village to less than one-half of its former size during the 1970s and early 1980s. This process continues.

By 1951 the village population had reached 207, and remained at almost the same level in 1961, evidence of some degree of economic and community stability despite the growth of better external links. In the two intercensal periods 1961–81, however, the number of inhabitants fell first to 160 in 1971 and then to 127. This rapid decline continued into the 1980s, and fewer than 100 persons inhabited the village at the close of 1986. As early as 1971 26 per cent of the households consisted of elderly widows living alone. Howdendyke had become a mere shadow of its former self. It was, quite recently, a thriving village of parents and children. Few children run in the streets and fields today.

Such evident deterioration immediately suggests questions. How did the village grow? What was it like to live there before this drastic transformation? How did this radical change come about, and who is responsible for it? And how did, and do, villagers react to the impending loss of their community and the growing deterioration of their environment? The goal of this book is to answer these questions, and in particular to try to elucidate the mechanisms by which such losses are inflicted in the name of 'progress'.

But, you may remark, this is a village which even at its peak had a population of little more than 200 persons. It is surely a mere drop in the bucket compared with the uprooting and attempted destruction of whole social and ethnic groups in Russia and Germany during the 1930s and 1940s, not to speak of the numberless Third World peasants who have been rounded up in 'resettlement schemes' by both colonial and indigenous governments since the Second World War. If there is to be a geography or history of eviction, surely the case of Howdendyke is a very minor one?

All of this is true. Yet a thorough study of such a small, obscure village has its advantages and benefits.

First, in terms of scale. Accustomed to seemingly endless reports of disaster, the modern citizen in our Western culture is unmoved by the five lines devoted in the newspapers to yet another ferry sinking, with the loss of 1,000 lives, in Bangladesh. He or she may even be left cold by a visit to Yad Vashem, where the annihilation of six million Jews is documented. These events are far from the reader in time, in space, and in experience. In contrast, this microscopic study of a small neighbourhood in Britain deals with the here and now, and, as we shall see, with what appears to be becoming a universal experience in an increasingly planned world.

Moreover, the story told in this book is not dealing with a past event, as is so common in social science writing, not to speak of history. Rather, it deals with a process which, at the time of writing, is in full flow and likely to continue for some years. Further, the narrative deals with the problems of people who, if not perhaps exactly like ourselves, are often very like our parents. And they speak in their own defence in their own words.

Besides being immediate, then, this microscopic study is also a microcosmic one. We are all familiar with the government official or businessman who promotes, for example, the siting of a new airport or military base in a rural area, and replies to protests regarding the nerve-shattering noise of low-flying jets by demonstrating that the new facility will relieve local unemployment. A noble goal indeed, but thus are noble ends subserved by very questionable means, and often against the will of those impacted upon by the development.

Here lies a major point of the exercise. This book is only one more piece in a growing literature which documents the deleterious impact upon local communities of modern developments engineered by regional or national interests – whether airports, military bases, urban renewal projects, public housing developments, or a host of other examples. One of the chief characteristics of such developments is the failure either to consult the wishes of the impacted population, or, having consulted, to consider them. The issue, then, is not merely that of public participation in the planning process, but of how far the public may take some control of their affairs, and how far regional and national, bureaucratic and corporate interests should prevail over the needs and desires of a relatively powerless local population.

The fundamental problems are clearly problems of ethics and power. It is my contention that, as in the case of Howdendyke, it is unethical for private enterprise, planners, and politicians to push through a development without even consulting the people likely to be impacted. Such power can, and will, affect you, the reader, unless perhaps you are an unassailable planner, politician, or corporate executive. Nuclear power stations may be located near your city, motorways be routed through your community, a noxious facility established in your street. Thus the overarching theme and title of this book is that it is quite possible, even within our form of parliamentary democracy, for the combined forces of elite power groups to legally plan a community to death. And, to add insult to injury, your protests against your community's being planned to death will be answered by the justification that such sacrifices are for the common good.

It will be clear by now that the story to be told in this book, despite being told by a well-established academic, is not a detached, value-free account. I do not believe such an account could be written, whether by a politician, a planner, a corporate executive, a villager, or myself. This is not to say that my account will be an unreasoned farrago of abuse levelled against power elites, but only that it will inevitably be coloured by the point of view of the author as the evidence is assembled and interpreted.

My own experiences have clearly shaped both the outlook and structure of this book. I am a Howdendyker. I spent the first eighteen years of my life in the village, and it was my permanent residence for a further three years while at Oxford. My mother was born in the village, and her father before her. After my mother died in 1971, I could not bear to revisit the scene of her life for almost a decade. On venturing back to the village in 1979, however, and happily reacquainting myself with former friends and neighbours, I could not but be struck by an air of dejection, despondency, and expectation in the village, matched by a number of house demolitions which had already destroyed several childhood landmarks and threatened to remove more.

Which brings me to the development of this book. My first reaction to the state of Howdendyke was on the lines of 'rescue archaeology'. I returned from Canada in 1980 with the intention of making a written and photographic record of the village, a 'rescue history', which would serve as a memorial to an obscure place soon likely to disappear. No one else seemed to be willing or able to do it.

The birth of my son, Gavin, in the interim, led to a second phase, that of a desire to record also my own life in the village. This autobiographical exercise, besides catering to a healthy sense of self-value, would also provide my son, should I not survive, with some knowledge of his father's background.

Both these phases involved public archival research and interviews with older Howdendyke residents. The historical phase, in view of the relative absence of public records, also demanded the investigation of property title deeds held by local businesses and owner-occupiers.

Phase three, which has grown to dominate the project, emerged from the former two phases, and was partly thrust upon me by the attitudes of both village residents and businesses (see the Appendix). First, those residents I interviewed for oral history purposes almost unanimously made unsolicited negative comparisons between the state of Howdendyke in the 1980s and a relatively much more pleasant recent past. They asserted, moreover, that nothing they could do seemed to be able to halt the changes being wrought in Howdendyke, nor could they even gain an idea of the goals of those responsible for the village's rapid decline. Above all, they were unsure of the identities of those responsible for the obvious deterioration of their lives and landscape. Most working-class people are not well-informed regarding political or planning processes, and hence the investigator generally finds that only an undefined 'they' are seen to be responsible.

As an academic, as well as a former Howdendyker, my forensic instincts were naturally stimulated by this discovery. My interest was furthered by contact with the two companies chiefly involved in industrial development, house demolition, and general land use change in Howdendyke. Executives of Hargreaves Fertilizers Ltd., successors to the Anderton regime, had been most accommodating of my request to make searches of their archives for the purposes of historical reconstruction. I am deeply grateful for this. On becoming apprised of the feelings of many Howdendykers, however, I returned to Hargreaves' head office, and spoke to two of the company's chief executives about the firm's plans and goals for its Howdendyke property. Although very courteous, these officials provided me with minimal information, and moreover made some rather negative comments about Howdendyke's housing and people.

But this was generous in comparison with my reception by the local manager of the second company, Humberside Sea & Land Services Ltd. (HS&L), who refused my initial request merely to peruse historical deeds relating to fields lately built over by the company, and later refused also a personal interview. At that time, 1980, I had not read the local newspaper archive, nor analyzed planning applications and reports relating to Howdendyke, nor spoken to many Howdendykers or even non-residents who were concerned about the village's apparent demise. I was, therefore, innocent of the probable high level of sensitivity of these companies, and particularly of HS&L, to research into their current activities, a sensitivity which no doubt arose from the irregular campaign of local protest against their industrialization of Howdendyke, a campaign which had been going on throughout the 1970s.

Six years later, I am, naturally, much more deeply acquainted with the story, and have interviewed most of the decision-takers involved. Yet as it stands, this account still tends to favour the point of view of the impacted villagers of Howdendyke. This apparent bias merely redresses a more general ill-balance. For planners, politicians, and private enterprise have no problem in obtaining public forums in which to express their point of view. Moreover, they have the power to compel the adoption of their viewpoints. The average working-class citizen, however, perhaps not well educated, and often poorly informed, with no organizational or financial support, no experience in formal expression, and no forum in which to express his opinions, is clearly at a grave disadvantage. This book allows such citizens to speak, to describe the effects of industrialization and village annihilation on their lives, and to make a plea for the right to be considered when the very existence of their community is at stake.

This was supposed to be a very brief introduction! Let me say, penultimately, that this book is written as far as possible in the normal language of educated discourse. I have no time for obscurantist academic jargon, which often serves to hide poverty of thought and aim, and usually prevents the average citizen from understanding the content. In contrast, I would like this book to be read by all those involved in its making – planners, politicians, business executives, and, above all, Howdendykers.

I wish, primarily, to tell a story. Those who feel the need to place that narrative, before its telling, in the appropriate philosophical, methodological, and substantive scientific contexts, should turn immediately to the Appendix, which is entitled 'A Much Longer, More General Introduction'. But if you wish to understand how Howdendyke grew (Chapters 2–5), what it was like to live there in the 1950s (Chapters 6, 7), how it came to be undergoing the process of slow but sure destruction, and what the villagers feel about this (Chapters 8–11), you should leave the appendix for later and go straight ahead.

I
Genesis

The business of the local historian ... Is to re-enact in his own mind, and to portray for his readers, the Origin, Growth, Decline, and Fall of a Local Community.

H. P. R. Finberg

The Fate of Towns and Cities is every jot as unstable as the State and Happiness of Men.

Camden

2

A local habitation and a name

> There be three things which make a nation great and prosperous: a fertile soil; busy workshops; and easy conveyance for men and commodities from one place to another.
>
> Francis Bacon

The village of Howdendyke is located on the north bank of the enormous reverse-S bend made by the Yorkshire Ouse half-way between the cities of Hull and York. It lies at the very centre of an extremely low-lying, formerly swampy region, which is known as the Humberhead Levels. Here the Ouse tributaries of Aire, Derwent, Foulness, and Don debouch, and the Ouse itself joins the Trent

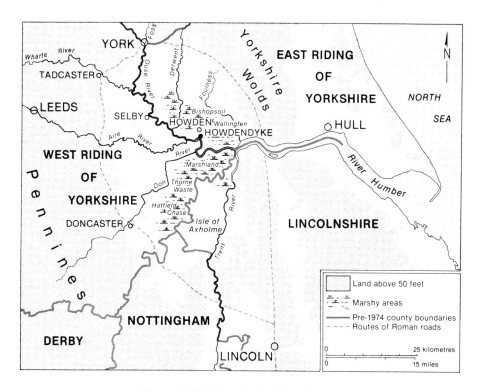

Figure 1. The Humberhead Levels *c.*1700

8

to form the River Humber (Figure 1). Although approximately 50 miles from the sea, the Humberhead Levels rarely rise more than 20 feet above sea-level. As the focus of Britain's largest river-system, with a total catchment area of almost 3,500 square miles, it is not surprising that the area has always been a relatively unpopulated marshland subject to frequent and devastating floods.

The Humberhead Levels

As the ice retreated in the last glacial phase, it was replaced by Lake Humber,

Plate 1. Location of Howendyke, centre right
(Crown copyright reserved)

which covered the present Humberhead region and far beyond to a depth of perhaps 100 feet (Palmer 1966). As Lake Humber drained away southwards, it left a huge swampy area now known as the Vale of York, the wettest part being the Humberhead zone south of the great line of morainic ridges which cross the vale near York.

Subsequently, the reinstitution of the Ouse-Humber river system filled the basin with estuarine and alluvial deposits, so that the solid geology now appears only as isolated sandstone islands on the fringes of Humberhead. The soils of Humberhead consist completely of alluvial deposits (known locally as 'warps') along the rivers which, despite natural levees, have always tended to flood, with wider areas of lacustrine sands and clays in the numerous interfluves. For several thousand years the zone stagnated in the form of a seemingly impassable marsh and forest tract. Until the present millenium it was more important as a sparsely-populated frontier zone than as an area of occupation.

Before the Iron Age, signs of occupation are absent in Humberhead and, indeed, are restricted to the very margins of the larger Vale. At the time of the Roman conquest the area was a Brigantian borderland, and in the Romano-British period seems to have incurred very few changes. Very significantly, the two major Roman highways which connected Lindum (Lincoln) with Eboracum (York) did not take the straightest, shortest route, which would have passed almost through the future site of Howdendyke (Figure 1). Instead, the western highway curved outward along the Magnesian Limestone belt, crossing the Don at Doncaster and the Wharfe at Tadcaster before swinging eastwards to York. The eastern highway, as if in mirror-image, followed the Lincolnshire limestone scarplands north to the Humber, and then curved gently westwards to York along the chalk edge of the Yorkshire Wolds and the mid-Vale moraines. Encircled by these civilizing influences, the Humberhead region remained backward and forgotten. Even though its rivers were highways between Eboracum and the North Sea, archaeological investigations have discovered hardly any evidence of Roman occupation of Humberhead, whereas both Roman and Anglian settlements were very common in the higher areas to west and east (Faull 1974, Loughlin and Miller 1979).

After the withdrawal of the Romans, Anglian invasions from the east gradually displaced the British, who eventually retreated beyond the Pennines. At this time Humberhead, true to its marshy nature, formed the border between the kingdoms of Deira and Mercia. Deira later gave way to Northumbria, whose very name confirms the Humber-Ouse system as a long-term political boundary. Yet such was the relative remoteness of Humberhead that it continued to form the eastern marchlands of the British kingdoms of Elmet and Loidis (Leeds) long after the subjection of adjacent, less marshy, lowlands to the Anglian invaders. Later the Humberhead Levels would provide the zone in which the three counties of Lincolnshire and the East and West

Ridings of Yorkshire abutted. Although the Humberhead Levels clearly form a geographical and even a social unit (Porteous 1982), it was not until local government reorganization in 1974 that the area was wrested from the piecemeal control of these three counties to became the Borough of Boothferry in the County of Humberside.

Archaeological and place-name evidence suggest that the latter part of the first Christian millenium was dominated by the gradual settlement of the area first by Angles (the English element) and then by Scandinavians and Danes. Most of the place-names of Humberhead derive from this period. English settlers chose the well-drained soils of natural levees or low gravelly ridges for their settlement sites, bequeathing us places with name suffixes such as -tun (Skelton), -ingtun (Eastrington), and -ham (Metham). Laxton, near the Ouse, suggests a salmon fishery. Arriving later, the Scandinavians occupied infill or less-desirable sites, identified by name suffixes such as -thorpe (Ousethorpe), and -by (Barmby, Asselby). It is significant that whereas place-names relating to hills or woodland are relatively scarce in Humberhead, the area has the densest distribution of marsh-related names (holm, carr, marsh, moor) in the Vale of York (Smith 1937).

The Domesday survey, exactly 900 years old as I write this, reveals the central Humberhead region around Howden as having a number of villages, but a great many of them were uninhabited and almost all were wholly or partially waste. William the Conqueror's devastation in the Vale of York seems to have been very effective in Humberhead, for the mapped evidence reveals that the district around Howdendyke had the largest concentration of villages 'wholly waste with no population' in the whole of the East Riding of Yorkshire (Maxwell 1962, 219). The area had little wood, meadow, or mills, but some fisheries were in evidence in 1086. Across the Ouse in the West Riding region known as Marshland the Domesday-derived maps are complete and absolute blanks, with not even village names, if any, being recorded (Darby 1962). One might speculate that William's particular devastation of this area relates to Harold's successful Battle of Stamford Bridge, at the northern edge of the Humberhead Levels, in 1066.

Imbanking and draining

By this time the central part of the Humberhead Levels, on the East Yorkshire side, and focussing upon the market town of Howden, had become known as Howdenshire. The history of Howdenshire from 1086 to the present day cannot be understood without constant reference to the problems of draining, flooding, and embankment, for much of Howdenshire lies below the high water level of the Ouse at ordinary spring tides. Sir William Dugdale's monumental *History of Imbanking and Draining* (seventeenth century; 2nd edition 1772) catalogues the seemingly endless battle to prevent the area's villages and fields from inundation by the overflowing Ouse, Derwent, Aire, Don, Trent, Derwent, and Foulness. By this time the Humberhead Levels had developed a number of subregional names: in Lincolnshire, the significantly named Isle of Axholme; in the West Riding, Marshland and Dikesmarsh; in the East Riding, Bishopsoil and Wallingfen.

From the eleventh century, the region was noted for ruptured river banks, the creation of sluices and levees, and even the diversion of rivers. The eleventh and twelfth centuries, however, were chiefly remarkable as a period of active drainage and settlement. Eight of the twenty-two township names in Howdenshire Wapentake are not mentioned before the twelfth or thirteenth centuries. Their names, such as Bellasize, Bennetland, and Clementhorpe, betray Norman origins; Gilberdike records the drainage efforts of one Gilbert. These efforts were encouraged by land grants made by Hugh de Puizet, Bishop of Durham, and Lord of Howdenshire (Saltmarshe 1920a, 1920b). The whole riverine zone was a salt marsh at this time, whence derives the family of Saltmarshe which inhabited their eponymous village, downriver from Howdendyke, from the late twelfth to the late twentieth centuries (Saltmarshe n.d.).

The effect of this colonization and reclamation scheme, begun in the late twelfth century, was that by 1285 agricultural production had greatly increased, and by 1379 the population of the district was almost equal to that of the present day (Saltmarshe 1920a, 1928, 1932). From the fourteenth century, however, the district suffered considerable depopulation, partially due to disease but more generally because of brutal de-peopling consequent upon the growing wool-production of the sixteenth century. Many small settlements in Howdenshire, such as Linton, Greenoak, Metham, Gunby, Cotness, Belby, and Thorpe were turned over to pasture and reduced to a single farmhouse, although their sites are visible on air photographs and sometimes marked by the remains of medieval moats (Beresford 1955, Beresford and Hurst 1971, Le Patourel 1973, Loughlin and Miller 1979). As with William the Conqueror, the Howdenshire area also incurred the wrath of Henry VIII as one of the chief foci of the uprising of 1536–37 known as the Pilgrimage of Grace.

Whereas attempts were made to further drain the adjacent marshlands of Lincolnshire and the West Riding in the early seventeenth century, remote Howdenshire had to wait until the latter part of the eighteenth century before significant drainage works were attempted. In the interim, most travellers had little to say about the zone. Leland, seeing the area about 1540, remarked on the River Derwent which 'at greate Raynes ragith and overflowith much of the Ground there about beying low Medowes'. Defoe, over a century and a half later, made similar remarks. While the late eighteenth century Market Weighton Canal helped drain the bogs of Wallingfen to the east, the common land of marshy Bishopsoil, a little north of Howden, was drained by two new cuts, one of which, Bishopsoil Near Drain, debouched into the Ouse at Skelton, about one mile downriver from Howdendyke (Figure 2). Subsequently flooding became less frequent and waterlogging less of a problem, and crops such as cereals, potatoes and flax began to take the place of the previously interminable pasture (Sheppard 1966).

Specializing in root crops, Howdenshire achieved some agricultural prosperity in the nineteenth century, thanks to the development of warping after about 1800. Warping drains were cut to lead silt-laden Ouse waters up to three miles inland, enriching the fields with layered accumulations of several feet of very fertile silt (Palmer 1966, Sheppard 1966). Warping continued well

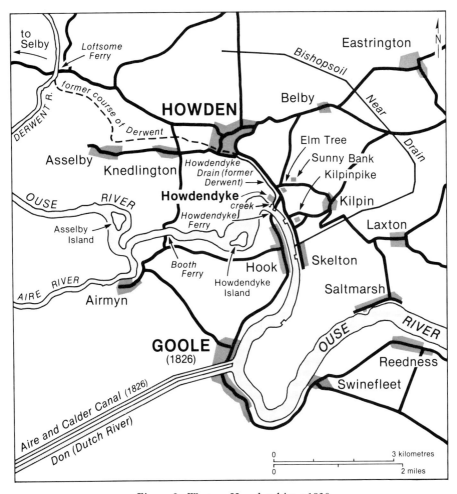

Figure 2. Western Howdenshire *c.*1830

into the twentieth century, by which time Howdenshire had developed a reputation for potatoes and other roots, with market gardening on sands and gravels. The effects of embanking, draining and the raising of land by warping proved spectacular; whereas the great floods of earlier centuries had covered the entire Humberhead Levels more or less indiscriminately, the high flood levels of 1947 devastated the Lower Aire, Derwent, and Ouse around Selby, but were of little moment in Howdenshire (Radley and Simms 1970).

The port of Howdendyke

The almost web-footed, stilt-walking, bogland denizens of the Humberhead were clearly a special breed, often resisting drainage schemes which would interfere with their relative freedom from authority and a local livelihood based on fishing and fowling. Howdendyke, however, was relatively less remote than many other Humberhead locations in medieval times, for it was closely connected with the town of Howden, little more than one mile away.

Howden has always been an important East Riding agricultural centre. The earliest detailed reference is a charter of King Edgar dated 959, in which the land boundaries of the manor of Heafuddene are very confusingly described, chiefly because of significant changes in river courses during the last thousand years (Farrar 1914, Hutchinson 1891). From the time of the Conqueror the agricultural district around Howden, known as Howdenshire, with its mills and fisheries, was granted to the See of Durham. The present imposing minster church of Howden dates from the twelfth century, and the nearby palace of the Bishops of Durham, where de Puizet died in 1194, is contemporaneous (Clarke 1850). The town housed at least two well-known medieval scholars, Roger de Hovedene and Walter Skirlaugh.

As early as 1200 King John granted the Bishop of Durham licence to hold an annual fair at Howden; this became a horse fair famous throughout Europe, and well-attended into the late nineteenth century. In both the fourteenth and the seventeenth centuries Howden appears to have been the fifth largest town in the East Riding (Neave 1979). Never the seat of significant industry, Howden served successively as manorial centre and market town until the late nineteenth century, by which time the growth of the nearby port of Goole had decisively eclipsed its economic base.

The place-name Howden is a compound of the Old English heafod (head) and denu (valley). This has been interpreted to mean a 'spit of land' (Smith 1937) and the valley in question is not that of the Ouse, over a mile away, but that of the River Derwent. Although the Derwent now flows into the Ouse some miles upstream, it is clear from ancient maps and charters that it once ran through Howden. In late medieval times there were apparently two distributaries, known as the Old and New Derwents, the latter possibly an artificial drain.

Detailed evidence from surficial geology and boreholes demonstrates that one Derwent distributary ran along the line of the present Howdendyke Drain from Howden towards Howdendyke (Gaunt 1980). At Elm Tree, just outside the village, however, the present drain takes an almost straight course to the Ouse about half a mile away (Figure 2). Yet the continuation of Howdendyke Road, which has followed the Drain to this point, forms a long meandering curve through fields and along Howdendyke's main street until it meets the Ouse at precisely the same point, now known as Howdendyke Creek. I infer from this evidence that the Derwent formerly ran from Howden through the present site of Howdendyke, which adds credence to the local legend that Tadcaster stone for Howden minster, coming via Wharfe and Ouse, was boated up the Derwent past Howdendyke to Howden. By the time of Saxton's 1577 map this old Derwent outlet had disappeared, a not uncommon occurrence in Humberhead where massive interference with river channels has been common since the Saxon era (Gaunt 1975).

The etymology of Howdendyke is now obvious. Known merely as 'the dyke' (or drain) in 959, it is variously spelled Houden Dyk, Houedendike, Howden Dyke, Howdendike, and Howdendyke in succeeding centuries (Smith 1937). Older modern residents still often refer to 'the Dyke'. The area now comprising Howdendyke village has been incorporated into the townships first of Skelton, and later of Kilpin, both of approximately equal size (very small) in 1086. Kilpin ('a calf-pen', 959) has always been an agricultural hamlet, whereas Skelton ('riverbank farmstead', 1086) has had moderate experience in fishing and shipping as well as farming (Jensen 1972, Smith 1937).

If vessels could navigate the Derwent as far as Howden, the need for a settlement at Howdendyke does not seem obvious. But as this distributary was silted up, stopped up, or abandoned, and the Derwent rerouted away from Howden in the late medieval era, Howden would clearly require access to the busy shipping lanes of Ouse and Humber, and the closest point was Howdendyke, only a little over a mile away along a raised causeway.

Some evidence that the Howdendyke Derwent filled up and fell into disuse is provided by the records of a commission of 1399, which complained that 'a certain watercourse, called Newe Derwent, from the end of Hovedene town, etc., from the way from Hale [currently Hail Farm] to Dykysmin [Dyke's mouth] was obstructed, and ought to be repaired by the towns of Hovedene, Knedelyngtone, Askylby, Kylpyn, etc....' (Dugdale 1772, 125). Most of these places admitted their liability and were fined, but there is no record of whether they actually scoured out the once-navigable dyke.

There is no mention of Howdendyke in the almost contemporary poll tax of 1377. The town of Howden at this time had a great variety of trades, whereas Kilpin was inhabited solely by husbandmen, labourers, servants, and weavers. The site of Howdendyke, however, was at this time apparently in Skelton township, and Skelton in 1377 supported, besides the usual agricultural occupations, two merchants and a ferryman. A second ferryman is included in the Howden list, and he and the lone Howden fishermen may well have lived at Howdendyke (Anonymous 1886, Saltmarshe 1932). The present settlement has therefore been at least the site of a ferry, and very possibly a port, for upwards of seven hundred years, although the earliest mention of 'Howdendyke' among local wills dates only from 1599.

Hearth taxes, land taxes and the like have been thoroughly searched for the post-medieval period, but yield meagre results, for it is impossible to separate entries relating to Howdendyke from the general lists for Howden, Kilpin, and Skelton. The only reference to Howdendyke's shipping activities in the sometimes garrulous Howden churchwardens' accounts appears in April 1655:

> Whether it were by the Salors neglect or want of water yt. the Ship called ye Constant Wher Richard Chapman of Holden goeth Master being fraught with three hundred qters. of Corn and other Necessaries touching her voyage set forward from Holdendike at Skelton … it hapned the said Vessel came foule upon some Stake or Pyle Whereby she received a Breach (then sinking) and thus caused great losse in the ship the corn and other pvision beside the hinderance of the present voyage. (*Howden Parish Registers*, vol. 1 (1593–1659), 324)

Accounts of the lower Ouse from the earliest times inveigh against obstructions to navigation (Duckham 1967). The most complete records for the early modern period are in fact those of the local Court of Sewers and of the Bishop of Durham, but these deal with watercourses and landing places rather than with shipping itself.

The Bishop of Durham's Howdenshire estate managers were owners of much of the foreshore at Howdendyke, which ownership was later vested in the Ecclesiastical Commissioners. Account books dating from the mid-fifteenth century demonstrate that Howdendyke was a flourishing small port at this time. From medieval times until the nineteenth century, when wooden jetties came into general use, the banks of the lower Ouse were studded with staithes. A staith consists of a hemispherical mass of earth and stone jutting out from the river bank, and faced with wood until the general use of ironstone facing in the early nineteenth century. Staithes can be made or extended by sinking alternate masses of woven willow staves and chalk or 'cliff' stone, and need constant repair because of river erosion. Depending on the state of the tide, vessels may approach the staith on either the upstream or the downstream side, and goods can be loaded or unloaded along plank walkways.

A late eighteenth century river map in the archives of the Bishop of Durham lists ten large and seven small staithes on the East Riding bank of the Ouse between Boothferry and Saltmarsh, a distance of less than ten miles. All ten large staithes were owned and leased out by the Bishop, and the three largest occupy the waterfront of Howdendyke (Figure 3). Nearly three hundred years earlier, however, there had been at least five separate staithes at Howdendyke, one known as Kylpyn Staith, the other four being the Magna Staith, West Ebb Stath, Est Floode Stath, and West Floode Stath, all at 'Dikesmyne'. All of these enjoyed extensive repair work in 1520, whereas many other Ouse staiths were neglected.

Howdendyke was clearly an important port for the Bishop's town of Howden in the early sixteenth century, and later record books show that Howdendyke's staiths always received a disproportionate share of the money available for repairs. In 1662 Thomas Young of 'Howden Dyke' was submitting expenses for repairs to pilings, but by this time the number of staiths had fallen, Howdendyke having only three (Ebb, Flood, and Kilpin). At this time the staiths were cone-shaped, 30 yards wide at the base, tapering through a length of 40 yards to a width of 6–10 yards at the crown. One of the most remarkable characteristics of these staith repair books is their continuity. The format for workmen's wages and details of wood utilized is the same in the early nineteenth century as it was in 1666.

We learn also that from at least the sixteenth century the Bishop was leasing the Howdendyke ferry and local fishing rights as a package, an arrangement which continued into the twentieth century, long after local salmon stocks had been devastated by massive pollution from West Riding factories upstream. The first known lease is dated 1574, but this simply reassigns the lease to Peter Holme from its previous tenant, Cuthbert Cowterd. At this time Howdendyke, at least that part around the Howdendyke Creek, may have consisted of only a single building and close.

By the early eighteenth century, however, the Bishop was leasing several land parcels and rights at Howdendyke. These included the Silver Pit fishery, a farm (later known as Ferry Farm), the Ebb and Flood staithes, Kilpin staith, a warehouse and storage ground, and:

> The Ferry or passage of water, with the fishing of Howden Dyke, with the Island or Sand Bed in the Ouse, abutting on the Ouse Carr ... and the Water Courses Rivers and Ditches within the Fishing, or the passage by Boat or otherwise in or upon the same River, extending from the River to a Stone Bridge in the town of Howden called the Brigg Gate, with all privileges to the same belonging. (Lease Book, 1755; same wording 1857)

Clearly, only the first part of the lease was operable, for the Howdendyke Derwent, now Howdendyke Creek and Drain, had long been unnavigable.

One Robert Claybourne was the farm and ferry lessee in the mid-eighteenth century. The intimate connection between Howdendyke and Howden is sparingly revealed in parish Visitation Books which, among endless fines and penances for fornication, refer in 1745 to Claybourne's failure to pay his church assessment. Four years later he was arraigned for 'keeping a Hogsty in the Churchyard'.

The significance of the Howdendyke waterfront to Kilpin township is seen in lists of churchwardens furnished by Kilpin to Howden minster. Although these Kilpin churchwardens were chiefly substantial farmers resident in Kilpin village, a coal merchant, Richard Ward of Kilpinpike, was selected in 1788, to be followed in 1789 by Robert Claybourne who held the office almost continuously until 1811. Thereafter the office returned to Kilpin farmers, except for a brief appearance in 1829–30 and 1833–4 by the merchant Richard Ward jun. of Kilpinpike, who we will meet again in the next chapter. Eighteenth century probates recorded for Howdendyke residents are of rare occurrence, attesting the settlement's very marginal existence prior to the early nineteenth century. In the period 1770–1817 only four probate records are extant, and relate to ferrymen, an innkeeper, and to Richard Ward the elder, coal merchant, the only one who had actually prepared a will.

With the growth of Howden as a market centre in the early nineteenth century, it appears that some of Howdendyke's old wooden staiths were extensively faced with stone. Accounts for 1811, for instance, include long lists of persons receiving 'staither's wages', while the ferryman, Charles Singleton, received payment for supplying wood to the value of several hundred pounds. Vast tonnages of 'cliff stone' were assembled, and by 1822 it was estimated that 'Howdendyke Ferry Staith' had absorbed 1320 tons of stone, and the 'Kilpin Pike Staith' 540 tons, while the 'Howdendyke Cryke Staith' still needed more. Predictably, most of this staith-refurbishing energy was directed towards the one Boothferry and the three Howdendyke staiths. Others, both up and downriver, were neglected and allowed to wash away unless given attention by local people.

A survey made about 1816 reported that the staiths at Howdendyke were in the best repair of all the Bishop's staiths, and that they drew respectively 7 feet (Kilpinpike) and 14 feet (Howdendyke) of water at low tide. 'Howdendyke Clough' (Creek) was reported to be 'much shalrer ... cliff [stone] here would be of infinite service'. By this time the fishing rights were worth very little and Howdendyke (Silverpit) Island, formerly 18 acres in extent and used for agriculture, had been eroded down to a mere 8 acres. The warehouse on the Flood Staith, by this time called Bishop's Staith, was 64 feet by 18 feet in size at mid-century; it housed a granary on its upper floor, most of which was let to Richard Ward of Kilpinpike.

By mid-century also Howdendyke Drain was silting up, largely because of defects in the clough or sluice where it opened into Howdendyke Creek. As residents of Howden complained that their health was suffering, a new clough was erected in 1840 and thereafter the ferryman was directed to regulate the sluice gate to permit the flushing out of the drain at high tides. This operation was still being performed by the occupant of Ferry House in the 1950s.

Until the development of Drainage Boards in the late nineteenth century, recommendations for the proper upkeep of staiths, cloughs and drains were made to those responsible by a Court of Sewers consisting chiefly of local landowners whose farming interests ensured their keen interest in thus preventing flooding and keeping in repair the means by which cargoes of fertilizers could be imported and crops sent away. Officially the Court of Sewers was enjoined to view and report on:

> All and singular the Banks Sewers Ditches Drains Watercourses Staiths Jetties Foreshores Rivers Cloughs Sluices Howles Tunnels Goits Calcies Bridges Streams and other works of Drainage and also all Trenches Mills Mill-dams Flood-gates Hebbing-wiers and other things which are Impediments Lets annoyances or obstructions to the Drainage. (Court of Sewers archive, 26 April 1834)

From the Sewers archive we learn that, in the early eighteenth century at least, the former Derwent was only two yards wide at the bottom. Nevertheless, this size made it the largest drain in the neighbourhood, and small vessels anchored in its mouth, Howdendyke Creek, just south of Bishop's Staith.

Howdendyke Creek and staiths continued in gradually diminishing commercial use throughout the nineteenth century. The last active industrial use appears to have been by H. B. Anderson's timber yard, on the south bank of the creek, which went out of business in 1900. By 1915 the old warehouse on Bishop's Staith was said to be 'untenanted for many years past. It was formerly used for warehousing goods in transit across the ferry but as the river traffic at this point has ceased it is useless and unsightly'. (Ecclesiastical Commissioners Howdendyke reports, 14 July 1915).

Although the staiths gradually fell into commercial disuse in the nineteenth century with the development of strong wooden jetties on heavy pilings, they had to be maintained to prevent excessive bank scour on this concave side of one of the biggest bends made by the River Ouse. Amazingly, the Ecclesiastical Commissioners continued to perform repairs to Howdendyke clough and staiths well into the twentieth century, frequently complaining that 'The current is very strong in this river, and carries away the cliff foundations [of the staiths] which if not renewed the superstructure of ironstone falls bodily into the river' (18 August 1903). Only in 1947 were the Ecclesiastical Commissioners relieved of any further responsibility. During the 1960s the outlet of Howdendyke Drain was diverted to debouch into the Ouse between the two staiths. As a result, Howdendyke Creek, scene of shipping activity for perhaps a thousand years, and in use as late as 1900, quickly silted up.

Location and name

The course of the Ouse between the confluence of the Aire and the Don (Figure 1) has always proved attractive for communication routes wishing to cross the major river. Until 1929 no road bridge crossed the Ouse below Selby, and two of the chief ferries were at Boothferry and Howdendyke. A number of eighteenth century cuts designed to circumvent Ouse bends, and at least one canal, were planned to have outlet at or near Howdendyke.

Whereas the Pocklington Canal, as planned in 1802, never arrived at Howdendyke, during the 1860s four projected railways from Goole to Hull planned to cross the Ouse, three just upstream of Howdendyke Island and one downstream at Skelton. The latter was selected and a bridge erected in 1869, unfortunately without passage for road vehicles. The Hull-Goole telephone line demanded a pylon on Bishop's Staith about 1890 (I climbed it before its removal in the 1950s), and in 1929 the severe inconveniences of Booth and Howdendyke ferries were circumvented by the construction of Boothferry Bridge, joining Goole and the West Riding with Howden and Hull. In the mid-1970s the M62 motorway arrived, to bestride the Ouse between Howdendyke and Boothferry like a colossus.

Most of these activities, although demonstrating Howdendyke's strategic location on the Ouse, did not actually assist the growth of the village. It is arguable that the building of the M62, and especially the location of an exit point only a half mile from Howdendyke, has had the most profound effect on the village since the arrival of George Anderton in 1857. These events are, however, left to later chapters.

It is appropriate here to note that the place-name 'Howdendyke' is one which has caused considerable confusion in the past. Many medieval Humberhead villages had roads or waggon tracks running down to staiths or pikes (small staiths or landings) on the Ouse. Thus the town of Howden had its dyke and staiths (Howdendyke), and the hamlet of Kilpin its pike (Kilpinpike). As shown in Figure 2, the tiny settlement known officially as Howdendyke lay within Howden township north of Howdendyke Creek. Howdendyke Drain and Creek was the boundary between Howden and adjacent townships, first Skelton and later Kilpin. A lane from the latter hamlet led to a small staith less than half a mile downstream from Howdendyke, known as Kilpinpike. Most significant for this story is the area between Howdendyke and Kilpinpike which, except for a possible warehouse and cottages at Kilpin Landing, consisted only of fields, the largest being known as Howdendyke Field (Figure 3) well into the eighteenth century.

The confusion of names is obvious. Officially, 'Howdendyke' refers to merely the very small settlement north of the Creek, which nevertheless is reached via a road through Kilpin township. According to the manuscript censuses of 1841–81, Howdendyke proper has never had more than six dwellings, and in

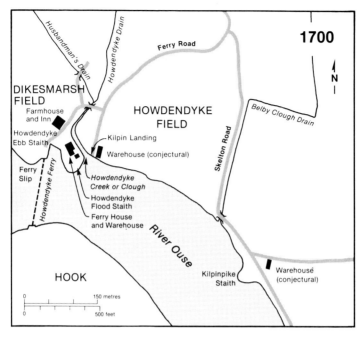

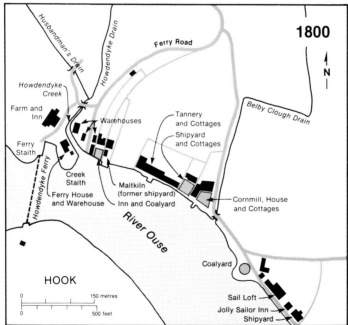

Figure 3. Howdendyke *c.*1700 and *c.*1800

living memory has comprised only Ferry Farm and Ferry House. The area is always included in the Howden township censuses, which renders research in historical demography tedious, for the rest of the village is in Kilpin township and parish.

'Kilpinpike' is the official name for the whole waterfront area of Kilpin township, including Howdendyke Field and the staith known as Kilpinpike. Nineteenth century practice, however, restricted the name Kilpinpike to the staith area at the end of Kilpin Lane. Beyond that staith the township of Kilpin gives way to that of Skelton, the main body of which hamlet is well downriver. For these reasons, and because the history of Kilpinpike staith has always been bound up with Howdendyke, I include it as part of Howdendyke in this study.

The no-man's-land between legal Howdendyke and Kilpinpike staith, mostly open fields until the late eighteenth century, should properly have been named Kilpinpike. Indeed, local directories display much confusion and contradiction over its naming well into the late nineteenth century. The situation was not informally resolved until the 1870s when George H. Anderton's rise to prominence as the leading local industrialist led to the common adoption of 'Howdendyke' for the whole waterfront settlement from the original Howdendyke to Kilpinpike.

In this study the name Howdendyke will be used to cover the whole settlement, as noted above. When Kilpinpike is used it will refer to the small group of houses at the eponymous staith, for these were separated by the width of three fields from the rest of the settlement until the 1970s. Elm Tree is a similar small group of houses one field away from Howdendyke on the Kilpin bank of Howdendyke Drain. It also is generally included in the designation 'Howdendyke'.

This confusing situation was not legally resolved until the early 1980s when a boundary change was instituted to bring the original Howdendyke, north of the Creek, into Kilpin parish.

3
The river port

Kilpin Pike [Howdendyke] is on the Ouse, and has several
wharfs and warehouses, with a considerable traffic in corn,
coal, &c., and a large tanyard.

W. White, *Gazetteer*, 1840

Beside the long established ferry and warehousing operation north of
Howdendyke Creek, the first record of activity on the Kilpin side of the Creek
occurs as late as a Kilpin terrier of 1706. At this time the triangle formed by
Ferry Road, Skelton Road, and the River Ouse consisted merely of an
approximately fifteen-acre open field divided into at least thirty-seven 'lands' or
strips, farmed by various tenants of the Athorpe family, chief landowners of
Kilpin parish since at least the sixteenth century. Of this large field, only about
half an acre was in non-agricultural use, consisting of a 'Ware house land',
probably at Kilpin Landing (Figure 3).

Shortly afterwards the township of Kilpin was enclosed and Howdendyke
field became a unitary close, farmed as one of the outlying fields of Kilpin
Grange. The first industrial enterprise to invade the field was a tannery erected
on one acre (two 'lands') fronting the Ouse by Robert Sutton, a Howden tanner.
This tannery was built before 1759, for in that year Robert Sutton died, leaving
it to his son Robert Sutton jun. He in turn transferred it to his upwardly mobile,
Cambridge-educated son, 'the Rev. Robert Sutton gent', Vicar of Howden, who
remained in control until 1831.

But for almost the whole of the eighteenth century only the tannery and
warehouse disturbed the relatively unchanging pattern of agricultural usage of
Howdendyke Field. The farm in whose purlieus the field lay changed hands
several times after its divestment by the Athorpe family in the 1720s, but not
until 1789 was the fifteen-acre close divided into two, a four-acre close along
Ferry Road on the upstream side (later the chief residential section of
Howdendyke), and the remaining eleven-acre field including the tannery. With
the contemporaneous sale of the latter field to speculators and entrepreneurs in
Howden, the scene was set for subdivision in 1792.

The last decade of the eighteenth century saw the resale of the 11-acre field
in three lots. While the bulk went to Thomas Tyas, variously described as joiner
and brewer and who built a malkiln, a small area in each riverfront corner was

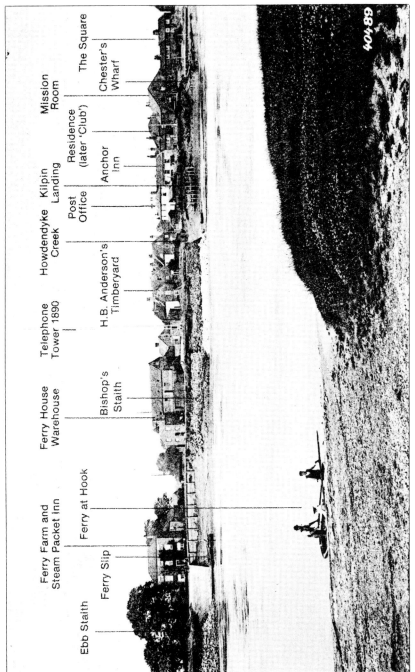

Ebb Staith

Ferry Farm and
Steam Packet Inn

Ferry Slip

Ferry at Hook

Ferry House
Warehouse

Telephone
Tower 1890

Howdendyke
Creek

Kilpin
Landing

Mission
Room

Bishop's
Staith

H.B. Anderson's
Timberyard

Post
Office

Residence
(later 'Club')

Anchor
Inn

Chester's
Wharf

The Square

68404

Plate 2. The River Port *c.*1900

sold off to other industrial interests. The upstream corner, with some newly erected cottages, went to John Nicholson, shipbuilder, while the downstream riverfront corner became the property of John Garlick and partners, including one Mr Pilling, who promptly erected a corn mill. By 1802 Tyas had given up a plot between tannery and corn mill to Richard Cuttill, a small-scale shipbuilder. Thus by the turn of the century the Howdendyke waterfront presented a discontinuous array of shipping and industrial enterprises, each with its own adjacent cottages. Three separate nodes were in evidence (Figure 3). The first, consisting of two inns, farm, ferry, shipyard, warehouses, coalyards, maltkiln, and cottages, clustered on either side of the Creek. The second, comprising tannery, shipyard, corn mill, and cottages, was a more purely industrial zone. Three fields downstream the Kilpinpike area was occupied by Richard Ward, merchant, as early as 1793, with a large house, coalyard, sail loft, and shipyard.

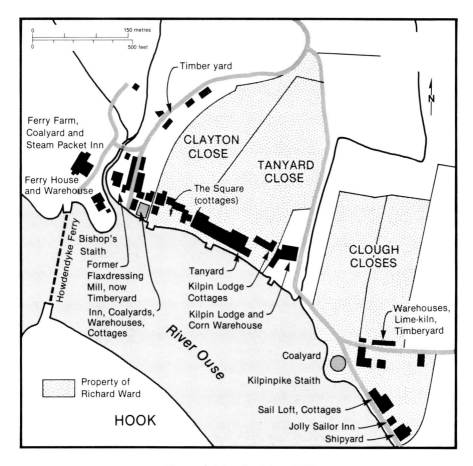

Figure 4. Howdendyke *c.*1850

At this point Howdendyke was almost wholly a waterfront village, and much of the waterfront housing extant in the 1960s was built in the last decade of the eighteenth century.

As warehousing, shipping, and the importation of bulky goods such as coal and timber increased throughout the first half of the nineteenth century, new small enterprises were added to the waterfront zone. These included a flax-dressing mill alongside Howdendyke Creek and a lime-kiln at Kilpinpike. The corn mill changed hands several times, becoming the property of John Singleton, merchant, in the early 1850s. It was Singleton, perhaps, who converted the cottages on the site into the unitary house, with some pretensions to style, which became known as Kilpin Lodge.

The chief change of the early nineteenth century, however, came via the development of Richard Ward's enterprise. Nephew of a master mariner who had become a Kilpinpike coal merchant by 1793, resident of the large house behind the staith or pike, Richard Ward inherited sufficient capital in 1817 to begin a series of property purchases which led to his becoming the chief, though modest, landowner in Howdendyke (Figure 4). By 1802 Howdendyke Field had become split into a number of smaller parcels. From 1823 Richard Ward began to purchase these either outright or after providing their owners with mortgages. The agricultural field – still by far the greater part of the area – the maltkin, Cuttill's defunct shipyard, the Kilpinpike shipyard, and the tannery had all become Ward property by the early 1830s. Although he also purchased fields between Kilpinpike and Kilpin Lodge, the latter, as well as the port complex around the Creek, was not engrossed by Ward, although he rented the ferry warehouse from the Bishop's lessees.

By the early 1850s, then, Howdendyke had become a thriving river port with several coalyards, shipyards, and industries forming a semi-continuous building line along the waterfront from ferry to Kilpin Lodge, together with Ward's outlier at Kilpinpike. There was still very little development away from the waterfront, along Ferry Road. This was to come with the arrival of the Anderton family in 1857, and under their influence the village had assumed much of its present form before 1914.

Shipping and shipbuilding

Fairly complete shipping registers permit a full account of Howdendyke's shipbuilding activities throughout the nineteenth century, and provide tantalizing glimpses of the small river port's shipping activities. If we assume that most of the estuarial and seagoing vessels built by Howdendyke shipbuilders were registered at Goole and Hull, the nearest large Humber ports, some indication of the village's shipbuilding activity from the late eighteenth century can be ascertained from the shipping registers of those ports.

Howdendyke was never more than a very minor shipbuilder. For the whole period from the 1780s to the turn of the nineteenth century the village's shipyards produced, on average, no more than one seagoing vessel every two years (Table 1) and these vessels were chiefly single-masted sloops or larger schooners of 40–100 tons burthen. Only in the later nineteenth century were brigantines and ketches of up to 150 tons built at Howdendyke.

Table 1. Seagoing vessels built at Howdendyke
and registered at Goole and Hull, 1782–1901

	Number of vessels built	Total registered tonnage	Average tonnage per vessel	Builders	Types of vessel
1782–91	1	45	45	Mann	sloop
1792–01	2	70	35	Cuttill	sloops
1802–11	4	281	70	Ward	sloops, schooners
1812–21	5	304	61	Ward	sloops, brigantines
1822–31	4	168	42	Ward	sloops
1832–41	3	118	37	Ward	sloops
1842–51	1	45	45	Ward	sloop
1852–61	6	543	90	Ward/ Banks	sloops, schooners, brigs.
1862–71	11	1435	130	Banks	sloops, schooners, brigs., ketch
1872–81	3	456	152	Banks/ Caiseley	schooner, brig., ketch
1882–91	9	850	94	Caiseley	ketches
1892–01	3	375	125	Caiseley	sloops, ketch

Source: Goole, Hull shipping registers.

The earliest references to shipbuilding are to be found in title deeds. At the turn of the eighteenth century at least two small riverfront plots in Howdendyke Field were sold to shipbuilders, John Nicholson (1792) and Richard Cuttill (1802). In 1791 a Kilpinpike shipbuilder named Richard Mann produced a 45-ton sloop, and Cuttill turned out two further sloops, the first in 1796. There is no record of Nicholson's work. In the last years of the eighteenth century, then, three small shipyards were building vessels chiefly for estuarial use. As there is no record of Nicholson, Mann, and Cuttill after the first decade of the nineteenth century, it is assumed that these small yards either were suddenly reduced to repairs and small boat-building, or, more likely, that the Howdendyke Field plots proved more suitable for other industrial uses, and eventually became adjuncts to the tannery site. Indeed, Nicholson sold out as early as 1801, and Cuttill sold his plot to Richard Ward in 1831.

After the turn of the century, then, only a single shipyard survived as producer of seagoing vessels. This yard, together with a long building used as a sail loft, was located in Skelton township just over the Kilpinpike boundary line. Successively run by Richard Mann (late eighteenth century), Richard Ward (c.1800–1850s), John Banks (1850s–1870s), and William Caiseley (1870s–1901), 'Skelton Shipyard' was responsible for fifty of the fifty-two Howdendyke ships registered in Hull and Goole in the nineteenth century.

The shipping registers, together with other documents, provide a wealth of information about Howdendyke's shipping and shipbuilding activities. The Mann family, like Nicholson and Cuttill, did not survive as shipbuilders. Richard Ward, however, was cast in a more substantial mould, and developed a small empire based on his large house at Kilpinpike.

During a long career spanning the first half of the nineteenth century, Richard Ward engaged in a variety of related enterprises at Kilpinpike. Taking over Skelton Shipyard from Mann, he turned out eighteen ships, chiefly sloops of about 50 tons burthen, in the period 1800–1852. The first three vessels were built for owners in Hull and Thorne, but thereafter Ward build almost exclusively for himself. There is no record of his registering vessels other than self-built ones during his long career as shipowner and merchant. With a half dozen or more vessels at any one time, Ward developed an extensive trade in bulk goods such as coal, timber, stone, and lime. He also bought the Howdendyke tannery and ran it during the 1830s and 1840s, and purchased the fields between Kilpinpike and Howdendyke proper. The remains of his coalyard on Kilpinpike Staith were to be seen until recently, and the large tract of land behind his imposing Kilpinpike house was devoted to a lime-kiln, a timber-yard, and a small row of cottages, long demolished, known as Woodyard Cottages.

Richard Ward appears to have been a self-made man with few pretensions. His vessels were almost universally given the homely names of daughters and relatives. Only with the *Tryphenia* in 1836 did he attempt something classical. The last vessel of the Ward fleet, the *Richard Ward* (1852) was built shortly after his death by his surgeon son. Although others of the Ward family remained in the Kilpinpike house after Richard's death, this son went bankrupt and the Skelton shipyard passed into the hands of one John Banks.

Banks, variously recorded as gentleman, timber merchant, shipbuilder, and shipowner, was a Howdenshire merchant who built and inhabited Howden Hall in the town of that name. Skelton Shipyard was only one of his many

Table 2. Seagoing vessels built in Howdendyke,
and registered in Hull and Goole, 1791–1901

Name	Year built	Registered tonnage	Vessel type	Owner	Builder
Mary	1791	45	sloop	of Hull	Mann
Providence	1796	38	sloop	of Hull	Cuttill
Mary	1800	32	sloop	of Hull	Ward
Friends	1802	70	sloop	of Hull	Ward
Merchant	1805	64	brigantine	of Hull	Ward
Yorkshireman	1808	94	brigantine	self	Ward
Nancy	1811	53	sloop	self	Mann
Huddersfield	1813	128	brigantine	self	Ward
Easter	1815	33	sloop	self	Ward
Bradford	1817	50	brigantine	of Stockwith	Ward
John	1819	48	sloop	self	Ward
Mary	1820	45	sloop	self	Ward
Sarah	1822	47	sloop	self	Ward
Ann	1822	36	sloop	self	Ward
Martha	1827	50	sloop	self	Ward
Susannah	1828	35	sloop	self	Ward
Tryphenia	1836	41	sloop	self	Ward
Elizabeth	1839	44	sloop	self	Ward
Jane	1841	33	sloop	self	Ward
Margaret	1845	45	sloop	self	Ward
Richard	1852	59	sloop	self	Ward (jnr.)
Fullerton	1854	172	brigantine	self	Banks
Saltmashe	1854	70	schooner	self	Banks
Brackenholme	1857	115	brigantine	local	Banks
Isabella Pratt	1859	60	schooner	local	Banks
James Pratt	1860	117	schooner	local	Banks
Babthorpe	1862	192	brigantine	self	Banks
Sarah & Jane	1863	96	schooner	self	Banks
Swallow	1864	116	schooner	self	Banks
Jane & Mary	1865	37	sloop	of Reedness	Banks
Howden	1866	120	schooner	self	Banks
William Cass	1866	104	schooner	of Cowick	Banks
John & James	1867	71	schooner	self	Banks
Brackenholme	1869	108	schooner	self	Banks
Cambria	1869	53	ketch	of Hull	Banks
Unity	1870	179	schooner	self	Banks
Superb	1871	159	ketch	of Goole	Banks
Merlin	1874	252	brigantine	self	Banks
Sparkling Glance	1878	142	schooner	local	Banks (jnr.)
Polyhymnia	1881	72	ketch	of Hull	Caiseley
Elite	1883	118	schooner	of Hull	Caiseley
Proserpine	1884	86	ketch	of Hull	Caiseley
Thalia	1884	79	ketch	of Hull	Caiseley

Table 2. cont.

Name	Year built	Registered tonnage	Vessel type	Owner	Builder
Parthenope	1885	90	ketch	of Hull	Caiseley
Metis	1886	90	ketch	of Hull	Caiseley
Egeria	1887	92	ketch	of Hull	Caiseley
Iris	1887	92	ketch	of Hull	Caiseley
Maude Mary	1889	77	ketch	Anderton	Caiseley
George Kilner	1891	124	brigantine	of Knottingley	Caiseley
Golden Wedding	1897	216	brigantine	of Knottingley	Caiseley
Hydro	1897	60	sloop	Anderton	Caiseley
Beatrice	1901	99	brigantine	self	Caiseley

Sources: Shipping registers for Hull (1804–1980) and Goole (1828–1980).

enterprises. Unlike Richard Ward, whose organization was very local and integrated, John Banks appears to have had a much wider reach. He built eighteen vessels also, but only half of these were for himself. His other customers were chiefly local merchants. For these Banks produced mainly schooners, while vessels for his own fleet included a number of brigantines (Table 2). Indeed, in contrast with Ward, Banks built only one sloop, and his two and a half decade (1854–79) control of the shipyard considerably increased the average size of vessel built in Howdendyke (Table 1).

Not content with self-built vessels, however, Banks contracted out much shipbuilding (Table 3). To his nine Howdendyke-built vessels he added at least sixteen other ships. Although some of these were not new when purchased, at least eleven of the sixteen were registered in the same year as built. From this we can infer that the Howdendyke yard remained very small and quite unable to produce either large vessels (over 150 tons) or more than two ships per year. In haste to build up his fleet in the 1850s, therefore, John Banks had a number of vessels specially built in shipyards as far afield as Stainforth (on the Don), Leeds, Hull, Sunderland, and later, Goole. The Sunderland builders were the Abbey family, some of whom may have relocated to Kilpinpike to become master mariners, importers of stone and gravel, and, eventually, masters of the Chemical Works' small fleet of sailing barges in the early twentieth century.

During the 1850s and 1860s, with a Howdendyke-based fleet of about twenty vessels, John Banks of Howden was the economic mainstay of Howdendyke. At least six of his vessels were co-owned by his sisters, his sons, and various local worthies, only one of whom, however, resided in Howdendyke. It is notable that Banks bought no more vessels after 1861, but continued to add to his fleet by building at his own yard. John Banks died in 1879, whereupon his daughter married H. B. Anderson, a Howdendyke timber merchant, who thereafter inhabited Howden Hall until 1900. As with Richard Ward, the last vessel of the

Banks regime was built by a son of the family, who thereafter sold the yard to one William Caiseley.

Caiseley was exclusively a shipbuilder rather than a shipowner or merchant. By the 1870s the Andertons, with their fertilizer factory built on the site of Ward's tannery, had become entrenched as Howdendyke's chief employer. Further, Howdendyke's role as a minor river port was already in decline, in conjunction with the declining fortunes of the town of Howden. Most of

Table 3. Seagoing vessels registered at Goole by Howden/Howdendyke owners, but built elsewhere, 1828–1980

Name	Year registered	Registered tonnage	Vessel type	Owner name	Owner domicile	Owner occupation
Howden	1834*	97	schooner	W. Carter	Howden	wine merchant
John & Ann	1842	38	sloop	J. Brown	Howden	saddler
Wm. Wells	1845*	70	schooner	R. Rockett	Howden	master mariner
Jane & Thomas	1847	40	sloop	T. Clayton	H/Dyke	innkeeper
Ann (?)	1850	44	sloop	J. Banks	Howden	gentleman
Sarah (?)	1850	43	sloop	J. Banks	Howden	gentleman
Ebenezer	1851*	52	sloop	J. Banks	Howden	timber merchant
Freebridge	1851*	100	schooner	J. Banks	Howden	timber merchant
Wave	1851*	197	brigantine	J. Banks	Howden	shipowner
Friendship	1852	42	schooner	J. Banks	Howden	timber merchant
John Banks	1853*	68	sloop	J. Banks	Howden	timber merchant
John Nussey	1853*	148	schooner	J. Banks	Howden	shipowner
Louisa's & Maria's	1855	67	schooner	J. Wells	Boothferry	farmer
Fanny	1855	37	sloop	J. Wells	Boothferry	
Wells	1856	67	sloop	J. Banks & others	Howden	shipowner
Laurel	1856	49	schooner	J. Banks & others	Howden	timber merchant
Victoria	1856	33	sloop	W. Watson & others	H/Dyke	master mariner
CPJ	1857	30	sloop	T. Pratt	H/Dyke	shipbuilder
Two Emmas	1859*	121	schooner	J. Banks & others	Howden	merchant
Thomas Hope	1859*	46	sloop	J. Banks & Thos. Hope	Howden & H/Dyke	shipowners
Wressle Castle	1859*	315	barque	J. Banks & sons	Howden	shipowners
Isabella Hartley	1859*	152	brigantine	J. Banks	Howden	shipowner
Surprsie	1860*	48	ketch	J. Banks & others	Howden	shipowner
Alice	1861	72	schooner	J. Banks & others	Howden	shipowner
William & Susamah	1864	34	sloop	J. Bankhouse	H/Dyke	coal merchant
Londos	1864	229	schooner	J. Wells	Boothferry	gentleman
Howdenshire**	1893	161	ketch	G. H. Anderton	H/Dyke	chemical manufacturer
Cupro**	1901	78	sloop	G. H. Anderton	H/Dyke	chemical manufacturer

* built and registered in the same year.
** registered at Hull.
Sources: Shipping registeres for Hull (1804–1980) and Goole (1828–1980).

Caiseley's output consisted of ketches for the Hull-based Holmes fleet, a change in focus in shipbuilding which mirrors the gradual loss of Howdendyke's shipping function. Perhaps symbolically, two of Caiseley's last five vessels were built for Anderton's, although that firm also had vessels built in Hull (Table 3).

After two decades of turning out ketches for others, William Caiseley had sufficient capital to build his last vessel, a 100 ton brigantine, for himself. On the basis of this he retired and closed down the shipyard, for no one wished to buy this small and antiquated outfit. Caiseley sold his tools to the Scarr family, who were to build a shipyard upriver of Howdendyke in 1903 (Chapter 4).

Except for a brief hiatus in 1902, then, Howdendyke can boast a continuous record of shipbuilding from the late eighteenth century to the 1960s. Its role as a port, chiefly importing goods for Howden and vicinity, however, although probably of ancient origin, reached its apogee in the mid-nineteenth century. During the two decades after Richard Ward's death John Banks' shipping enterprises were matched, at a very much smaller scale, by John Wells of Boothferry with at least five vessels, and at least four Howdendyke inhabitants with a single vessel each (Table 3).

These latter four illustrate most tellingly the small-scale enterprise common in Howdendyke before the arrival of the Andertons. Their occupations are given as innkeeper, master mariner, coal-merchant, and shipbuilder. Other evidence, including family histories and deeds, demonstrates that individual Howdendyke families were engaged, like Richard Ward, in many of these trades simultaneously. The Watson family, for example, kept the Anchor Inn, ran a coalyard and a grocery, and owned a vessel captained by William Watson in 1856. Similarly, the lessors of the Bishop of Durham's ferry combined this operation with farming Ferry Farm and keeping the Steam Packet Inn. A fifth entrepreneurial family, the Chesters, moved across the river from Hook and set up a shipping business with ancillary boat-building on Nicholson's former site in Howdendyke.

Most of these shipping concerns, however, seem to have gone out of business by the 1880s, and much of their warehouse and other building property was taken over by the Andertons, as described in the following chapter, which also relates the final demise of Howdendyke as a port in the late nineteenth century.

Population change

Howdendyke's economy before the 1850s was inextricably intertwined with that of Howden, for the village's chief function was to act as Howden's port, chiefly for the bulk import of timber, coal, stone and the like. A reconstruction of the demography of Howden parish (a very large area including Kilpin) using early parish registers, was undertaken, revealing that the district contained a stable population of perhaps 2500–3000 people during the period 1551–1641, after which statistics become unreliable. In the eighteenth century, adjusting for nonconformists, we again find a stable population of about 2000. The first census assigned 1552 persons to Howden town alone in 1801.

Howden's quiet career as an important country town came to an end with the draining of the nearby waterlogged land commons of Wallingfen and Bishopsoil in the late eighteenth century. Commons and open arable fields were enclosed, some new settlements appeared, and agricultural production rose dramatically. Howden residents responded by rebuilding, using brick and tile from newly-established brickworks. The old town consists chiefly of brick and pantile buildings of the period 1770–1850 (Neave 1979).

Economic prosperity meant population growth not only for Howden but for its port. During the two decades 1801–21 Howden grew rapidly, but Kilpin parish grew twice as fast, increasing by about one-third in each decade (Table 4) and reaching a population of 476 in 1861 after six decades of almost continuous growth. Only a small proportion of this growth can be accounted for by agricultural expansion in Kilpin hamlet and the establishment of a brick and tile works at nearby Sunny Bank. The chief reason for the more than doubling of Kilpin parish's population in the period 1801–1851 was the growth of

Table 4. Population change 1801–1981

Census year	Goole	Howden	Kilpin parish	Howdendyke*	Intercensal changes of 10% and over			Houses, Kilpin parish	
					Howden	Kilpin parish	Howdendyke	Occupied	Empty
1801	294	1552	183					36	1
1811	348	1812	243		+17	+33		49	3
1821	450	2080	318		+15	+31		56	–
1831	2203	2130	349			+10		58	–
1841	3571	2332	393	238	+10	+13		86	6
1851	4619	2491	385	251				89	10
1861	5937	2507	476	338		+24	+35	100	–
1871	7700	2355	395	265		–17	–22	91	6
1881	10687	2192	332	196		–16	–27	67	29
1891	15416	1960	393		–11	+18		95	6
1901	17120	1975	376					92	6
1911	20916	2007	420			+12		93	–
1921	19679	2052	385					95	–
1931	20885	2154	333					?	?
1941	–	–	–					–	–
1951	20293	1931**	649**	207				195	–
1961	20010	2282	537	195	+18	–17		180	–
1971	19926	2605	484	160	+19	–11	–18	155	–
1981	19830	3270	360	127	+26	–26	–21	–	–

* Figures derived from Ms. Census returns 1841–81 and 'social reconstruction' survey 1951–81
(see Appendix).
** Significant boundary changes.

Source: Census.

Howdendyke as Howden's port, with a direct connection by water to the nearby port of Goole, founded in 1826.

After the 1820s, however, Howdendyke's rate of growth slackened somewhat, to receive a second boost with the arrival of George Anderton and his conversion of Ward's defunct tannery into the Chemical Works in 1857. The correspondingly dramatic rise in population of 35 per cent in the 1851–61 decade is the only occasion in which Kilpin parish (which increased only 24 per cent as a whole) received the dignity of a special note in the census tables: 'The increase in population in Kilpin township arises from the conversion of a large tannery (unoccupied in 1851) into a manufactury for agricultural chemicals'.

This conversion took place at a most opportune moment. For with the arrival of railways at the ports of Selby (1834) and Goole (1848), these towns gradually began to usurp the role of Howden as trading and distributive centre, via Howdendyke, for the agricultural region of Howdenshire. Howden's few industries began to close down; a sacking factory in the 1830s, its tanneries in the 1850s, and a flax factory in the 1860s.

With the arrival of Howden's first railway in 1840, Howdendyke's shipping function was threatened at the very moment of its most rapid growth. And with the phenomenal growth of Goole from a hamlet of 450 people in 1821 to a thriving port of over 10,000 by 1881, Howden's role as a regional market centre also declined (Porteous 1969, 1977b). After 1851 Howden's population first stagnated, then began a decline not arrested until the mid-twentieth century; in 1951 its population of 1,931 was the lowest since 1841. Despite the shipping efforts of John Banks, it is likely that Howdendyke would also have stagnated, had not George Anderton appeared on the scene.

Nevertheless, Howdendyke's population did fall by 22 per cent in the period 1861–71, consequent upon the disengagement of labour brought in specially by George Anderton to build the Chemical Works. The half decade following 1857 must have given Howdendyke a 'construction boom town' appearance, soon lost with the necessary reduction of construction labour and reversed in the decade 1871–81 when the riverport's population fell by 27 per cent to a figure, 196, much below that of the pre-Anderton era. The decline in port functions, migration to Goole, teething troubles at the Chemical Works, and the prevailing agricultural depression, with a consequent fall in demand for fertilizers, all contributed to this drastic fall of 42 per cent from the 1861 peak. In 1881 Howdendyke had twenty-nine vacant houses, a trough of depopulation not to be experienced again until the 1970s. Many of these houses, however, were the result of a common Howdendyke waterfront activity, the conversion of redundant warehouses, granaries, and stables into cottages. In turn, several adjacent cottages were frequently knocked together to make a large house. Several of the houses of The Square and alongside the Creek can claim this kind of history, including the village pub (the Club) and Post Office.

Taking the latter, my home in the period 1943–65, as a case-study, we find some evidence of an early warehouse on the site in the late eighteenth century. As a 'warehouse containing several chambers or granaries and a cellar' conveniently located alongside the Creek and Kilpin Landing stage, it was owned by John Barker, one of Howden's many small investors in Howdendyke in the late eighteenth century. By 1814 four cottages and a coalyard had appeared, and in 1835 these were acquired by Robert Howe of Howden, corn factor and precursor of the Singletons in the corn mill and cottages which were to become Kilpin Lodge. In 1837–41 the property was sold to the Little brothers, Howden wheelwrights and timber importers, who had established timber yards nearby. By the time the property passed into the hands of the Claytons – a Howdendyke family engaged in innkeeping, shipping and coal import – in 1847, the four cottages had been knocked into two. Sold by the Claytons for £210 in 1866, the building had by that time become one large dwelling-house and was converted into a grocery and post office (1875) by the Goole owner. In 1896 relatives of the Claytons recovered it, but sold it to Charles Mell, my grandfather, in 1918 for £200.

Because of the frequency of such conversions, and the difficult nature of the title deeds which serve as the only evidence, no accurate written or cartographic account of Howdendyke's early housing is possible. It is clear, however, that the building of the Anderton factory in 1857–62 did not occasion much house-building, for the large temporary population was accommodated by the 'doubling-up' of families, by the taking in of lodgers (clearly indicated in the 1861 census) and by the conversion of increasingly-redundant waterfront warehouses into cottages.

After the nadir of 1881 Howdendyke's economy and population recovered sharply, refilling most of the empty houses by 1891. Thereafter the village's rather stable population history becomes independent of that of the declining town of Howden. Only after the 1950s, when it became a commuter town, a planned growth node, and began to attract light industry, did Howden show remarkable population increases, matched by an equally rapid fall in Howdendyke's population after 1961 (Table 4). An explanation of these trends, which had led by the mid-1980s to the destruction of over half of Howdendyke's dwellings, awaits part III of this book.

Howdendyke at mid-century

The earliest land tax assessment to give property descriptions, that of 1826, depicts a Howdendyke-Kilpinpike riverfront zone of scattered clusters of houses, cottages, warehouses, and the by now 'unoccupied' corn mill, the adjacent house (Kilpin Lodge) being already the home of the Singleton family. The tannery is not mentioned, and according to the census was possibly not in operation in 1851. Except for a short-lived flax-dressing mill, then, in the latter part of the first half of the nineteenth century, Howdendyke seems to have been much more an import-distributing river port than an industrial centre.

Table 5. Occupational structure 1811–31, (%)

	Howden			Kilpin parish		
	Agriculture	Trade	Professional/ other	Agriculture	Trade	Other
1811	28	56	16	51	49	0
1821	26	49	25	38	21	41
1831	26	56	18	26	62	26

Sources: Census.

Table 6. Occupational structure, males over 20 years in 1831, (%)

	Howden	Kilpin parish
Agriculture: occupiers employing labourers	2	6
Agriculture: occupiers without labourers	1	4
Agriculture: labourers	23	28
Non-agricultural labourers	10	25
Servants	2	1
Professionals	8	0
Retail, trade, handicrafts	44	36
Manufacturing	0	0
Other	10	0

Source: Census.

Early census details confirm this (Tables 5, 6). Whereas Howden's particularly market town mix of agriculture, trade, and professional occupations changed little in the period 1811–31, the parish of Kilpin saw a sharp relative decline in agriculture and other occupations in favour of 'trade'. By 1831 Kilpin parish's males were occupied chiefly in trade (largely shipping), agriculture, and as labourers (chiefly riverside porters, coalyard and timberyard workers). The lack of manufacturing in both Howden and Kilpin is obvious but not remarkable in this agricultural zone. Figures 5 to 8, derived from the Kilpin and Howden tithe maps of 1841 and 1846, place Howdendyke in perspective. Between the extensive estates with big fields on either side, a swathe of land consisting of smaller fields with a large variety of small owners reaches from Howden towards the Ouse at Howdendyke. It is noteworthy that, except for Richard Ward, most of the landowners are not the occupiers, leasing to tenants being the normal procedure for both major and minor landowners. Ward owns most of Kilpinpike and Howdendyke Field, but does not fully occupy the latter.

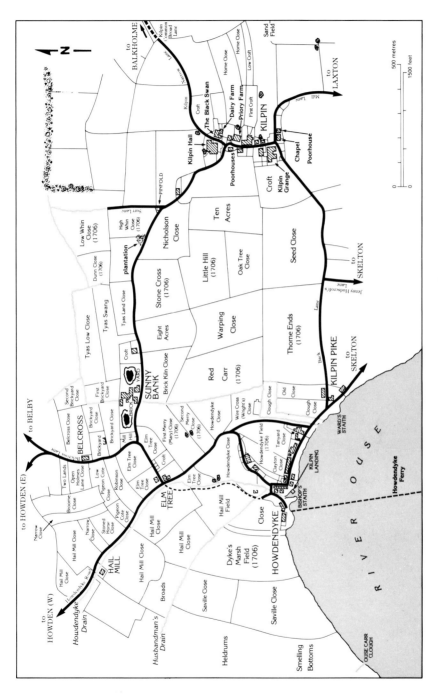

Figure 5. Place names c.1840

37

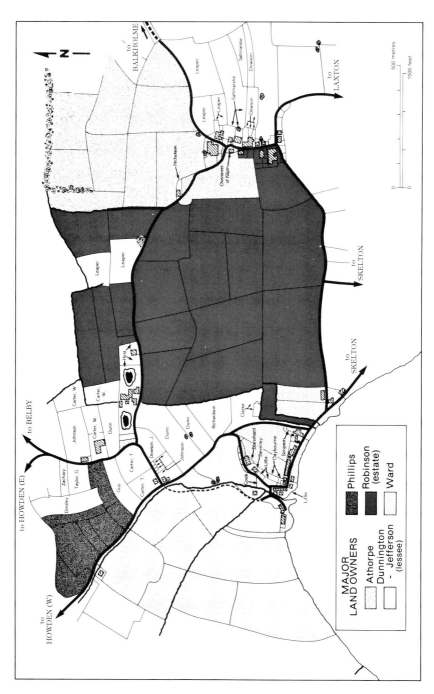

Figure 6. Landowners *c*.1840

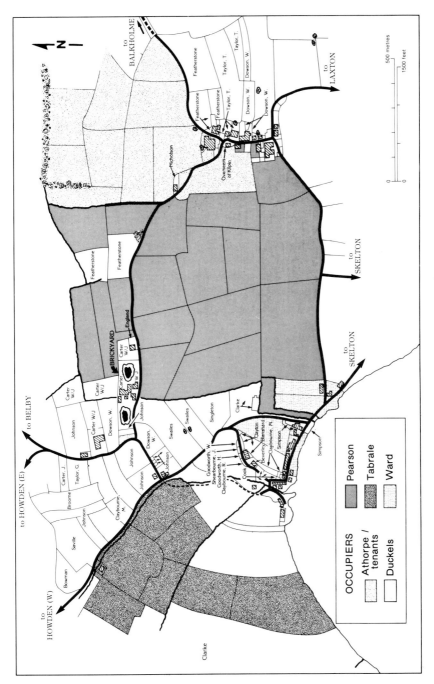

Figure 7. Occupiers *c.*1840

39

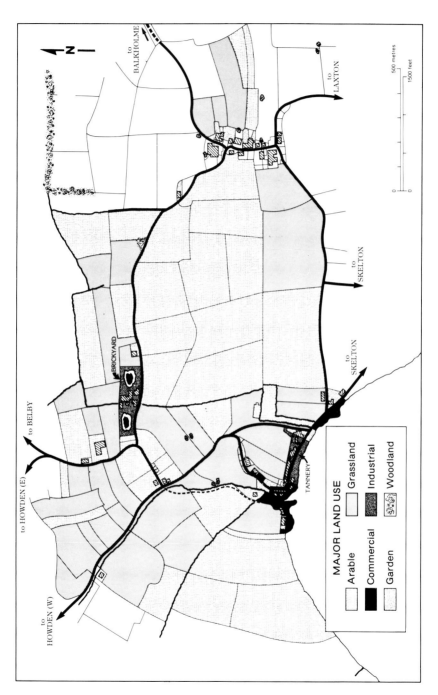

Figure 8. Land use *c*.1840

Kilpin, with its wholly agricultural character, and Sunny Bank, a small brickyard settlement, contrast strongly with the industrial and commercial Howdendyke. All these settlements, however, are lost in a sea of arable and grassland, the latter especially common in the swathe of small fields between Howden and Howdendyke.

Early directories dating from 1821 to 1855 depict a settlement apparently growing in size but changing little in character. By the late 1840s Howdendyke, with Kilpinpike, had become very much the bustling riverport, with the constant arrival and departure of cargo vessels, a daily carrier to Howden, twice weekly 'market boats' to Goole and Hull, an active ferry, and daily calls by steam packets plying the Ouse and Humber between Hull, Goole, Selby, and York.

The settlement was dominated at mid-century by Richard Ward, vessel owner, coal and lime merchant, and shipbuilder, of Kilpinpike, and by the Singletons, corn factors and general merchants, of Kilpin Lodge (Figure 4). Both large and small entrepreneurs engaged in a wide variety of activities, the smaller ones combining innkeeping with shopkeeping, farming, or coal distribution. At least five coal merchants had riverside yards in 1840, including Ward, Clayton (Post Office area), Watson of the Anchor Inn next door, Howe the corn merchant, and Duckles of the Steam Packet Inn, who was also ferryman and farmer. At the latter's coalyard John Mell, my great-great-grandfather, heaved coal for a living. At least two timber yards were in operation, one of them also specializing in the import of iron. The only real industry appears to have been the tannery, operated by Richard Ward's sons, Westoby and Richard jun.

Of the five inns, only the Jolly Sailor at the Kilpinpike end of Skelton, and the Steam Packet (or Ferry Inn) at the extreme upriver end of the village, retained their names throughout the century. On the Kilpin side of the Creek, there were probably three inns, the Blue Bell, the Anchor, and Clayton's King's Head which later became the Lord Nelson. A further public house was to be found at Elm Tree. More solid refreshment was available from several stores, one run in conjunction with the Lord Nelson, and a butcher. Feet could be shod by a shoemaker, and from 1848 at least the use of a warehouse as a chapel and Sunday school permitted the contemplation of higher things.

The 1841 and 1851 manuscript census returns remind us that these entrepreneurs comprised only a small proportion of Howdendyke's population. In both years the most common occupational category was a river-related complex made up of shipowners, seamen, sailors, mariners, master mariners, watermen, boatmen and ferrymen. Of sixty-nine persons with listed occupations in 1841, thirty (44 per cent) were engaged in these river-going pursuits. The same percentage (thirty-four of seventy-eight persons) prevailed in 1851. Add to these the shipwrights, merchants, merchant's clerks, corn factors, timberyard sawyers, wharf labourers (porters) and innkeepers (who, as we have seen, were also master mariners, coal merchants, or ferrymen) and the proportion of the occupied population directly employed in river-related trades reaches 62 per cent in both 1841 and 1851. Add to these again, the non-basic occupations relying upon these river trades, as well as the domestic employees of Richard Ward and the Singletons, and the port-related occupied population of 1851 becomes 88 per cent of the whole. The remainder of the working population consisted, at both dates, of no more than two or three tannery labourers, an equal number of shipyard workers, a dozen farmers, yeomen, and farm labourers, and sundry individuals such as a stonemason and a brickmaker. A number of inhabitants without occupations were retired mariners, mariners' wives (the husband being 'from home') or sailors' widows, further adding to the prevailing nautical flavour.

From the late 1830s to the early 1850s, then, Howdendyke was a remarkably stable riverport. A glance ahead at the 1861, 1871, and 1881 census manuscript data, however, reveals a rapid fall in the number of river-related trades (Table 7), especially among the seagoing fraternity, which had almost disappeared by 1881. This rapid change in fortunes is ascribable not merely to the construction of the Anderton Chemical Works in 1857, but to the general decline in the trading function of the mother town of Howden.

Table 7. River-related occupations, Howdendyke, 1841–81

Occupations	*1841*	*1851*	*1861*	*1871*	*1881*
Sailors, mariners, seamen	26	25	9	5	1
Ferrymen, watermen, boatmen	3	2	3	5	1
Shipowners	1	2	0	0	0
Shipwrights & shipyard workers	1	1	2	3	3
Sawyers, timber-yard labourers	5	12	1	4	3
Coalyard labourers	2	4	2	3	0
Tanyard workers	3	2	1	0	0

Source: Manuscript census returns 1841–81.

Howden censuses reveal, tellingly, a fair number of resident mariners, sailors, shiphands, and watermen in 1841 (five) and 1851 (seven), with ten tanners in the latter year. By 1861 only two sailors and one tanner remained, matched by at least two persons with employment at the new Howdendyke Chemical Works. One of these was the owner, George Anderton, who resided at 72 Hailgate in Howden town before relieving the Singletons of Kilpin Lodge in 1862. By 1871 there were still three sailors and a ferryman in Howden, but these were now outnumbered by six chemical workers. It appears that the long-established dominance of Howdendyke by Howden was being reversed by the 1860s.

As previously noted, Howden's market and trading functions were in decline by mid-century. A contemporary document (undated, but c.1850) in the archives of the Bishop of Durham notes, in relation to the Bishop's lands at Howdendyke:

> The value of these lands rests entirely upon their agricultural character, the town of Howden not being increasing in population. Its inconvenient railway accommodation has shut it out almost entirely from trade except for the Horse Fairs, and its Corn and Cattle Market which some years ago was of rather high reputation in the vicinity has been attracted to Selby mainly in consequence of the ready River and Railway communication to that place.
>
> The ferries of Howdendyke and Booth at present derive their value from being on the route to the Town of Goole a prosperous and rising Shipping Town on the south side of the River Ouse but a line of railway is now in course of completion from the Hull and Selby Railway to Goole which will still further deprive Howden of the small amount of commerce which it still enjoys ... [Even] the value of the Ferries will be reduced.

It is clear that George Anderton and industrialism reached Howdendyke just in time to prevent the village's inevitable stagnation.

4

The Anderton era

The role of the entrepreneur in industrial location has been
neglected. In many cases it was the decision of an individual,
acting on imperfect information, which was responsible for
the foundation or reviving of an industry.

P. S. Richards

Industrial location theory demands an aggregate view. Yet an individual
industry may be the brainchild of an individualistic entrepreneur. This was
often the case before the twentieth century, and is true of Howdendyke. For
after 1857 this small river port, inhabited chiefly by minor entrepreneurs and
only partly in thrall to Richard Ward, John Banks, and others, was transformed
almost into a company village by scions of the energetic Anderton family of
Cleckheaton.

Advent

James Anderson was a citizen of credit and renown. Though not eke a train-
band captain, he achieved fame in the West Riding of Yorkshire woollen district
by helping his father George put down the Chartist-inspired 'Plug Riots' of
1842. James and George were members of a prolific family which still inhabits
the wool textile manufacturing region between Bradford and Dewsbury (Figure
9). During the late eighteenth century John Anderton and his son Joseph were
considered to be 'fathers of the wool trade' in the Bradford area. Joseph's son
George (George I), having seen an advertisement for the sale of machinery in
Cleckheaton, moved to that town and set up a worsted spinning factory there in
1819 at age twenty-one. It still exists.

According to a former workman (Harrison 1903) and the acknowledged
dean of local historians (Peel 1893), George I was a mover and shaper. His
work-related exploits include the invention of new wool-combing machinery
and the extension of his factory from two looms in 1819 to a mill employing
109 women, 102 boys, 96 girls, and 80 men by 1851.

He was equally active socially, being immersed in the liberal Non-conformist
tradition of the nineteenth century north. Heavily involved in agitation for the
Reform Bill of 1832, he got up a banquet to celebrate its passing. He helped

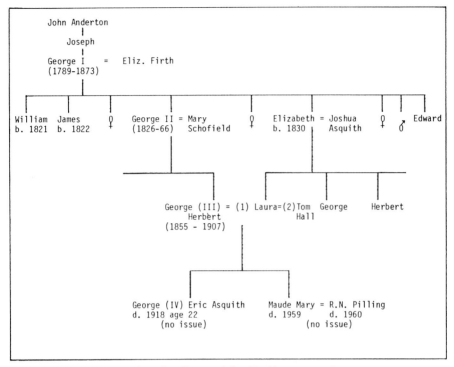

Figure 9. Selected pedigree of the Cleckheaton (to George II)
and Howendyke (from George II) Andertons

Source: Anderton archives

build schools, a gasworks, and sundry other Cleckheaton institutions. He assisted during a local 'famine' in 1839, built a chapel opposite his mill, helped end church rates in 1842, and in the same year assisted his son James in putting an end to the Plug Riots. A member of the Anti-Corn Law League, he induced both Cobden and Bright to speak in out-of-the-way Cleckheaton.

His portrait betrays a stern but genial patriarchal authority and determination. A number of Anderton character traits, expressed in the works of George I, are evident in the way his son George II and grandson George Herbert (George III) reorganized Howdendyke. First, George I lived, as was then becoming uncommon, on the site of his industrial premises. Indeed, a former, perhaps somewhat sycophantic, workman noted that 'the good saintly old man and his wife ended their days at the top of the Mill Yard, joining to their warehouse' (Harrison 1903). Typically, their home was known as 'Providence House'. This patriarchal location policy, the owner's house adjacent to his warehouses, was exactly reproduced in Howdendyke and continued until the death of George III's only surviving child, Mrs Maude Mary Pilling, in 1959.

Second, George I's tradition of paternal interest in, and therefore control of, his workers continued through succeeding generations in Howdendyke. Third, George I's role of prominent public involvement (as Justice of the Peace, etc.) was carried on by his Howdendyke descendants. Above all, the Andertons were, according to their Non-conformist lights, zealous developers of both family fortunes and community well-being:

> He was a man of punctuality, at one time his son James after he was married did not come [to the works] till breakfast time, he met him at the Wharehous landing, he said James where as thow been this morning, his ancer was, Father i over slept my-self; thow had no zeal, or thow would have been in time. (Harrison, 1903)

Harrison's apogee of encomium rounds off my consideration of this paragon:

> ... and I beg to say that it would be hard to put a finger on one blot in his life ... by his inherent worth, he gathered around him as much esteem and respect as any man ever lived in this town or neighbourhood. He had the political, social, and religious well-being of the community at heart ...

Cleckheaton soon proved too small a scene of enterprise for the burgeoning Anderton family. George's third son, George Anderton Jr. (George II) was first apprenticed in a local dye-house, and then transferred to a small plant adjacent to his father's Victoria Mill as a manufacturing chemist and drysalter. As Harrison (1903) inimitably relates, George II wanted to expand:

> The premices he ockupied at his fathers Yard became far two small ... he Removed to Kilpin Lodge, Howden, to commence business there of some-what of a different kind, he was not spared to live long their, And in the prime of life he was called to lay it down on Dec. the 17th 1866, aged 40 and we laid his remains to rest in The Cleckheaton Cemetery.

George II's widow remained and the Howdendyke business passed to his son George Herbert (George III).

When George II moved to Howdendyke he was not entering an entirely unknown environment. Like his father, he saw an advertisement, this time for the sale of Richard Ward's Howdendyke tannery. He may have seen it during a visit to the area, for his father had a number of connections with Goole, the Aire & Calder Canal Company's company town founded a little downriver from Howdendyke in 1826 (Porteous 1969, 1977). In particular, George I was a director of the Lancashire & Yorkshire Railway Company, which soon connected Goole with the remainder of the West Riding, and also of the Goole Steam Shipping Company. George II therefore had ready-made connections in

George Anderton I

George Herbert Anderton

Mrs G. H. (Mary) Anderton

Mr and Mrs R. N. Pilling

Plates 3-6

Plate 7. Howendyke Ferry *c.*1890

Plate 8. Bishop's Staith and, left to right,
Chemical Works, Kilpinpike, Sail Loft, and sloop, *c.*1900

the Lower Ouse area, and good reason to leave Cleckheaton, for he could not be accommodated in the firm, George Anderton & Sons, in which his two elder brothers were partners, and which still flourishes today in Cleckheaton.

Both George II and his younger brother Edward moved from textile chemicals into vitriol (sulphuric acid) manufacture and finally into fertilizer manufacture, though Edward soon left Howdendyke to set up his own small empire, the West of England Bone & Manure Company, in Cornwall. Born in 1826, the year of the founding of the port of Goole, George II was at the ripe age of thirty when he arrived in Howdendyke in 1857 to spend the last decade of his life in beginning the process which was to transform the village's economy and way of life.

The Ouse Chemical Works

George Anderton was able to take advantage of the bankruptcy of Richard Ward jun., declared in 1855, three years after his father's death. At a public auction in Howden held on 19 May 1857, George Anderton was the highest bidder, paying £2500 for four lots. These four lots covered over 11 acres (Figures 4, 10), and included both parts of Howdendyke Field, by this time known as Clayton Close and Tanyard Close. Besides houses, cottages, and an inn, the purchase included the defunct tanyard. In 1860 Anderton mortgaged his Howdendyke properties for £5000 and used the capital to convert the tanyard into a chemical fertilizer factory.

George Anderton II's Ouse Chemical Works began by producing a variety of chemical products, but from the beginning there was a heavy concentration on chemical fertilizers for agricultural use. During the third quarter of the nineteenth century the demand for synthetic fertilizer products grew tremendously as more farmers came to adopt the principles of Victorian 'high farming'. Originally introduced by university-educated farmers, and involving a battery of improved techniques, including model farms, steam ploughs, pedigree stock, deep drainage, and artificial manures, high farming was very gradually adopted by the average farmer, especially with regard to new techniques of drainage and fertilizing (Mingay 1977). And with the demand for these two operations, brick and tile works (as at Sunny Bank, Kilpin) and fertilizer factories (as at Howdendyke) developed or expanded from the 1830s onwards.

Despite a high degree of resistance on the part of traditionalist farmers it eventually became common for farmers to believe that 'with drains, steam-ploughs, and artificial manure, a farmer might defy the weather' and the more adventurous were soon able to engage in 'a scientific discourse on ammonia and the constituent parts and probable value of town sewage as compared with guano' (Jeffries 1890, 9, 66). And 'many men who would not listen to the lectures of professors, or read the articles of chemical experts, were worried by persistent agents for the sale of patent manures into giving them a trial' (Horne 1980). George Anderton employed such agents from the first, and his Howdendyke fertilizer factory, set in the midst of a fertile rural district and well-placed for the import of raw materials and the distribution of products by river, was readily able to take advantage of what has become known as the Second Agricultural Revolution (Thompson 1968).

The conversion of Richard Ward's tannery into a fertilizer works, however, was not without difficulty. Local newspapers record a number of major accidents in the period 1857–61, the first five years of operation. During the first months of construction, a gale blew down the brick pillars supporting a lead cistern to be used for holding sulphuric acid, killing one workman (*Goole & Marshland Gazette*, 2 November 1857). A few months later, eight men were

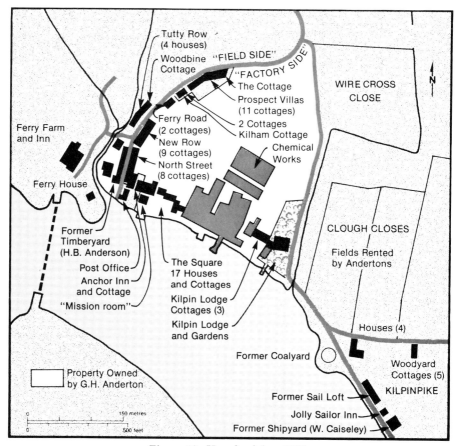

Figure 10. Howdendyke *c*.1900

killed, although the newspaper report is more concerned with the exploits of William Duncan Wright, the original 'Steeple Jack,' in completing an extension of the 130 feet chimney (*Goole & Marshland Gazette*, 1 January 1861). Part of the vitriol chamber collapsed again in 1861 (*Goole & Marshland Gazette*, 1 June 1861). Nevertheless, by the early 1860s the Ouse Chemical Works was in full production, in competition with other small factories founded earlier or contemporaneously in York (Richardson's, 1824), Hull (Milestone's, 1845), Beverley (Tigar's, 1848), Goole (Tillage Co., 1870), and elsewhere. Newspaper advertisements of this period demonstrate also that chemical fertilizers were in competition with more traditional sources of manure, such as guano imported from Peru. Indeed, as late as the 1930s the Goole Tillage Company proudly pointed out that some of their manures contained a small proportion of the now rare organic Peruvian guano.

By the 1880s 'Andertons', the 'Vitriol Works', or the 'Chemical Works', as it was variously known, was employing about seventy workmen, rising to 100 after the turn of the century. A number of company characteristics, especially relevant in the story of Howdendyke's destruction after the 1960s (Chapters 8–11) were apparent almost from the beginning. As early as 1870 the Andertons leased the fields between Kilpin Lodge and Kilpinpike, and in the 1880s local shipyards were producing seagoing vessels for the firm's small fleet. Indeed, so successful did Andertons become that by the 1890s the firm was exporting some fertilizers to Germany, the original source of artificial fertilizer technology, and where the family had connections.

Some indication of the range of products can be obtained from the firm's advertising brochures, the earliest extant being that of 1897. At this time, forty years after the foundation of the firm, 'Geo. H. Anderton's Ouse Chemical Works' was able to deliver, carriage paid to the farmer's nearest railway station or river wharf, a great variety of manures, including Dissolved Bones (33 per cent phosphates, 3 per cent ammonia), Dissolved Bone Compound No. 1 and No. 2, Superphosphates Nos 1, 2, and 3, Nitrophosphate, Special Top Dressing Manure (for barley, oats, wheat, grass, or clover), Special Turnip Manure ('I have paid special attention to having good fertilizing ingredients both for bringing the plant to the hoe and continuing its growth to maturity') and Special Potato Manure ('the result of a study of many years' experience ... well adapted to bring the Tuber to perfection in all its stages').

The firm was incorporated in 1903 as George H. Anderton Ltd., whereafter the advertising schedules become somewhat less personal. Inexplicably, the trade mark adopted consisted of an Indian elephant in profile facing left. The product was now advertised as 'Anderton's Celebrated Manures'. Despite the loss of German potash supplies in World War I, fertilizer production grew with the wartime drive towards increasing nationally produced food supplies.

During the 1920s, when the firm was increasingly directed by Richard

Norman Pilling who in 1915 had married the deceased G. H. Anderton's only surviving child, Maude Mary Anderton, the variety of products increased yet again. Traditional fertilizers, such as 'old-fashioned' dissolved bones, were supplemented by products specially designed for locally staple root crops, such as turnips, mangolds, and sugar beet, with as many as four types of potato manure (for sandy soils, for medium loams, for heavy land, and for heavy warp lands).

The next decade, under the direction of Mr Pilling, saw a complete rebuilding of the Chemical Works, the installation of the latest American granulating machinery, and the purchase of Ferry Farm (the former Steam Packet Inn) for use as an experimental farm. The folksy, locally-produced advertising slogans of the 1930s deserve a page to themselves (Table 8), the most popular being 'Anderton's Fertilisers – They're Wizards in the Soil'. A brochure of 1954–55 aptly sums up what seems to have been Anderton policy for a century: 'We do

Table 8. A selection of Anderton advertising slogans from the 1930s

Anderton's Manures for every crop you grow
Specialists in Fertilizers for over 60 years
Anderton's helps the Underworld
Be Wise and Fertilise
At the Root of All Good Crops – Anderton's Fertilisers
A starving crop cannot pay
Anderton's aids your pocket through your land
A well-fed crop is a joy to the eye
Feed your crops and have a harvest
Fertility means prosperity
For EVEN CROPS use WELL-BALANCED COMPOUNDS
An old firm with new ideas – Anderton's
You cannot buy better fertilisers than Anderton's
Anderton's Fertilizers cover the countryside
Don't be put off with anything – insist on Anderton's
Here, there, and everywhere – Anderton's Fertilisers
The best is always worth it – Buy Anderton's
Fertilize and economise with Anderton's
You want the best fertilisers – use Anderton's
For Quantity and Quality use Anderton's
The Fields are Fertile with Anderton's
Don't say 'Fertiliser', say Anderton's
Anderton's Fertilisers grow more – better
For 'fruitful' results, use Anderton's
Your land will thank you for Anderton's
Sound dealing and top quality at Anderton's
Feed your crops as you would your stock
Anderton's Fertilisers – They're Wizards in the soil

Source: G. H. Anderton Ltd. advertisements.

not spend vast sums of money on paper advertising; it has always been our policy in building up our business to increase our sales year after year by giving farmers the results they look for.'

Minutes of the annual board meetings of George H. Anderton Ltd. survive from 1908 onwards. Only three directors were appointed, and Mrs Laura Anderton and her future husband Tom Hall had complete control. The years immediately preceding World War I were marked by the construction of new plant, the extension of jetties, the erection of new sheds, and the refurbishing of the company's two sailing keels *Cupro* and *Hydro*. By 1919 Maude Mary Anderton had married Richard Norman Pilling, and both became directors in that year. In 1920 Mrs Pilling took control of 3994 of the 4000 shares. From that year the board of directors was an entirely family affair, comprising Mrs M. M. Pilling, her husband, and the former Laura Anderton and her husband Tom Hall. As in the periods 1867–76 and 1907–18, the firm was officially controlled by females, with the active assistance of husbands or relatives.

With the retirement of the Halls in 1928, the directorate was further simplified, with Mrs Pilling acting as Chairman and her husband as Managing Director. From this date all shares were owned by the Pillings and the firm became, once again, a simple family affair. Thereafter the minutes provide very little information except for the purchase of the motor barge *Colwick* in the 1930s, sailing keels having became redundant. Only in 1954 did assets become divided, first among six relatives, then by the formation of a holding company in a bid to avoid future death duties. In 1958 the firm amalgamated with a long-established York fertilizer and seed business, Henry Richardson and Company, the result being known as Anderton-Richardson Fertilizers Ltd.

The decline of Howdendyke as a port

The Ouse Chemical Works soon became the chief employer in Howdendyke. Whereas the eponymous hamlet of Kilpin parish remained almost wholly agricultural throughout the 1841–81 period, the far bigger village of Howdendyke radically changed in industrial structure (Table 9).

Even with the inclusion of the residual category (retired, annuitant, independent, widowed and pauperized persons), three occupational categories comprise about two-thirds of all occupied household heads in each of the five census years. But whereas shipping, together with associated shipbuilding and distribution services, dominates 1841 (51 per cent) and 1851 (46 per cent), these directly river-related services had fallen to only 26 per cent of all occupations in 1861, eclipsed by agriculture (33 per cent) and almost matched by chemical manufacture (20 per cent).

The 1861 Census clearly demonstrates an ongoing occupational transition begun with the arrival of George Anderton II in 1857. Pre-Anderton

Table 9. Head's industrial group , 1841–81, (%)

Howdendyke						Kilpin				
1841	*1851*	*1861*	*1871*	*1881*		*1841*	*1851*	*1861*	*1871*	*1881*
2	2	2	2	0	Professionals	0	0	0	0	0
19	16	33	10	14	Agriculture	76	80	68	76	80
0	2	1	2	0	Shipbuilding	0	0	0	0	0
0	0	20	33	34	Chemicals	0	0	0	5	0
13	18	13	19	23	Distribution	0	5	0	0	7
38	26	12	12	13	Shipping	0	0	0	5	0
13	16	15	15	9	Services	0	5	16	9	0
0	2	0	2	2	Personal services	0	0	0	0	0
15	18	4	5	5	Residual	24	10	16	5	7

Source: Censuses 1841–81

Table 10. Occupational types in Howdendyke 1841–81

Ouse Chemical Works	*Shipping and Shipbuilding*	*Distribution*
Owner	Shipowner	Coal merchant
Manager	Master of vessel	Corn merchant
Time keeper	Ship's carpenter	Timber dealer
Clerk	Joiner	Clerk
Coachman	Copper plate maker	Coal porter
Groom	Sailor, seaman, mariner	Labourer
Fireman	Boatman, waterman	
Docker	Ferryman	
Engine driver		
Millwright		
Fitter, engineer		
Lead burner		
'Hands', labourers		
Night-watchman		

Source: Censuses 1841–81

Howdendyke was a mosaic of small entrepreneurs engaged in tanning, shipbuilding, and the import and distribution of coal, corn, timber, iron, stone, sand, and gravel. All these were predicated upon the role of Howdendyke as port for the market town of Howden, a role it had served time out of mind (Chapter 3). As a small port connected with both the river traffic and European trade, Howdendyke in the 1840s and 1850s experienced a tide-based rhythm, its life regulated by the arrival and unloading of ships, by the arrival of carriers to meet those ships, and by the well-attended launchings from small shipyards.

These traits continued, although in a subdued fashion, into the late nineteenth century. Ship arrival again dominated economic life after 1968, although the last launch of a Howdendyke-built vessel occurred not long after mid-century. But from the 1860s this essentially small-scale activity, with only the rare employer having more than ten workers, was altered for ever by Anderton enterprise. By 1871 the Anderton family firm employed sixty men and three women in industrial, metal-related capacities totally unlike the wood-based craftsmanship and seamanship which prevailed in Howdendyke before 1861 (Table 10). Class structure also changed, as the semi-skilled craftsmen of the shipping era to 1851 diminished both absolutely and proportionally with the growth of unskilled factory labour to 50 per cent of the village workforce by 1861 (Table 11). As small entrepreneurs disappeared, the upper-middle class was proportionately reduced, although both middle-class and skilled workers increased with the development of the Anderton factory. Throughout the era the hamlet of Kilpin remained agricultural, with a stratum of middle-class farmers and a workforce of agricultural labourers traditionally, though unjustly, categorized as 'unskilled'.

Table 11. Head's socioeconomic group, 1841–81 (%)

Howdendyke						Kilpin				
1841	*1851*	*1861*	*1871*	*1881*		*1841*	*1851*	*1861*	*1871*	*1881*
5	3	3	2	2	Upper Middle	5	0	0	0	0
2	5	10	7	9	Middle	19	25	16	24	33
16	16	21	25	30	Skilled	0	15	16	9	7
43	48	15	15	9	Semi-skilled	5	0	0	5	0
34	28	51	51	50	Unskilled	71	60	68	62	60

Source: Censuses 1841–81

Although the distribution of imported materials continued into the twentieth century, these services were much reduced after the mid-nineteenth century. The founding of the port of Goole in 1826, and the subsequent development of railway lines to both that port and the town of Howden, were severe blows to Howdendyke's role as a river port. Corn, coal, and iron, in particular, were bulky goods very suited to rail transportation, and could readily be delivered to Howden railway station which was more centrally placed than Howdendyke for distribution both to Howden itself and to the Howdenshire district. Further, coal supplies via rail proved to be more reliable than by river, for the three decades from the mid-1850s to the mid-1880s were marked by severe floods and freezes. During floods, when water lay up to two feet deep within Howdendyke's main street, coal carriers had great difficulty in moving their carts. During freezes, Howdendyke ferry could not be worked (although individuals were sometimes able to walk across the Ouse) and coal vessels were unable to reach the port, leaving Howden residents without supplies. Further, Howdendyke's small shipyards producing wooden vessels rarely over 100 tons burthen, became increasingly redundant in the age of steel.

It is not surprising, then, to find evidence of a decline in Howdendyke's distributive trades during the transition from river to rail between the 1840s and the 1880s. From the early 1850s local newspapers contain a number of advertisements for the lease, often followed by an attempted sale, of wharves, warehouses, coalyards and shipyards, and of stocks of stone, coal, timber and iron. In 1870 James Jackson, a Howdendyke coal merchant, attributed his bankruptcy to 'want of trade'.

The deaths of a number of entrepreneurs with small shipping, shipbuilding and industrial interests at Howdendyke also hastened this decline. From the death of Richard Ward in 1852 to that of John Banks in 1879, small river-related entrepreneurs declined in number at Howdendyke. By 1862 John Singleton had abandoned Kilpin Lodge to the Anderton family, given up his multifarious interests in the distribution of corn and other goods, and, perhaps perversely, become a 'dealer in artificial manures' for Tigar's of Beverley.

The Ouse Chemical Works, clearly, was established just in time for the increasingly redundant river port to reorient itself towards a more land-based economic base. For after the 1860s Howdendyke was to become a basically one-industry community, with one-third of all household heads directly employed in the Chemical Works, and with a majority of those in the 'distribution' and 'shipping' categories in close connection with chemical manufacture. For Anderton's became an important multiplier factor in Howdendyke, employing the services of nominally independent shipbuilders, vessel operators, sack-makers, basket-weavers, brick-makers, carriers, coal and timber merchants, builders and eventually, farmworkers.

Only two small shipyards, Caiseley's at Kilpinpike and Chester's in the heart of Howdendyke village, and the timber yard of H. B. Anderson on Howdendyke Creek, retained a measure of economic independence. All these operations continued into the 1890s, but did not reach the twentieth century. During the Depression G. H. Anderton Ltd. was able to purchase not only much of the Howdendyke land and housing belonging to these firms, but also Ferry Farm, which had lost part of its *raison d'être* with the closure of Howdendyke ferry in 1929.

Two other economic trends are worth noting. When Howdendyke could be characterised as a completely 'open' village, before the 1870s, it supported a variety of services, including several public houses, a butcher, a bootmaker, several general shops, a barber, a tailor and the usual complement of dressmakers, seamstresses, and milliners. Indeed, in 1851 over 16 per cent of the occupied population were engaged in such services. Such occupations were strongly related to Howdendyke's role as a river port, as were the 18 per cent of household heads classed as 'residual' in 1851, some of them non-employed sailors' wives, their husbands absent aboard ship. This residual class rapidly dropped between 1851 and 1861, to one quarter of its former strength, as more of the male population were employed, on land, in the Chemical Works. After a lag of almost a generation, the service population suffered its greatest decline in the 1871–81 period, a combination of easier access to nearby Howden town, the growth of rural deliveries by Howden merchants, and agricultural depression resulting in lay-offs at the Chemical Works and a fall in Howdendyke's population (from 265 in 1871 to 196 in 1881) below the threshold required for many of these small specialist service trades. By the early twentieth century, only three small general stores remained.

The connection with Howden remained of great importance, but reversed itself in the 1860s. By 1871, no longer of great importance as Howden's river port, Howdendyke had become a major source of employment for Howden and district. Traditionally a market town with no major industries or large employment sources, Howden came gradually to rely upon Howdendyke as an important supplier of jobs. Of the sixty men employed by Andertons in 1871, no more than twenty were Howdendyke residents. The importance of Howdendyke for Howden's social and political, as well as economic, life is outlined in the following chapters.

Demographic changes

From the 1830s to the 1850s Howdendyke's population hovered around the 250 mark. The sharp rise to 338 in 1861 was occasioned by the influx both of workmen engaged in the construction of the Ouse Chemical Works and of prospective employees of the fertilizer factory. By 1871 the population had fallen back to a more normal figure of 265, and by 1881, with the loss of traditional economic mainstays and the onset of agricultural depression which depressed the fertilizer market, the population had fallen to less than 200 (Table 12). In that year at least twenty-nine village houses were unoccupied. Revival came with the new century, but the population of the village remained little more than 200 into the 1960s, whereafter it began a precipitous decline, the causes of which are analyzed in detail in the third part of this book.

It is instructive, throughout the period 1841–81 for which manuscript census returns are available, to compare the demographic characteristics of industrial Howdendyke with those of the much smaller agrarian hamlet of Kilpin close by. There are some similarities. Throughout the 40 year period, Kilpin households were larger, one of the chief differences being the existence in Kilpin of large farm households involving several live-in labourers and servants (Table 13). This is confirmed by an analysis of the size of the head of household's actual family (Table 14), which demonstrates that Howdendyke had relatively more families, though not more households, in the 'over 9 persons' category. The average number of children per family was approximately two throughout the period in both villages (Table 12). In both places households were dominated by married males, with widowed females usually forming the second largest category (Table 15).

Despite the rapid expansion of Howdendyke in the construction period 1857–62, Kilpin consistently displayed a larger proportion of families sharing accommodation (Table 16). Again, only in 1861, when 21 per cent of Howdendyke households contained lodgers, did Kilpin have proportionately fewer households with lodgers than Howdendyke (Table 17). Except for lodgers, most of whom were single men, no severe housing shortage appears to have existed at Howdendyke.

Overall, agricultural Kilpin's households were more diverse than those of Howdendyke. A Kilpin household was much more likely to include another sharing family (Table 16), lodgers (Table 17), relatives (Table 18), and domestic servants (Table 19). Throughout the period, few major Howdendyke industrialists actually lived in the village; John Banks and H. B. Anderson were successively residents of Howden Hall. Other entrepreneurs kept few servants; in both 1871 and 1881 the Anderton household had only two live-in servants, a cook and a housemaid. By contrast, Kilpin farmers had traditionally kept live-in house servants as well as farm labourers.

Throughout the period, Howdendyke's total population was never less than twice, but never more than three times that of Kilpin (Figures 11, 12). The greatest absolute discrepancy appears in 1861 when Howdendyke, at the peak of its construction phase, had 338 inhabitants to Kilpin's 122. Except for this

Table 12. Number of children of head (%)

	Howdendyke					Kilpin				
	1841	1851	1861	1871	1881	1841	1851	1861	1871	1881
0	21	26	22	23	23	24	35	24	38	27
1–2	41	43	37	40	36	33	25	40	38	40
3–5	32	30	31	31	27	33	30	24	24	27
6+	6	1	10	6	14	10	10	12	0	6
(mean)	(2.1)	(1.9)	(2.2)	(2.0)	(2.5)	(2.3)	(2.2)	(2.2)	(1.2)	(2.1)

Table 13. Persons per household, 1841–81 (%)

	Howdendyke					Kilpin				
	1841	1851	1861	1871	1881	1841	1851	1861	1871	1881
1	7	3	3	3	4	0	0	8	19	0
2	16	17	14	13	21	19	30	8	10	20
3–5	50	56	55	66	41	48	35	48	38	46
6–8	23	21	21	15	27	14	25	32	19	27
9+	4	3	7	3	7	19	10	4	14	7
(mean)	(4.2)	(4.1)	(4.7)	(4.2)	(4.7)	(5.2)	(4.9)	(4.3)	(4.9)	(4.9)

Table 14. Persons in head's family, 1841–81 (%)

	Howdendyke					Kilpin				
	1841	1851	1861	1871	1881	1841	1851	1861	1871	1881
1	9	10	7	8	4	9	0	12	28	13
2	21	28	18	16	25	19	40	20	19	13
3–5	44	41	55	63	43	48	35	48	43	60
6–8	24	21	17	11	21	24	20	20	10	13
9+	2	0	3	2	7	0	5	0	0	0
(mean)	(3.9)	(3.6)	(4.0)	(3.8)	(4.3)	(4.1)	(4.1)	(3.9)	(2.8)	(3.9)

Table 15. Household type, 1841–81 (%)

	Howdendyke					Kilpin				
	1841	1851	1861	1871	1881	1841	1851	1861	1871	1881
Married male	79	74	78	81	80	76	90	76	62	80
Single male	5	0	1	0	0	0	0	0	5	0
Widowed male	0	3	8	2	4	5	5	4	24	7
Married female	5	2	3	6	2	0	0	0	0	0
Single female	0	0	0	1	0	0	0	4	0	0
Widowed female	11	21	10	10	14	19	5	16	9	13

Table 16. Another sharing family, 1841–81 (%)

	Howdendyke					Kilpin				
	1841	1851	1861	1871	1881	1841	1851	1861	1871	1881
No	98	98	99	100	100	100	90	96	95	100
Yes	2	2	1	0	0	0	10	4	5	0

Table 17. Number of lodgers per household, 1841–81 (%)

	Howdendyke					Kilpin				
	1841	1851	1861	1871	1881	1841	1851	1861	1871	1881
0	95	92	79	87	89	76	85	84	71	80
1	0	2	13	8	4	14	5	4	10	7
2+	5	7	8	5	7	10	10	12	19	13

Table 18. Number of relatives per household, 1841–81 (%)

	Howdendyke					Kilpin				
	1841	1851	1861	1871	1881	1841	1851	1861	1871	1881
0	87	82	82	94	93	67	85	64	71	73
1	11	16	12	6	7	33	5	24	14	27
2+	2	2	6	0	0	0	10	12	15	0

Table 19. Number of domestic servants per household, 1841–81 (%)

	Howdendyke					Kilpin				
	1841	*1851*	*1861*	*1871*	*1881*	*1841*	*1851*	*1861*	*1871*	*1881*
0	95	95	96	81	96	86	90	96	81	80
1	3	3	1	9	0	0	5	0	9	13
2+	2	2	3	10	4	14	5	4	10	7

Table 20. Head's age, 1841–81 (%)

	Howdendyke					Kilpin				
	1841	*1851*	*1861*	*1871*	*1881*	*1841*	*1851*	*1861*	*1871*	*1881*
Under 35	23	26	35	23	23	29	20	16	14	20
35 – 54	48	38	36	50	45	33	45	36	33	40
Over 54	29	36	29	27	32	38	35	48	53	40

upswing in 1861 – largely a brief response to expanding Howdendyke's need for accommodation – Kilpin shows a steady decline in population throughout the period accompanied by the gradual shrinking of the base of its population pyramid from its most 'normal' position in 1841.

In contrast, Howdendyke's pyramid approaches 'normality' most closely in 1861 and 1871, with a severe contraction, due to agricultural depression and the release of labour, in 1881. Throughout the period Howdendyke's population remained considerably younger than that of Kilpin, where heads of households over the age of fifty-four comprised approximately half of all household heads in 1861 and 1871 (Table 20). The population pyramids confirm the relative youthfulness of Howdendyke's population.

Equally great contrasts are to be found in the origins of the populations of the two places (Tables 21, 22). Throughout the period, between one half and

Table 21. Head's birthplace, 1851–81 (%)

Howdendyke					Kilpin			
1851	*1861*	*1871*	*1881*		*1851*	*1861*	*1871*	*1881*
1	10	13	16	Howdendyke	0	4	0	0
25	5	3	0	Kilpin	30	16	24	27
15	15	14	21	Howden	0	4	5	7
1	1	0	2	Goole	0	0	0	0
25	32	34	18	Within 7 miles	45	40	43	20
15	17	16	25	Within 15 miles	15	24	19	33
8	5	5	5	Agricultural East Riding	10	8	0	0
7	6	8	11	Industrial West Riding	0	0	0	7
3	3	7	0	Rest of U.K.	0	4	9	7
0	6	0	2	Foreign	0	0	0	0

three quarters of Kilpin's population were born either in the hamlet or within 7 miles of it. There were no foreigners, and very few from any part of Britain other than the largely agrarian East Riding of Yorkshire. In contrast to this high degree of localness, Howdendyke's population was rather cosmopolitan in both pre-Anderton and post-1857 eras. The census entries for 'Kilpin' and 'Howdendyke' are ambiguous, but even in 1841 the village of Howdendyke had little more than a quarter of its population born in the parish. From 1861 this proportion diminished to approximately 15 per cent and remained there into the 1880s.

For, unlike agricultural Kilpin, the riverport of Howdendyke in 1851 drew a considerable proportion of its population from among the Howden-born, there being a natural connection between a market town and its port. After 1851, however, those born in Howden and within 7 miles rose from 40 per cent to almost 50 per cent, demonstrating that the boom caused by the development of chemical manufacturing was of greatest benefit to the immediate district. Yet dynamic Howdendyke's net was cast much wider than static Kilpin's. Heads of households born more than 7 miles away rose from one-third of the total in 1851 to 43 per cent in 1881. Those originating in the industrial West Riding, in other parts of Britain, or abroad rose from 10 per cent in 1851 to 15 per cent in subsequent census years. Relatively cosmopolitan in the immediately pre-Anderton era, Howdendyke became much more so in the decades immediately after the establishment of the Ouse Chemical Works. In particular, management and skilled tradesmen had to be brought in by George Anderton II as local people had no experience of factory work in general, or chemical manufacture in particular.

In many ways the Howdendyke of 1871 and 1881 was not demographically different from that of 1841 and 1851. Once the crowded construction years around 1861 were over, the chief differences were that the population was younger than before, contained very few old people, and was considerable more

Table 22. Head's wife's birthplace, 1851–81 (%)

Howdendyke					Kilpin			
1851	1861	1871	1881		1851	1861	1871	1881
0	0	8	13	Howdendyke	0	11	0	0
18	5	2	0	Kilpin	22	33	25	17
7	18	18	16	Howden	0	0	25	0
0	2	0	0	Goole	0	0	0	0
27	38	40	44	Within 7 miles	56	33	33	25
14	11	14	10	Within 15 miles	17	17	17	42
16	14	10	7	Agricultural East Riding	5	6	0	0
7	4	4	7	Industrial West Riding	0	0	0	0
9	2	2	3	Rest of U.K.	0	0	0	17
2	6	0	0	Foreign	0	0	0	0

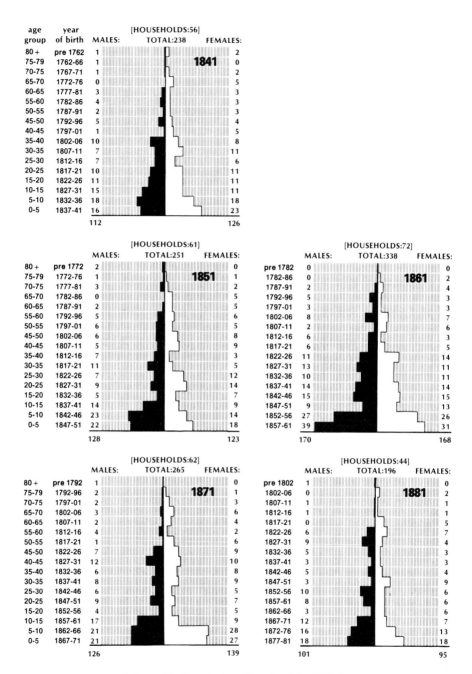

Figure 11. Population, Howdendyke 1841–81

The Anderton era

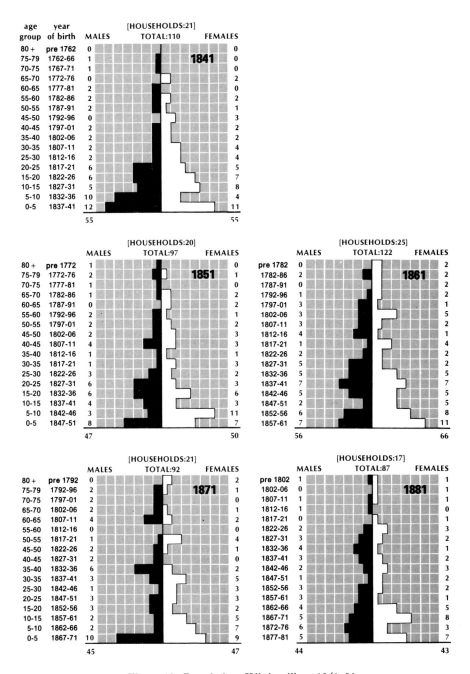

Figure 12. Population, Kilpin village 1841–81

63

cosmopolitan. In short, the Howdendyke of the early Anderton years displayed a number of the characteristics associated with boom towns and new towns throughout the industrial world. The consequent changes in social class structure and especially, occupational structure, have already been noted.

Scarr's Shipyard

With the loss of traditional shipyards, distributive trades, and some services, early twentieth-century Howdendyke looked to the Ouse Chemical Works for economic survival. The only important employment alternative after 1900 was a small shipyard upriver of Ferry Farm.

As had occurred with the Andertons, a family firm of Beverley shipbuilders branched out as sons could not be accommodated in the original plant. Three sons took shipyards at Beverley, Hessle, and Howdendyke. The Howdendyke yard, inherited by Tom Scarr, was begun in 1902 at the half-way point between the firm's chief customers in York and Hull. Tom Scarr also inherited the Howdendyke shipbuilding mantle by purchasing Caiseley's tools. Originally run as a family firm, it became D. E. Scarr Ltd. in 1934 when Donald Scarr took over.

Scarr's shipyard reached its zenith very early. Its employment peaked at about thirty men before World War I. Thereafter the number of employees stabilized at about twenty, falling during the Depression and again in the 1950s. Until its closure in 1968 the yard never again employed more than fifteen men, and at times the number fell below ten. I was a labourer in the yard for six months in 1962, followed by two months as chief clerk (there was only one clerk). Except for the brief decade of expansion before World I, at no time did Scarr's shipyard provide more than one quarter the number of jobs available at the Ouse Chemical Works.

Beginning by building traditional Humber keels, the yard quickly moved to the construction of Thames barges, seagoing lighters, and 150-ton steam vessels, increasingly in steel rather than the English oak beloved by Banks and Caiseley. By the 1920s one of the chief products was sailing sloops for a Goole shipping firm, but these gradually gave way to motor barges in the 1930s (Table 23). After World II a number of vessels of up to 250 tons deadweight were built, but the competition of larger yards soon reduced the yard to 'bread and butter' repair work and the building of the occasional yacht.

The closure of the yard in 1968 came with the retirement of Donald Scarr. The yard was in irretrievable decline, for the Admiralty, its best customer, had decided no longer to contract work out to private yards. Further, traditional barge traffic on the Ouse was rapidly dwindling. On the other hand, several firms were seeking deepwater river berths for the unloading of imports from ocean-going vessels. Howdendyke happens to have one of the deepest berths,

Table 23. Vessels built by Scarr's Shipyard and registered in Hull and Goole, 1903–68

Decade	No. of vessels built	Registered tonnage	Average tonnage per vessel	Vessel types
1902–11	17	1863	109	lighters
1912–21	5	758	152	lighters
1922–31	24	2137	89	sloops, lighters, barges
1932–41	2	151	75	lighters
1942–51	2	259	130	barges
1952–61	10	1051	105	barges
1962–71	2	30	15	yachts

Source: Hull and Goole shipping registers 1900–80 (there are no surviving company records).

with up to 30 feet of water at low tide, between Goole and Selby. One such firm offered Donald Scarr a good price.

This development, involving the search by import distributors for sites for private river wharves whereby they could avoid dock dues in major ports, was to have profound effects upon Howdendyke. The process is described in part III of this book.

Towards a closed village

Rural historians commonly make a distinction between the 'open' village with many owner-occupiers and small entrepreneurs, and the 'closed' village where land-ownership is dominated by a single employer who rents tied dwellings to his tenants (Mills 1972, 1980). Quite naturally, liberal historians tend to favour the dynamic open village, often radical in politics and nonconformist in religion, over the static, establishment atmosphere which often prevailed in so-called 'feudal' villages during the Victorian era.

Howdendyke was clearly an open village in the pre-Anderton era. Several coal merchants, shipbuilders, and timber yards were in active competition. Much housing was owner-occupied. No single person or firm dominated either employment or housing, although a number of persons had considerable standing. These included: Richard Ward of Kilpinpike, shipowner, shipbuilder, coal merchant, and tanner; the successive tenants of Ferry Farm, who farmed over 30 acres, operated the ferry, had local fishing rights for salmon, and doubled as landlord of the Steam Packet; other publicans, who habitually kept grocery stores or were coal merchants, or both; and H. B. Anderson and John Banks, Howden residents but operators of sawmill and shipyard respectively. For the workpeople of Howdendyke, a variety of opportunities were available in both employment and house-renting, and there was always the lure of river and sea-going life.

For all directories indicate that at mid-century Howdendyke was very well-connected indeed to nearby towns. Market boats left up to three times per week for Hull. Steam packets plying between the towns of Hull, Goole, and Selby passed the village daily and were always ready to pick up or discharge passengers. Special excursion boats from Goole inevitably took on passengers from Howdendyke pursuing their day-trips to York, Spurn Point, Hull, or the Trent. Later in the century this traffic declined, especially with the development of two railway stations at Howden and a third at Saltmarshe on the Hull-Goole line which crossed the Ouse on a bridge built in 1869 between Howdendyke and Goole.

Howdendyke was considered sufficiently important for a sub-Post Office to be inaugurated in 1875, and in 1893 an enterprising individual set up a waggonette service which ran three times daily between Howdendyke and Goole via Howdendyke Ferry. These innovations, however, did not compensate for the gradual loss of immediate river connections to large cities. In fact, it could be argued that until the rise of car ownership in Howdendyke in the 1960s, largely bus-less twentieth century Howdendyke was relatively more isolated from its region than it had been a century before. This isolation increased in the 1930s when the ferry became defunct.

Both the decline of traditional river trades in the Railway Age and the immense developments inaugurated by George Anderton II began the trend towards a closed community from the 1860s. A comparison of several directories over two generations illustrates the trend (Table 24). Clearly, both alternative employment sources and specialist services were severely reduced by the turn of the nineteenth century, the first in response to Howden's reorientation from river to rail, the second in response to population decline and the increasing use of services provided by the town of Howden. By the early twentieth century Howdendykers, should they wish to work and shop in the village, had the choice of two stores and the Post Office for shopping and the Chemical Works and the small shipyard for employment.

Howdendyke never became a fully 'closed' community in terms of employment, although it was clearly dominated by the Chemical Works which almost always employed at least four times as many people as Scarr's shipyard. Nor was the village ever fully 'closed' in terms of housing ownership, complete one-entrepreneur ownership being prevented by the building of eight council houses in 1936 and a further eight twelve years later.

It is impossible to ascertain whether the Andertons ever envisaged complete control of land and housing in Howdendyke. Certainly, the company built few new houses. From the 1870s, however, George III and his successors made strenuous efforts to extend their property holdings. Data gathered from the East Riding County Deeds Registry in Beverley, from Howden Manor Court records, and from deeds now held by BritAg Ltd., suggest that three separate

Table 24. **Towards a closed community: Howdendyke/Kilpinpike 1831–1937**

Facility	Directory year	1831	1846	1858	1864	1879	1887	1892	1928	1937
	Population (est.)	(230)	(240)	(320)	(320)	(200)	(220)	(220)	(220)	(200)
Shipbuilders		2	2	2	2	2	2	1	1	1
Tanners		1	1							
Chemical manufacturers				1	1	1	1	1	1	1
Timber merchants		2	2	2	2	1	1	1		
Coal merchants		3	5	3	2	2	1			
Corn merchants		1	1	1						
Seed merchants					1					
Sand, lime, stone merchants		1	1	1			1			
Butchers		1	1	1	1					
Blacksmiths				1	1					
Coopers				1						
Shopkeepers		1	1	3	3	3	3	2	2	2
Post office and grocery							1	1	1	1	1

Sources: Yorkshire and East Riding Directories.

thrusts comprise most of George III's property purchases. First, and least important from our point of view, George III purchased a large number of farms, fields, and other property in a variety of scattered locations within the Howdenshire district. Most of these were sold off in 1904. Second, successful efforts were made to take control of the rival Tigar's Fertilizers of Beverley, which was finally absorbed in 1924.

Most important for Howdendyke was the third thrust, which seemed to embody a determination to control as much property and housing in Howdendyke as possible (Figure 10). In the late nineteenth century most of Howdendyke's dwellings were located on the riverfront from Kilpinpike to Ferry Farm. North Street, leading from Kilpin Landing and the Post Office, towards Howden, was lined by Anderson's timberyard and cottages on one side, and by a row of cottages on the other. Further from the river were Tutty Row (five houses, with Woodbine Cottage) and Prospect Villas (twelve terrace houses including The Cottage), both erected after 1860 with the growth of the Ouse Chemical Works.

From the late 1870s George III began systematically purchasing all Howdendyke's waterfront property (Table 25). Almost all the former warehouses and cottages of the Square were in his hands by 1889, and in 1900 H. B. Anderson's timberyard, warehouses, sheds, and cottages on North Street were bought. Some of these warehouses were demolished, and three new company houses built. A little further north, the Andertons built New Row (nine cottages) in celebration of Maude Mary's wedding to R. N. Pilling.

After George III's death in 1907, the directors of George H. Anderton Ltd. continued their drive towards complete control of the village and its environs. In 1915 and 1923 the last two buildings in the Square, one of them the Anchor Inn, were bought. In 1909 Kilpin Brickyard and cottages, its brickpond long the source of Ouse Chemical Works water, was purchased, to be followed in 1917 by four of the Prospect Villas.

The last two privately-built houses to rise in Howdendyke (Ouse Cottage and Studley House, Elm Tree) were built by a farmer in 1911. These were purchased by G. H. Anderton Ltd. in 1945, culminating a burst of Depression-era purchases which brought Ferry Farm, houses at Elm Tree, all of Tutty Row (five houses), and many fields adjacent to Howdendyke into company control.

After 1945 only The Cottage (purchased 1947), the seven remaining cottages in Prospect Villas (1952), and Kilham Cottage (1954) remained for the

Table 25. Anderton property purchases 1857–1966

Date	Description (see Figure 4)	From
1857	Inn and Clayton Close (4.5 acres)	Tyas et al.
1858	Tanyard, house, cottage (The Square) and Tanyard Close (6.5 acres)	Ward jnr.
1860	Kilpin Lodge Cottages (former shipyard)	Cuttill
1862	Kilpin Lodge (former cornmill and cottages)	Singleton
1887	Cottage (former warehouse), The Square	Greenwood
1889	5 Cottages (former warehouse), 3 cottages (former houses) in North Street	Little/Miller
1889	2 houses, Ferry Road (former timber yard)	Little
1889	Cottages and land, North Street	Little
1900	Wharf, timber yard, cottages (0.5 acre)	Anderson
1909	Kilpin Brick yard (Sunny Bank)	Carter
1915	Cottage, opposite post office	Schofield
1917	4 cottages and land (part of Prospect Villas)	Watson
1923	Anchor Inn	Watson
1930	Ferry Farm and Steam Packet Inn (32 acres)	Scott
1932	Tutty Row (3 houses)	Tutty/Cooper
1932	Woodbine Cottage	Cooper
1936	Wire Cross Close (4 acres)	Shaw
1941	Shop in Tutty Row	Cooper
1945	Studley House (Elm Tree) and Ouse Cottage (Howdendyke)	Blyth
1947	The Cottage (Ferry Road, end of Prospect Villas)	Hall
1952	Remaining 7 cottages, Prospect Villas	Smithson
1954	Kilham Cottage (Ferry Road, 'factory side')	Hall
1964	Area of rubble, former cottage (Ferry Road, 'factory side')	Beverley

Source: East Riding Deeds Registry, Beverley; BritAg. deeds.

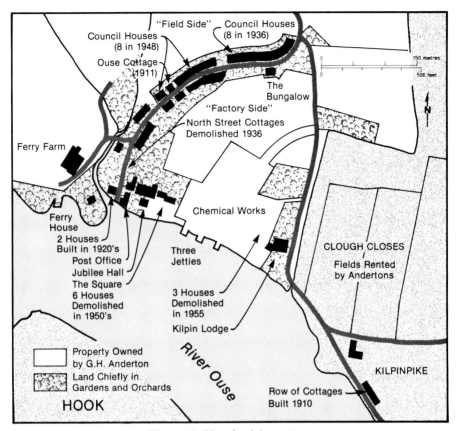

Figure 13. Howdendyke *c.*1955

company to buy. A handwritten company memorandum relates to the latter two properties and demonstrates the general Anderton policy of fairly low rents:

> 29 July 1952
>
> Mrs ⸻ asks
> Do we wish to buy Prospect Villas, H. Dyke? Thinks they would be cheap (£175-200). Let at 4/6 per week (one 5/6) inc. Rates – 7 cottages –
> (would then own the who [sic] Triangle excepting for Mr Hall's cottage).
>
> Sat. Aug. 9th
>
> Mr P. phoned Mrs ⸻ who promised us first refusal.

Except for a small area of rubble, bought in 1964, G. H. Anderton Ltd. was now sole controller of Howdendyke, with the exceptions of Kilpinpike and the Post Office (five houses, four owned by the Mell family), Ferry House (Ecclesiastical Commissioners) and sixteen Council houses. And, in particular, the company had sole control of works, field, and all housing situated within the triangle formed by the roads leading into and around Howdendyke (Figure 13).

Hardly had the 'whole Triangle' become Anderton property when Mrs (1959) and Mr (1960) Pilling died. It is not possible to ascertain what use, if any, they intended to make of their almost total control of the village of Howdendyke. According to a niece, the Pillings hoped that Eric Hall, a young relative, would take over the business for them, but he refused. No one else in the family was able or willing to continue G. H. Anderton Ltd. as a family firm. 'When they knew Eric was not interested in the works and they were both getting older they both seemed to lose heart.'

The use made of the 'whole Triangle' by their successors, however, has resulted in the destruction, at the time of writing, of more than half the village's housing and the general demoralization of the community.

5

Masters and men

In Memoriam
George Herbert Anderton
(Howdendyke)
This Memorial was placed here by the
employees of the Ouse Chemical Works
In Loving Memory of
Their Devoted Master and Friend
November 20th. 1907

Memorial tablet,
Howden Minster

Mainstream Victorian history threads a broad channel between two extremes. At one side the Scylla of the *Supermensch*, beloved of Nietzsche and Carlyle, faces on the other the Charybdis of the inexorable economic processes propounded by Marx and Engels. As almost everywhere, the history of Howdendyke clearly involves both.

On the one hand, historical processes rendered extremely likely the decline or even demise of Howdendyke as a river port in the century 1850–1950. Both goods and passengers were more readily handled by rail and road with the coming of the successive railway and early motor ages; Howdendyke's shipping and distributive functions correspondingly declined. Small wooden ships lost ground to steel vessels in the late nineteenth century; the closure of small shipbuilding yards and the opening of Scarr's shipyard on modern metal-working lines is Howdendyke's contribution the spirit of the age. And as working peoples' horizons widened with improvements in transportation, local services declined. The only constant, it seemed, in the Howdendyke of 1857–1959, was the Ouse Chemical Works.

Here the social scientist's second hand comes into play. For the Ouse Chemical Works cannot be regarded as some monolithic, faceless business enterprise. On the contrary, the factory and what increasingly became its village was the creation of a single family and, for the formative period 1876–1907, of a single man.

Eighteenth- and nineteenth-century British history includes an unbroken thread of capitalist benevolence, based on a fairly rigid class structure. Nonconformist industrialists, and Quakers in particular, were keen to rehouse their workers in good, often rural, conditions. Although this may have been a management ploy ('the content worker is a good worker'), a strong vein of religious enthusiasm and genuine charity was also involved. The villages of Bournville (Cadbury), New Earswick (Rowntree) and many others remain as testimony to this desire to extend the benefits of capitalism beyond the capitalist's drawing-room. This benevolence, however, was largely confined to small towns and 'country mills', for suburban owners quickly lost contact with and feeling for their workers (Dennis 1980). The Anderton family, staunch nonconformists before their arrival in Howdendyke, were very much a part of this tradition of benevolent capitalism and did not lose it when, in the rural environment of East Yorkshire with its great landed estates, they naturally became Anglicans.

Social life in Howdendyke

On reading reports of newsworthy Howdendyke activities from the 1850s to the 1920s, I not unexpectedly found them little different from those of other Howdenshire villages, with the exception of river-related stories. I was most charmed to find that the events most likely to be reported by the newspapers in the 1870s were not very different from those I witnessed or heard of as a child in the district in the 1940s and 1950s, the chief difference being a gradual reduction in violence over the years. Indeed, from the evidence of surnames, it appears that in many cases the same families were involved.

Late nineteenth-century Howdendyke had its share of arson, particularly rick-burnings, drunken brawls, poaching, straying cattle, mad dogs, and the like. Particularly related to the river are incidents of drowning, especially of children falling from jetties while playing; inquests on waterlogged corpses were held in the Jolly Sailor Inn at Skelton or the Steam Packet at Howdendyke. As a child I was not allowed to view river-borne corpses but clearly remember a childhood friend drowning in the river near my home.

Some evidence of an almost defunct rural traditionalism appears in a report of an incident of 'riding the stang' in 1887. This old custom involves the forcible riding of the victim, usually a malicious gossip or adulterer, through the street upon a hurdle or field gate to the general ridicule of the populace. In this case the victim was an un-named woman, and the urban(e) reporter expressed surprise at the continuance of such a custom which by the 1880s had become 'interesting to read about, but more honoured in the breach than the observance' (*Goole Weekly Times*, 19 August 1887). It is quite likely that the participants had also blithely attended the village's regular 'service of song' held at the Congregational Sunday School some time earlier.

Despite the words of the well-known hymn, the daily round and common task rarely furnish all we need to ask, and moreover are not reported in the newspapers. There are few reports of any kind of social event before the arrival of the Andertons, and they chiefly relate to the formation of a branch of Howden's Independent Chapel at Howdendyke, probably in the 1840s.

As befits a settlement of small entrepreneurs, nonconformists dominated Howdendyke in the pre-Anderton era. As I have noted, the Cleckheaton Andertons were strongly imbued with the Liberal, Nonconformist tradition, but although remaining Liberal in politics into the twentieth century, the Howdendyke Andertons had taken on the protective colouration of middle-class Anglicanism by the 1860s. Nevertheless, many of their workmen remained staunch Independents, Congregationalists, or Primitive Methodists; Howdendykers were especially strong supporters of the latter sect. Howden's Primitive Methodist baptismal registers for the period 1873–1937 record that an average of 14.4 per cent of baptisms were of persons from Howdendyke and Kilpinpike, rising to 25 per cent in the period 1892–97. Most of my Mell relatives were baptised as Primitive Methodists.

All of these related sects used a small building known generally as the 'school room' in Howdendyke. Wesleyans were accommodated by a small chapel in Kilpin hamlet, while a further chapel, unused during the period 1868–1883, was located downriver in the hamlet of Skelton.

From the 1840s at least, regular Independent and Congregational Sunday School services were held in the schoolroom (for regular schooling Howdendyke children walked to Howden). Most Congregational Sunday School treats were held in Howden, but major religious events, after performance at the Howden chapel, were reenacted at Howdendyke. Thus, in the 1880s, Howdendyke chapelgoers enjoyed oratorio performances of *Abraham, Elijah, Elisha,* and *Ruth*. The congregation for the latter was so large that many had to stand outside to listen. Through the 1880s and 1890s the 'schoolroom' was variously known as the 'mission room' and even the 'town hall', a rather lofty designation for a village of 200 people. Rebuilt in 1889 and furnished with electric light by G. H. Anderton as early as 1890, it was the scene of meetings of the Temperance Band of Hope, Mothers' Meeting, Congregational Sunday School, Primitive Methodist Sunday, harvest festival and Easter services, missionary meetings, and performances by Howdendyke choir, as well as more secular 'entertainments', 'Penny Readings', parties, and dances.

The Jubilee Hall, as it was known after 1935, continued in regular use into the 1960s for parties and dances, but its religious function ended after World War II. Many older Howdendykers have fond memories of Sunday schools and services in the 'schoolroom', and recall the homeliness of lay preachers, particularly the one whose nose-picking son always accompanied him, leading to pronouncements such as: 'And the Lord said unto Moses – get that finger down your nostril!' More legitimate secular amusement was derived from Howdendyke Feast and the village football club. The feast, an unremarkable village fair until the transformation wrought by G. H. Anderton in the late 1870s, was rarely noted in the district newspaper unless some magnificent brawl ensued or drunken revellers fell from the ferry and drowned. The fair barely survived the nineteenth century but the football club, victorious throughout the district in the 1880s, expanded to two teams and remained in good fettle until World War II, after which it was replaced by a village cricket team.

But whereas Sunday schools, football, and the fair were weekly, seasonal, or annual events, normal social life revolved around work, home, and pubs for men, while women chiefly relied on the shops and seasonal agricultural work for relationships outside the home. This sexual division of social lives, men in factory and pub, women in shops and fields, continued well into the 1950s.

Masters: the Anderton family

Industrially, as we have seen, Howdendyke was gradually transformed after 1857 from a port village of many small entrepreneurs into a factory village dominated by a single major employer. Furthermore, that employer gradually became the driving force behind formal social activity in the village.

Because of its riverside position, Howdendyke has always been subject to flooding caused by exceptionally high tides, river icing, or severe storms. The 'precautions' described by a newspaper report of 1874 were probably similar to those taken by the riverside residents of the 1940s and 1950s, chiefly consisting of wooden boards ('dam-boards') placed in prepared slots to block the front door and made watertight by sand-bags. In severe winter storms, these precautions were insufficient, and residents suffered great distress. Before the arrival of the Andertons such distress was relieved by the concerted action of local worthies. In 1855, for example, the Howdendyke Soup Kitchen fed about fifty poor families with beef, bread, and soup paid for by local entrepreneurs and made by Mrs Duckles of Ferry Farm. With the rise to ascendancy of the Andertons these collective charitable enterprises became the prerogative of a single family (Figure 9).

The growth in importance of the Anderton family in Howdendyke and district was slowed by the sudden death of George Anderton II in 1866 at the early age of forty. George II had spent only ten years building up his Ouse Chemical Works, and did not occupy Kilpin Lodge until the Singletons vacated it in the early 1860s. He found time, however, to continue the Cleckheaton tradition of benign employer-worker relationships in the form of large Christmas parties such as the one held in Howdendyke on Christmas Eve 1861. Workmen and wives, totalling 132 in number, proposed the health of Mr and Mrs Anderton:

Mr. Anderton replied on behalf of himself and lady. The Rev. Geo. Richards, of Howden, then gave an able address on the desirableness of cultivating good-feeling between employer and employed. Dr. Hartley proposed the health of the men, their wives and families. The rest of the evening was spent in a highly agreeably manner, all feeling their increasing obligations to their generous employer, who, in the midst of the comforts and luxuries of his own home at this festive season of the year was not unmindful of those beneath him in the social scale, to whom he thus afforded so much enjoyment and gratification (*Goole and Marshland Gazette*, 1 January 1862).

This paternalist social tone, very appropriate to the mid-Victorian context, became the norm for the Andertons during the remainder of their 100 years as chief employers of the villagers of Howdendyke.

Although George II had clearly made the acquaintance of local physicians, lawyers, industrialists, and churchmen by 1861, a social ambience which was to characterise the family into the 1950s, the Anderton name did not become prominent in Howden social circles for a number of years. Indeed, the report of a Howden 'society ball' of 1860 contains the names of several worthies with business interests at Howdendyke, including H. B. Anderson the timber merchant, John Banks the shipowner and shipbuilder, and John Singleton, general agent and merchant, of Kilpin Lodge. A directory of 1864 lists fifty-two 'gentry and clergy' in the Howden district, only ten of whom merit the title 'Esq.' and only one, Mrs Westoby Ward, resident in Howdendyke.

George Anderton, in fact, achieved greatest notice in the local newspaper by dying unexpectedly, aged only forty, on 17 December 1866 (*Goole and Marshland Gazette*, 1 January 1867). His body left Howden for burial at Cleckheaton at the head of a cortege of nearly one hundred people, including forty employees of the Chemical Works, many residents of Howden, and members of the St Cuthbert's (Howden) lodge of Freemasons.

His son, George (III) Herbert Anderton, born 16 May 1855 at Cleckheaton, received little notice until his coming of age in 1876. Educated at Huddersfield College, Owens College, Manchester, and in Germany, George III inherited the management of the Chemical Works from his mother and uncle at the age of twenty-one. On 16 May 1876 the 'houses and vessels at Howden-dyke and Kilpin-pike presented a very gay appearance as a compliment to the Anderton family who are held in very high esteem by the inhabitants' (*Goole and Marshland Weekly Times*, 19 May 1876). At a select gathering at the Half Moon Hotel, Howden, George III accepted a gift from his workmen as a sign of esteem not only towards himself but toward his mother. The vicar then eulogised Mrs Anderton for her work in carrying on and expanding the Chemical Works while a widow, while at the same time not neglecting her religious duties nor her helping of 'suffering humanity'. H. B. Anderson, owner of Howdendyke Sawmill, proposed 'success to the Howdendyke chemical works' which, despite some recent drawbacks seemed now well on the road to prosperity. He also proposed the health of the workmen and their wives, while the works manager re-emphasized the importance of making 'the Howden-dyke chemical works beneficial both to employer and employed'.

Little more than a year later Mrs Anderton married a Mr Brook and moved to Huddersfield, and shortly afterwards George III was offering 'good wages' to a prospective cook. The marriage was again the occasion of great festivities. Howden minster bells pealed and flags flew from its tower. A party of Cleckheaton Andertons joined the usual Howden society throng of churchmen, physicians, solicitors, businessmen, and the inevitable H. B. Anderson. On arriving at Kilpin Lodge, the wedding party was received with 'great cheering', and 'Several small cannon were fired off on the banks of the Ouse. Flags and banners were displayed from shops, houses, and vessels, and gave undoubted proof of the very high esteem [in which] the lady is held by all classes' (*Goole and Marshland Weekly Times*, 7 September 1877). The workpeople and their wives were regaled yet again at the Half Moon.

With the removal of his mother closer to the family fold in the West Riding, George Herbert Anderton came into his own in Howdendyke. A very energetic and capable young man, he first employed his talents in organizing social events in Howdendyke, later turning to Howden and the district in general. The only known blot on his character appears to be a five shilling fine for allowing his dog to stray at a time when a mad dog was terrorizing the neighbourhood. More positively, George III took over the old Howdendyke Feast with its small scale athletic sports and reorganized it as the Howdendyke Athletic Sports Festival in 1878.

Until he turned his talents to organizing sports venues in Howden after 1881, Howdendyke Sports became an important regional event. Held in an Anderton field adjacent to the works, and featuring a 'dancing booth', a fireworks display, a splendid brass band, and performers on the flying trapeze and slack rope, Howdendyke Sports and Gala attracted people from the whole district, who converged upon the village by river, road, and footpath. In view of the rather luxurious prizes, designed by the Skipton jeweller Fattorini, competitors for the athletic events came from as far afield as Selby, Huddersfield, Sheffield, and Hull. Mindful of the probable semi-professional status of some of these 'amateurs', certain races were restricted to workers at the Ouse Chemical Works and those residing within eight miles of Howdendyke. For the gentry there was hurdle jumping, the first race in 1878 being won by the horse of none other than George Herbert Anderton. This embarrassment was avoided in future years. Although partially eclipsed by George III's growing interest in Howden Show and Sports, Howdendyke Feast and Sports continued into the early twentieth century as an important summer event in the district.

The five-year period 1876–80 – which began with George III's coming of age and the remarriage of his mother – culminated in George's own marriage in January 1880 to his cousin Laura Elizabeth Asquith, resident of Morley in the West Riding and kin to the Asquith political family. The reader will by now be unsurprised to learn that a celebratory dinner was given to over one hundred workmen and their 'wives and sweethearts', that the workmen presented a handsome gift, that the bridegroom's mother was eulogised yet again, or that the workpeople, via the manager of the Chemical Works, expressed their opinion that Mr Anderton was 'a bright genial young man' who 'had won their esteem' (*Goole Weekly Times*, 16 January 1880). Hyperbole rules OK in Victorian local newspapers, yet it is likely that George III was highly regarded by not a few of his employees.

After his marriage George devoted less time to sports in favour of the more sober and elevating occupations of presiding over 'entertainments' in the schoolroom, giving magic lantern shows of his trips down the Rhine, and instituting the annual Howdendyke Children's Christmas Party, begun in the 1880s and continued well into the 1950s. George III must have been fond of children. At Howden minster bazaar in 1892 he presided over the toy stall. In 1890 over 150 children attended the village children's party, which had been preceded on Christmas Eve by the annual dinner for over 130 workmen and their wives. At this latter event:

> Mr W. W. Mellor proposed the health of Mr Anderton, whose unvarying kindness and generosity were known to and appreciated by every one connected with the works of which he was head. Mr Anderton responded in a most genial manner stating that no master had better staff than the men in his employ. (*Goole Weekly Times*, 2 January 1891)

In this atmosphere of mutual congratulation George III proposed a toast to those employees who had been employed in the works for over thirty years. There were eight such employees, two of whom, Tom and Charles Mell, were my great-grandfather and his brother.

A further institution, guaranteed to bind Maude Mary Anderton, George III's daughter, to the hearts of Howdendykers, emerged in 1888. The Sail Loft at Kilpinpike was festively arrayed to celebrate the second birthday of Miss Anderton, and over 140 employees and spouses were entertained, George III and the workers again mutually endorsing 'the cordial relations that had always existed between them' (*Goole Weekly Times*, 23 March 1888). These birthday celebrations continued through Miss Anderton's childhood, with over 200 children being 'regaled with a sumptuous tea' in March 1897 on Maud Mary's eleventh birthday.

As early as 1889 the infant Maude Mary launched the eponymous ketch from

Caiseley's shipyard to become one of the Anderton fleet. She was an only child for a decade. A son, George (IV) Eric, was born in 1895 amid great rejoicing.

From the late 1870s George III expanded his horizons. Along with his friend H. B. Anderson, his father before him, and other Howdendyke entrepreneurs such as John Banks, George became a Freemason, later becoming Grand Swordbearer. By 1890, when he became East Riding County Councillor for the Howdenshire Division (elected unopposed) he was also president of the Howden Liberal Council, the Howden St. John's Ambulance Association, and the Howden Literary and Scientific Association; vice-president of the Howden Horticultural Association; installing master of the Freemasons; a leading light in the Howden Branch of the Church Missionary Society and superintendent of the church Sunday school at Howdendyke; trustee of the Howdenshire Savings Bank; captain of Howden Cricket Club; and extremely active in an array of amateur theatricals, magic lantern shows, lecturing, and the organizing of 'entertainments'. In 1893 George followed the Cleckheaton tradition by becoming a Justice of the Peace. As befitted his senior economic and social role in the district, he become vicar's warden of Howden Minster in the 1880s while the more elderly H. B. Anderson undertook the more junior role of people's warden. The occupation of both Howden churchwarden positions by two Howdendyke industrialists for over two decades amply testifies to the importance of Howdendyke in the district during the generation before World War I.

Despite these widening interests, George III found time to rebuild the schoolroom at Howdendyke in 1889 and confirm its use by all religious denominations, although in practice it was utilized chiefly by nonconformist sects. He organised trips for his workmen, including a day-trip by rail and sea to the Isle of Man, a feat which would be remarkable even today. Always keen on technological improvement, he had installed both electricity and telephone in the Chemical Works and Kilpin Lodge by 1890, although, as we shall see in later chapters, such marvels had not reached the rest of the village by 1948. Every year he sent both 'lurries' and 'rullies' to convey Howdendyke children to nonconformist Sunday school treats at Howden.

If the general ambience seems Dickensian, with George III as Cheeryblye, the fault may lie with the sugary encomiums of local newspapers. Yet the list of mourners at George III's funeral in 1907 takes up over a column of newsprint, and records only notables and trades people, for 'the employees of the Ouse Chemical Works were present in very large numbers, almost to a man, and many of the residents of Howdendyke and neighbourhood, the names of whom it would be almost impossible to mention' (*Goole Times*, 29 November, 1907). It is significant that the memorial plaque affixed to the wall of Howden minster by his employees describes George Herbert Anderton as 'master and friend'.

The sheer consistency of the reports of George III's character, through

Plate 9. Masters: Mr Richard Norman and Mrs Maude Mary Pilling (née Anderton), centre, with relatives, friends, and management at their ruby wedding, 28.12.1955

Plate 10. Men: Charles Mell jnr. (centre) with cycling mates, *c.*1900

Plate 11. Ferryman Abbey with Ouse salmon, *c.*1920

Plate 12. Villagers outside the Anchor Inn, *c.*1918

generations of reporters from the 1870s to 1907, suggest an extraordinary geniality and a highly developed paternalist sensibility:

> He was a thorough businessman of great energy and tact, and as an ideal employer of labour he will always be remembered and loved. No one ever heard of disputes between master and men at Howdendyke; on the contrary, his employees never knew how to sufficiently sound the praises of their kind-hearted and beneficient master. (*Goole Times*, 22 November 1907)

Disraeli, promoter of just such industrial relationships in his novel *Sybil*, would have been proud. George Herbert Anderton, I believe, can fairly be entered in the company of those Victorian industrialists for whom a free economy meant an economy operated in the spirit of Christian justice, and entrepreneurship involved a conscious moral dimension. It was only with the twentieth century severing of the connection between industrial capitalism and Christianity, suggests Paul Johnson (1977) that capitalism took on the oppressive role which so manifests itself in Howdendyke today.

But George III's death did not sever the connection, which continued in Howdendyke until the 1950s. For here history almost repeats itself. George II died at forty, left the works to his widow, who later remarried when George III proved old enough to manage the firm. George III, in turn, died at fifty-two, leaving the works to his wife, the former Laura Asquith, who afterwards married her cousin Tom Hall. Like George III, George IV was left fatherless at an early age, and the works was managed by his mother and stepfather. But instead of inheriting the Ouse Chemical Works on his majority, as did his father, George IV found himself in Flanders fields and died there, age twenty-two, in the last months of World War I. At this point the Ouse Chemical Works, for the third time, devolved upon a woman.

Maude Mary Anderton, in her early thirties in 1918, was already married to Richard Norman Pilling, who soon became Managing Director of the company. While Mrs Pilling carried on the tradition of her mother, being active in charities such as the Red Cross, and other groups as various as the Poultry Association and the Imperial League, it was as if the mantle of George III fell directly upon the shoulders of R. N. Pilling.

He rapidly became a county councillor, a magistrate, a member of Kilpin parish council, president of Howden Football Club, a member of Howden Tennis Club, a freemason, and engaged in other pursuits reminiscent of George Herbert Anderton, although he was not active in 'entertainments' that continued to be held in the village hall into the 1960s. He also stepped into George III's shoes as vicar's warden of Howden minster for the period from 1947 until his death in 1960. It was Mrs Pilling, however, an Anderton by birth, who chiefly carried on the Anderton social regime, somewhat modified by changing times and mores, into the late 1950s.

Men: the Mell family

In sharp contrast to the bourgeois Andertons, the Mell family were prolific but illiterate labourers who had inhabited the parish of Eastrington since at least the very early seventeenth century. Generations of John, Robert, and Thomas Mells worked as farm labourers at Newland, Hive and Sandholme, all hamlets within easy walking distance of Eastrington parish church and less than ten miles from Howdendyke (Figure 2). John Mell of Eastrington, *fl.* 1670–1730, begat Thomas Mell (1728–1778) also of Eastrington, who begat, on Ann Parker, the younger Thomas (1763–1823), who in turn begat at least eleven children on two wives.

His second son, John Mell, was baptised in Eastrington church on 19 January 1798. An illiterate farm labourer, he nevertheless travelled as far as Hull to marry Isabella Harrison in 1823, and by then was resident in the town of Howden. John is variously described as a labourer or porter, and Isabella as a farm labourer. During the 1840s the family moved to Howdendyke, where John was employed by various coal merchants as a 'coal porter'. He continued in this heavy work well into his seventies, dying of 'old age and apoplexy' on 26 May 1876, a week after the coming of age of George Anderton III.

John and Isabella had at least ten children between 1824 and the late 1840s. They appear as a single family in the census schedules of 1851 and 1861. But by 1871 at least three of the sons had generated their own families, making four Mell households in all, yet totalling only sixteen of the population of 265. In 1871 John, aged 74, was still heaving coal, and his sons Richard (33) and Charles (34) were also porters. By contrast, the third son, Brown (36), who had by far the largest household, of seven persons, was an agricultural labourer, and had so far broken the tedious Mell mould to call two of his children Calonia and Carrick.

Brown is a suspicious character. Alone of John's children, he has left no record of birth or baptism. Born in the early 1830s, he is very probably the Thomas Mell who died in September 1901 and in whose grave-plot in Howden churchyard are buried my mother and father. The mysterious Brown, according to the evidence of his children's marriage certificates, appears to have changed his name to Thomas in the late 1870s. He was, apparently, my great-grandfather.

Some indication that, like all families, that of the Mells was good and bad in parts, is revealed by local newspaper accounts of the 1870s and 1880s. Most of them appear to involve Brown/Thomas, his children, or his brother Richard. In 1878 George Mell, a farm servant and probably Brown's fourth child, took a fellow labourer to court on a charge of assault. Two years later his uncle Richard spoiled his evening at Howdendyke Sports by engaging in a brawl with two Goole butchers who were awaiting the ferry. According to the ferryman, while Richard was pinning one of the butcher brothers to the ground, the other

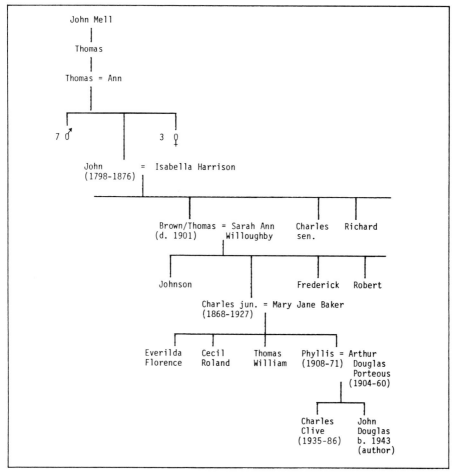

Figure 14. Selected pedigree of the Eastrington (to John II)
and Howdendyke (from John II) Mells

brother was continually 'bunching' him about the body and head. Ferryman and
fishermen helped pull them apart, and at the subsequent Howden petty
sessions hearing the upper butcher was fined one pound, though the
magistrates felt that all were very probably drunk. A little later in the year
Johnson Mell, Brown's eldest son, was summoned and fined for committing
'malicious injuries' on a door. It appears that, while drunk, he had kicked in the
front door of his father's neighbour, James Alcock.

After the death of John in 1876, worn out with coal-heaving, Isabella was
moved to Howden workhouse, despite having at least three sons in the village. I
make no apologia for this, except to note that early in the next century when
plans were made to close the workhouse, many residents complained on the

grounds that given poor wages, large families, and small houses, the workhouse was the best place for aged parents who could no longer work. Evidently, the brothers made some contribution to Isabella's upkeep, although a maintenance order of one shilling a week had to be assessed on Brown/Thomas in 1882. Isabella died of old age two years later. In 1885 Thomas was again in court for assaulting the same James Alcock, although countercharge was made by Thomas' wife that Alcock had assaulted her son Frederick. Frederick was apparently 'brayed' by Alcock for throwing a stone at him. The magistrate was evidently of the opinion that neighbours at loggerheads should solve their own problems, called both charges 'paltry', and dismissed them.

There is evidence then, of a brawling, litigious sort of Mell, quite unlikely to be considered respectable by more staid villagers. This accounts for my discovery, whilst doing genealogical research in the early 1980s, of whole families of local Mells, closely related to my own, who were never acknowledged by my own family. Besides the awkward Brown/Thomas, his oldest son Johnston stands out as an unusual character. In 1896 either his wife or daughter (the newspaper report is garbled) committed suicide by poison. Twice married, Johnson Mell was the local 'strong man', renowned for heaving heavy fallen cranes from prostrate bodies, and so esteemed for his hard work at a Goole timber yard that his employer left him an annuity.

Other Mells proved more staid and sober. Charles sen., son of John, worked for Andertons almost from the inception of the firm. He also had a pig-rearing business (in 1886 his premises were declared free of swine fever) and kept a small grocery, probably in the dwelling known as The Cottage. His nephew Charles Jun., Brown's third son and my grandfather, also worked at the Ouse Chemical Works, first as a labourer and finally as timekeeper. Whereas the fourth son, Frederick, became a cobbler and fathered numerous progeny, Robert, Brown's fifth son, went into business and no doubt pleased the more respectable Mells greatly by becoming Lord Mayor of Hull.

Charles Jun. (1868–1927) married Mary Jane Baker, a shoemaker's daughter from Goodmanham in the Yorkshire Wolds, in 1893. Of their six children, two died young. The sixth was my mother Phyllis (1908–1971). Charles Jun. proved to be a leading light in Howdendyke, organizing football teams, riding in penny-farthing bicycle races, and assiduously remaining Church of England despite his wife's addiction to Primitive Methodism. Although both his father and mother were illiterate, Charles and his wife were competent writers. The only surviving letter of Charles to Mary Jane provides some flavour of Howdendyke life at the turn of the century:

Howdendyke 31 December 1901

Dear Wife,
    I arrived home quite safely and found everything alright. Pigs and dog alright and in normal condition. I was very fortunate in catching a good connection

arriving at Selby at 11:10 and departing at 11:15 so you will see that I had only five minutes to wait getting home about 1 p.m. Well dear I commence work to-night Tuesday so if all be well I shall be on at nights all the week so that if you care to spend the remainder of this week with the dear ones you are quite at liberty to do so then if they kill the pig this week you will be able to bring it along with you on Saturday and if you contrive to get to Howden station about 3 oclock it can come up with the bus and then transfer it to Hatfield's carrier and than I can meet it at the corner. I think there is nothing fresh at the Dyke work not very brisk. Mother got home yesterday and she baked me a loaf and a cake or two and if I want anything cooking she says she will do it for me. So me dear, I shant hunger and there is no need for you to worrit but enjoy yourself as well as you possibly can. Hoping the dear children are behaving themselves better than they did and that Rob's arm is still improving and that all dear ones are in good health. I remain

your loving Husband sending you
all my love and best wishes for a bright and
prosperous New Year.

Chas Mell Jnr.

The turn of the century appears to have been a time when astute labouring folk, in Howdendyke at least, were able to accumulate capital by assiduous saving, and become house-owners and shopkeepers. Three families stand out here. The Manns were famous throughout northern England for Richard Mann's almost embarrassing success at flower shows, exhibiting plants grown in his own nursery. The Tuttys were grocers and owners of the four houses known as Tutty Row and the adjacent Woodbine Cottage. Charles Mell purchased Howdendyke Post Office and Shop in 1918, and three of the four houses, formerly Richard Ward's, at Kilpinpike in 1926. All these people or their families worked as labourers at Andertons, but carried on small money-making operations in their spare time. Charles was ably assisted by Mary Jane who first market gardened and then became village postmistress and shopkeeper.

It is interesting to note that when Kilpin Parish Council was formed in 1894, Charles Mell jun. was the first to be nominated. Thirteen nominations were made. Of these, George Herbert Anderton, H. B. Anderson, and a group of farmers, publicans, and market gardeners all nominated each other. Indeed, of the thirteen nominations, four were made exclusively by the Anderton/Anderson team, while Anderton and Anderson were chief nominators of each other. On the other hand, the Mell family was involved as nominators of four labourers, including Charles Mell, at the Ouse Chemical Works. The remaining three nominations also formed a group, largely pro-Anderton, consisting of the works manager, Chester the shipbuilder, and Richard Mann, Anderton employee and florist. For reasons ungiven, two Mell-nominated candidates were considered ineligible to stand.

The first Kilpin Parish Council finally consisted of nine members, of whom eight (Anderton, Anderson, farmers, works manager, publican, shipbuilder, and Richard Mann) could firmly be said to be pro-establishment. The only labourer elected was Charles Mell jun. The latter then found himself the only person to vote against Anderson as vice-chairman, Anderton naturally being elected chairman. Thereafter Charles showed little dissent, and with the deaths of Anderson in 1900 and Anderton in 1907, went on to become one of the longest-serving members of the council (1894–1927). His son Cecil Roland Mell also served on the parish council from 1935 into the 1950s.

Charles did not reach sixty, dying suddenly in 1927. Each of his four surviving children inherited a house; as one son had moved away, his dwelling was occupied by Mary Jane, my grandmother. Phyllis, my mother, inherited the Post Office. In the 1940s and 1950s then, I grew up in an extended family of several separate but closely interconnected households (see Chapter 6). By the 1970s, however, my mother's generation had all but died out, and of my own generation all had moved out of Howdendyke. With the death of Phyllis Mell, 'who was born in the village, had kept the village store and post office for 35 years, and was an active member of the life of the community . . . , Howdendyke lost one of its best-known and respected residents' (*Goole Times*, 10 September 1971). I often urged my mother to write about Howdendyke, but she always refused. Perhaps she knew too much.

The Mells preceded the Andertons as Howdendykers, and lasted longer. They had a fierce independence of spirit, which did not prevent some of them from taking Anderton employment, though none of them inhabited Anderton houses. Their pride was more of a reaction against dependency rather than against the Andertons themselves, for the century of Anderton/Pilling rule in Howdendyke was quite benign.

In choosing the Mells as an example of the 'men', I have not chosen the extremes. There were many families more illiterate, less respectable, and even more brawling than the Mells. I have, however, provided a background for the reader's better understanding of the geoautobiography which follows.

II

Chronicles

But now the sounds of population fail ...
No busy steps the grass-grown footway tread,
But all the bloomy flush of life is fled.
  Oliver Goldsmith, *The Deserted Village*

We should undertake a topoanalysis of all the space that has
invited us to come out of ourselves ... each one of us should
make a surveyor's map of his lost fields and meadows.
  Gaston Bachelard, *The Poetics of Space*

6

The living village: a geoautobiography

Childhood is not a thing which dries up as soon as it has finished its cycle. It is not a memory. It is the most living of treasures, and continues to enrich us without our knowing it ... Woe to the man who cannot remember his childhood ... he is dead as soon as it leaves him.

Franz Hellen

Although I was born, for parental convenience, in the city of York, I spent the first twenty-one years of my life in Howdendyke. The Porteous family, which could not agree on the spelling of its surname (Portas, Portus, Porteus) until the twentieth century, came south from the Scottish moors of the upper Tweed, were domiciled in inland County Durham as tinkers in the seventeenth century, and reached York in the late eighteenth century to become farm labourers, cobblers, engineers, and railwaymen (Porteous, 1980). My father, a plumber, came from York in the 1920s to do a job at Kilpin Lodge. Going to the Post Office, he met my mother, Phyllis Mell.

The Mell family had always been rural and even today their nation-wide distribution is heavily concentrated on the Humber and its Yorkshire and Lincolnshire tributaries. In an extensive research study (Porteous, 1982) I was able to connect almost all known Mells, nation-wide, for the period 1538–1980 into four major 'clans', the three largest of which cluster in what is now the largely rural Borough of Boothferry. Probing the pre-1538 period (Porteous, in press) by exhaustively (and exhaustingly) reviewing all parish registers in the area, I was able to infer that the surname Mell originated in the township of West Cottingwith in Thorganby parish, about twenty miles up the Ouse and Derwent from Howdendyke. There are records of Mells in this parish in 1295, 1339, 1514, and 1563.

Migration to other East Riding areas followed, but well into the eighteenth century most Mells remained 'place loyal' (Porteous, 1985) to the small low-lying flood zone, scarcely forty miles across, between the first ripples of the Pennines on the West and the chalk scarp of the Lincolnshire and Yorkshire Wolds on the east. A major focus formed in Howdenshire as early as the late sixteenth century, centring upon the parish of Eastrington, whence came John

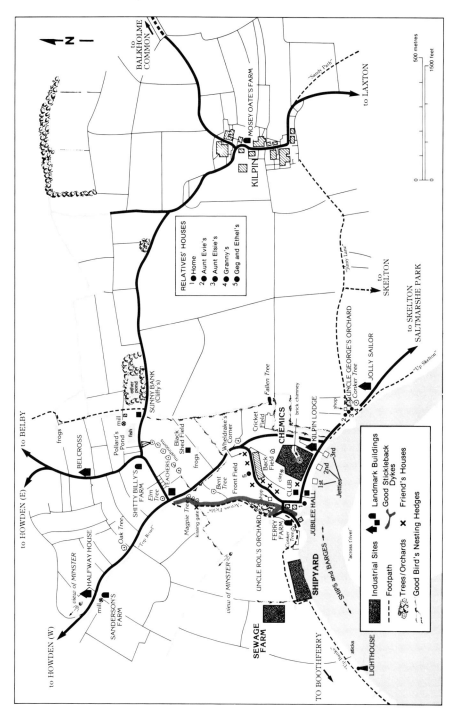

Figure 15. Childscape c.1950

89

Mell, the first of the family to settle in Howdendyke in the mid-nineteenth century. A century later, despite much out-migration, Howdendyke was still well-populated by Mells.

As we have already seen (Chapter 5), the Mell family were village independents. My grandfather, a Chemical Works labourer turned timekeeper, and my hard-working grandmother Baker, cook and gardener, saved enough to purchase Howdendyke Post Office in 1918 and three of the four houses at Kilpinpike in the 1920s (for the fate of these houses see Chapter 9). My great-granduncle, Charles Mell Sen., apparently kept a shop and by marriage linked the Mells to other, more prolific, Howdendyke families. My grandfather, Charles Mell Jun., and my uncle, Cecil Roland Mell (sonorous names for a labouring family), served on Kilpin Parish Council for many years. At a time when most villagers were tenants, chiefly of Andertons, the Mells were remarkable in their stubborn desire to own their own houses in this 'company village'.

I grew up, in the 1940s and 1950s, in an extended family (Figure 15). Two sets of aunts and uncles and my grandmother occupied the Kilpinpike houses, a cousin lived in the village, and my mother was the village postmistress (my father, astonishingly stubborn himself, commuted by bicycle and rail to York). In a small community the village postmistress is the central vortex of the continuous flow of information. As acting postmaster, shop assistant, and postman from about age eight, I was in an excellent position to know the village, its inhabitants, and their houses (many had no mailbox).

This is not the place for an extensive geoautobiography. But in the absence of oral history (see Appendix) and the almost total lack of documents, my own recollections must serve as a basis for understanding the nature of village life immediately before the changes that were to come in the 1960s (Chapters 8–11). A complementary, more objective view, is to be found in the following chapter.

I begin with a brief evocation of 'the days before'. This is followed by three essays which establish the Ouse Chemical Works as the work focus of the village, the Post Office as the chief focus of information flow, and the village's rather tenuous links, in the 1950s at least, with the outside world. Once these major themes are established, some notion of village life can be gained from a series of short vignettes.

The days before

It is as if the late 1940s and 1950s in Howdendyke were the 'days before' everything. They were the days before street lighting; we groped about, used the moon, took a flashlight. The days before sewage systems and water closets; to use the can was not a euphemism. The days before the British working classes took to cars; we walked, we ran, we biked, hitched lifts in lorries. The days before paid holidays; we never went very far from home. The days of a six-day working week; when did we last see our fathers? The days before television; whatever did we do with ourselves?

And above all, the days before electricity. The days before the washing-machine; red-armed women using tubs and washboards, possers, dollies. The days before clothes driers; a winter kitchen full of steaming clothes, drying on the clothes-horse before the coal fire, absorbing the only heat available to keep us warm. The days before central heating; you huddled to the single coal fire, front roasting, back freezing, capillaries bursting and discolouring in women's legs. The days before hot water heaters and baths; what the back-fire boiler couldn't heat came from the kettle on the copper and you bathed laboriously on Fridays in a tin tub before the fire. The days before refrigerators; shopping every day. The days before the electric stove; food cooked in the coal oven (which was warm enough when the cat got out) or directly on the coal fire. There is a fine art in boiling and frying over live coals. And toasting too, a dangerous enterprise,

I came to North America at age twenty-four. At twenty-five I first turned on a television set (I had often turned them off) and learned to drive a car (car-driving was not a puberty rite in the days before, when there were haystacks aplenty). In North America I found that the normal household goods of my recent childhood were 'antiques', 'collectibles', or museum pieces – fish knives, flat irons, paraffin lamps, stone hot-water bottles, iron bedsteads, jugs and bowls and washstands. When 'progress' came to Howdendyke in the late 1950s, we threw all this old stuff into the river; these were the days before 'ecology'. Thirty years ago; a generation. The days before.

T'Chemics

T'Chemics reared a tall black chimney, streaked with white, above the village. You could see it from any angle. It was our dreaming spire. Below it huddled the low factory buildings, fronting the river, and around the works spread village and fields. 'Ouse Chemical Works' it said on a board near the office, but to us it was t'Chemics.

Uncle George worked at t'Chemics. No one else in the family did. But nearly everyone in the village worked there. Every morning t'Chemics' whistle blew, every lunch-time twice, and again at knocking-off time at night. You could set you watch by those whistles, if you had a watch.

I grew up seeing men, and women clad in sacking aprons, disappear into t'Chemics every day. But I knew little of what went on within. One day, when I was eating Aunt Evie's rhubarb pie and Uncle George was looking benevolent, I asked him: 'What do you do in t'Chemics, Uncle George?'

'He's a bagman', said Aunt Evie with some asperity.

'What's a bagman?'

'Why, I take bags off elevator and see they're all tied up', broke in Uncle George. 'Then I wheel 'em across to stack, with a sack-barrow.'

'Do you do that all day, then?'

'Well, we has us drinkings and dinnertime', said Uncle George.

'Aye, he moves hundreds of bags every day', chimed in Aunt Evie. 'Hundreds of bags every day. Your granddad, that's my dad, you never knew him, he was timekeeper.'

'What's timekeeper?'

'Why, he sits in an office with a collar and tie on and clocks men in in a morning and clocks 'em out at night.'

'Didn't he work, then?'

'Your granddad work? He did nowt else, *and* your grandma. They were always working. They worked and saved. He was a working-man who got to be timekeeper and bought Post Office and these three houses.'

But granddad was long dead, so I returned to Uncle George.

'What's in all them bags, Uncle George?'

'Fossit, me lad.'

'What's fossit?'

'It's tillage. It's what you put on t'land.'

'Why do you put it on the land?'

'You put it on t'land to make stuff grow.'

'How does it make stuff grow?'

'Because it's fossit. That's what fossit does.'

'But why do they call it fossit? I've never heard tell of fossit.'

'It's a chemical, like. It's tillage. It's what they spread on t'land to make crops grow. I use cowshit meself.'

Uncle George rarely swore, and it signalled the end of that topic. It was years later before I equated t'Chemics' product with superphosphate.

Most of the raw materials for t'Chemics came upriver by barge. Three jetties lunged from the river front of the factory into the Ouse, and all vessels tied up at one of these. Big cranes with grabs hauled up fine white powders which sometimes spread in a light, penetrating dust all over the village. This was at the First jetty, relatively new and made of concrete.

Second jetty had two storeys; the men at t'Chemics called it Tay Bridge. Pulleys from the top storey let down huge wicker baskets which were hauled up again full of rough raw materials. The baskets were made of willow, and held together with rope. They were like potato-baskets, the kind you used for tatie-picking, but bigger. Eventually they wore and broke, cascading a cargo of heavy materials among the shovellers in the ship's hold below. Discarded baskets were slung into the river, to rot away in the mud. Long after baskets were abandoned in favour of cranes and metal grabs, you could seem them poking out of the mud at low tide, for all the world like strange, stranded, seabirds' nests.

Third jetty was different again. It had a little railway whose tracks looped at the end of the jetty. Small rail waggons were filled from the barges and carried materials into the works. We liked to play on this miniature railway and when a train of empty tubs was left unattended on the line, it was our joy to clamber from tub to tub and even to uncouple the tubs from each other and push them around the track. This led to much cursing and complaining to mothers by the workmen. 'Keep away from that third jetty', cried the mothers, 'It ain't safe.' 'It's dangerous', said Mother. 'You could be crushed between those waggons.'

But we liked Third jetty best, because at low tides barges would tie up there for the night before going further upriver. Some of these barges carried peanuts to the oil-crushing factories at Selby, miles upstream. When such a barge put in, youths converged. Bargemen were besieged.

'Hey mister. Any monkey-nuts?'

'Gi'us some monkey-nuts, mister.'

'Have you any spare?'

'Mister, gi'us a few.'

Sometimes a sack of unshelled peanuts was heaved up from below. We fell upon its contents with ferocity. At other times we would be asked, rudely, why we couldn't get enough monkey-nuts at home. Others told us to bugger off. One bargee would shout: 'Monkey-nuts? Ain't got none. Monkeys ain't been laying this week.' But even more fascinating than the monkey-nuts were the bones. Huge barge-loads of partially-crushed bones were shipped into t'Chemics, there to be further ground into fertilizer. They were probably animal bones, but tales were spread of human bones dug up from the battlefields of Flanders and brought over from Indian famines.

If you were very careful, you could creep into t'Chemics, past the millmen at their drinkings, and clamber into the metal hoppers below the crushing machinery. Each hopper was as big as a fair-sized room, and as deep. Crushed powdered bones, a fine grey dust, fell in a steady stream from a central chute into each hopper. You had to wait until a hopper was almost full before venturing in, because you had to be able to reach the rim in order to get out again. And you had to stay near the edge and avoid slowly sinking into the powder which lay ten feet deep below you.

Treading powder, anxiously avoiding the steady fall from the overhead chute, our shoes filling with gritty particles, our eyes smarting, our hair and skin itching, we searched for bones. Sometimes small bones miraculously survived the crushers and fell with the powder into the hoppers. They seemed mostly to be teeth. Honour was satisfied when each member of the group could show two or three teeth. Bone searching was rather an ordeal, but once it had been suggested, no-one would back out of the adventure. Thankfully we heaved ourselves out of the hoppers, crept past the millmen yawning in their oil stained overalls, and felt the fresh river air on our faces. Shaking ourselves free of the clinging dust, beating each other's sweaters and trousers, we went home with our trophies. The fertilizer ate small holes in our clothes, which our mothers put down to moths.

T'chemics was full of white powdery dust. It made you cough and prickled at your skin. It also covered the outsides of the factory buildings and on windy days it blew across the village and women hastily took in their washing. It collected on window-panes and sifted through doors and cracks. Women complained: 'We can't never keep nowt clean in this village.' 'It's tillage. It's good for you. Makes you grow,' said the men. And, with a finality that could not be refuted: 'Where there's muck there's brass.' With all that muck we should have been rich.

Post Office

Our village had two streets. One ran in from the nearby town, originally to the ferry that used to ply from the landing near our house. This road was known as Ferry Road, but became North Street as it approached the river. We played cricket in the middle of it, moving our wickets of old bricks only when the occasional vehicle came through. The other street ran along the river bank fronting the agricultural fertilizer factory known as t'Chemics.

The two streets ran at right angles to each other, and met at the village Post Office on the river bank. Our shop and Post Office was thus the focus of the village. Nearby was The Square, an open space fronted on one side by old houses, on the others by the river, the Jubilee Hall and the village's only pub, The Ouse Chemical Works Working Men's Club and Institute. Workmen passing on their way to both Club and Chemics called in the shop for cigarettes. During working hours womenfolk came in for postal orders, biscuits, tea, stamps, flour, and patent medicines. Every day the mail was dropped here at seven a.m. and then delivered throughout the village.

You could tell it had been an old shop. A directory mentioned the Post Office in 1879, and old Johnny Fleming, its proprietor, left draught-excluding souvenirs in the form of shirts stuffed in cracks and newspapers pasted to walls, all neatly covered with wallpaper. Under the shop's front window stood two huge wooden flour bins, now full of junk, lidded over, and covered with piles of biscuits, tins of crisps, packets of tea.

The back wall of the shop was a mass of narrow shelves and tiny wooden drawers. None of these drawers held anything of value, and some were stuck shut by repeated paintings. The shelves supported packets of tea, biscuits, bottles of soft drinks, large and small, and packets of flour. Lyons' tea came in several qualities, distinguishable by the colour of the packet. The teabag had not been invented; when my mother first saw one, she thought it was a convenient method of measuring out tea leaves for the pot. Smith's Crisps came in greaseproof paper packets packed in airtight cubic tins. Each packet contained salt in a twist of blue paper; it was often damp.

Over the empty drawers hung cardboard placards on which small glass bottles were secured by means of elastic. These were patent medicines; people swore by them, and probably at them too. Parkinson's Pills, of Burnley, were clearly able to restore almost the dead to life. Each type of pill was good not for a single ailment only, but for two. 'Liver and Kidney' pills jostled with 'Head and Stomach' and other dual reminders of the human interior. All were whitish-grey in colour and sugar-coated. Buf if you sucked off the sugar, they were universally foul within. 'The wuss they taste, then better they are' said the old folks.

Cigarettes reposed on a shelf behind the counter. Their variety reflected individual tastes; Capstan Full Strength, for example, was kept for a single customer only. Most had romantic, old-fashioned names – 'Player's Weights', 'Navy Cut', 'Wild Woodbine', 'Robin', 'Passing Clouds'. The cheaper ones were sold in open packets of five, but some people asked mother to break even these packets so that they could purchase one or two cigarettes at a time. In time you learned what individuals preferred, and they had only to ask for 'ten cigs' for you to unerringly pick the correct packet from the shelf.

The counter was a massive affair of wood, about ten feet long, four or more feet high, and several feet wide. On the house side it was full of drawers and recesses in which dad kept his tools and mother kept string, paper bags, and sundry oddments. Most of the Post Office items, and the till, were in a capacious central drawer. Some drawers were empty and remained so for years. We discovered that they were open at the rear to the large central recess in the counter quite by accident. A long-unopened drawer one day began to squeak and was hurriedly opened to reveal the cat and a litter of newborn kittens.

The shop and the Post Office were supposed to operate separately. For shop goods people paid irregularly. When I served in the shop some customers were more inclined to pay cash. Others simply asked me to 'put it on t'bill' or 'chalk it up'. Perhaps half the village had 'tick', for no small shopkeeper in a rural village could afford to operate without such a credit system. On Fridays wives rolled up to pay off their bills of the previous week. By Monday all their money had gone and they were 'on tick' again. Mother had no regular account books, but kept records on the backs of envelopes, on pieces of scrap paper, on old cigarette packets. All these were thrust into a counter drawer and pulled out for totting up on Fridays.

The Post Office could not officially give 'tick'; it was subject to sudden audits on the part of the central postal authorities. So people had to pay on the spot for their stamps, dog licenses, television licenses, and postal orders. Pensioners came on 'pension day' for old age, disability, and war service pensions. At one time elderly people were given coupons for tobacco.

Mother was the village scribe. She had left school at fourteen, like most people of her age, but was superbly literate, mainly through self-study. Some villagers, on the other hand, were either illiterate or unable to put pen to paper effectively. Many official forms had therefore to be referred to Mother. Hardly a day went by without someone bringing in a form for her to complete. In this way she gained a lively appreciation of people's lives and circumstances, which appeared only to increase her tolerance.

Some were apparently unable to complete even their football pool coupons. These were diligently completed, under direction, by Mother, and the postal order written, the material inserted in the envelope, the stamp licked and affixed. In time some villagers came to regard this as normal Post Office service. 'Why don't you pay for the postal order, as well?' I would ask in exasperation. 'Not many need it doing' said Mother; 'some are old and some are daft'.

Other people came into the Post Office with strange requests. The Stamp Book held perhaps twenty types of stamp with face values from a half-penny to a pound; most people asked to buy 'a stamp'. Some insisted on purchasing 'post lorders' (postal orders), and on the few occasions that registration was required, the request was often for a 'red-chested envelope'. Pre-stamped envelopes were always known as 'stamped, addressed envelopes', although Mother only addressed them if requested.

Few people in the village had telephones, perhaps a half-dozen at most. The rest of the population had to rely on a tall red public telephone kiosk which stood eccentrically at the far end of the village from the Post Office. Many people would not walk so far, and some simply could not master the technique of using a public telephone, with all those forbidding knobs, dials, and A and B buttons. This led to a heavy demand for use of the Post Office telephone which was supposed to be used for official business only, except for a limited number of 'private calls'.

Good nature usually prevailed. Calls had to be placed through the operator as a 'private call' and the phone then transferred to the suppliant. You could speak forever on a local call for fourpence (my record with one girlfriend was two and one-quarter hours). But this sometimes led to a customer abusing the privilege by spending half an hour on the wrong side of the counter.

For the very old and faint-hearted, Mother actually made the calls and relayed messages. These were transferred line by line from the customer, over the counter, to Mother who then acted as both translator and social facilitator. For example, an old lady wanted to speak to her son Fred. After Mother had made the connection, she reported:

'It's your Fred's wife, Annie. Fred's out.'

'Oh is it? Is he? Well.'

'Do you want to tell her anything?'

'Well, ask her if she's alright.'

'Are you alright, Enid? (Pause) She's alright, Annie.'

'Well, I'm glad to hear that, I am that.' (Pause).

'She says what do you want to tell her? She's baking.'

'Baking, is she? She's always baking, is that Enid. I think our Fred's done well for hisself, I do.'

'She says she's going out in half an hour, to the shops.'

'Off to the shops. Well. That Enid, she always was a worker. Our Fred don't do a hand's stir in that house.'

'Annie---'

'Oh, tell her me and his dad want our Fred to come round and mend that broken window.'

'Enid, the message is: Annie wants Fred to come and mend the broken window. (Pause). She says she'll tell him. She hopes your're well.'

'Tell her I'm as good as can be expected.'

'She's as good as can be expected. (Pause). She says cheerio.'

'How much is that?'

'Fourpence.'

'Fourpence? By, don't it cost a lot just to talk for a minute on them phones?'

Links

Time did not seem important to us. Clock hours were not often referred to, even by adults. Time for work and time for school were the points around which our lives revolved. There were also: time for dinner; time for tea; opening time; and time for bed. All these were daily times.

Most other times were weekly times, such as pay-day, and time to pay off 'tick'. Travelling retailers came once a week at a regular hour. Shitty Billy Austwick brought produce by horse and cart from his nearby farm (Figure 15). And on Fridays came the fishman from Hull, the butcherman on Tuesdays, the greengrocerman on Wednesdays. Twice a week came the van from Rambla Bakeries of Beverley, piloted, naturally, by the Ramblaman. At one time we were even visited by an evil-smelling mobile fish-and-chip shop from far-off York, although this remarkable phenomenon (fish-and-chipman) did not last long. But for children Sundays was the important day, for after lunch there came the ice-cream man. A refrigerator-less village, we waited eagerly for Doubtfire's mobile ice-cream van with its locally-made icy-cooly announced by a hand-rung bell.

'Run out and get two bobs' worth in this dish', said Mother.

'Can I have a cornet, mam, as well?'

'Aye, a cornet as well, lad.'

'Two bobs' worth in here please, and a tanner cornet with some red juice on.' It was often difficult to decide between a cornet with red juice and a sandwich with chocolate wafers. But we liked the red juice. It was an extra.

If the ice-cream man was late we could watch for him along the river. From our backyard wall, which ran along the inner side of the river bank, you could stand and look for several miles downriver along the curving bank. A dark brown or shiny silver river, a blue and white sky, and in between the lush green of trees, farms, and high river bank. Against this green background, the white dot of the ice-cream van could be spied two or more miles away near Skelton Bridge, and we could enjoy the anticipation as it crept along the river bank road with frequent stops for customers. After the ice-cream man had gone, Sundays always seemed a little flatter.

You could also watch for the bus coming along the same road. Even though the Lincolnshire Road Car Company's buses were deep green, you could distinguish them as a moving green object against a static verdant background. You had to watch for the buses. They were not always on time and sometimes a driver would miss out our village altogether. But mostly they came right into the village and turned round in North Street about fifty yards from the Post Office. Then you could travel to Howden (two miles) or even to Goole, five miles away, across the river, a foreign place in a different county where people used different words for things and kids called 'goodies' 'spice'.

The buses came on Wednesday and Saturday afternoons, and Saturday evenings. On other days, or if you missed one, you had to walk or bike. No one had a car. The Pillings had two, but they owned t'Chemics. A few had motorbikes. No one went very far. Mother and Father visited my grandparents in York, but most people were content to visit Howden or Goole once a week with occasional trips to Hull. To get to York you took a taxi two miles to Howden (no morning buses), then a bus ten miles to Selby, then a second bus fifteen miles to York. The twenty-five mile journey took about two hours each way, for these were country buses with frequent stops. But York was worth it. Where else had castles, walls, battlements, tall church towers, and narrow windy streets. Besides, I had been born there, in the Purey Cust Nursing Home within the grounds of York Minster. And you can't be more Yorkshire than that.

Not only did we have relatively few contacts with the outside world, we were also poorly supplied in terms of modern conveniences. Public utilities were a long time reaching Howdendyke. In our village in the 1940s, a few houses, including our own, had gas lighting. Most had 'tilley lamps', and our shop did a brisk trade in paraffin.

People brought their own containers and we measured out the paraffin in gallons and half-gallons. Serving paraffin was a nuisance. It meant you had to leave the customer alone in the shop while you went down to the coalhouse in the backyard. Consequently, I was often called upon to serve the paraffin while Mother kept the customer company in the shop. The paraffin reposed in a five-foot high metal container. One day the cat fell in and drowned. When the drum was half-empty and I had to lean right in to scoop up the liquid I often feared the same fate. Below half-empty I could not reach, until I learned to tip and swivel the heavy drum. The whole business was dirty and smelly. I was glad when electricity came.

I was not the only one. One old lady became deeply enamoured of the electricity system. Naked lamp bulbs were hung from her cottage ceilings during the installation period, and blazed all day and night for several days thereafter. Finally, while delivering the mail, Mother approached her and tactfully asked how she liked the new electric light. 'Ee, I do like that 'lectric', she replied. 'It saves a right lot of messing about with them tilley lamps. And doesn't it last a long time?'

Everyone used coal as the main source of heat. The coalman came weekly, and coal was rationed. Life was cold during strikes or if the coalman didn't come. Those with small houses were lucky. A coal fire and range in one room could readily heat that room to roasting point and take the chill off the adjacent room and the two bedrooms above. But our house had six rooms beside the shop, and a coal fire was regularly lit only in one, although one other downstairs room and one bedroom had fireplaces. Back-fire boilers provided hot water in some houses, such as ours, but never very much and never dependably.

Going to bed in winter was an agony, but a normal, regular agony. Bedrooms were freezing, sometimes damp. Blankets and eiderdowns were piled on in geological layers; hot water bottles or a wrapped hot brick were de rigeur. We must have held the world record for speedy undressing, donning pyjamas, and leaping into a very cold bed. You soon warmed up the bed by body heat, but any exposed skin surface was liable to go blue with cold. Yet it was impossible to cover everything without smothering. An ear and nose had to be left exposed as the temperature plummetted. Luckily we had not heard of central heating and so envied no one. This was life.

Six vignettes

These vignettes, chosen with difficulty from a wide-ranging selection, are meant to provide some flavour of the denizens of Howdendyke, including myself as a child, relatives, pigs, cats, and working men.

My home (primary school essay, 18 May 1954, age 10)

My home is the Post Office at Howdendyke. It is a fairly big house and nearly two hundred years old. It has seven rooms in it, and there is a shop door, a front door, and a back door. In the house there is a scullery, a kitchen, a sitting room, and a shop. There are also three bedrooms in order of size there is small one a medium sized one a very large one. The scullery has just been built (the other one was made of wood) and it is the most modern place in the house. We have not got a pantry but a big cupboard for food. We have just got a new sink and a pedestal wash basin. There are shelves on one side of the room on which are all the cups, plates, saucers etc. In the kitchen my father has pulled the old fireplace out and put a new one in. The new one has a lot more modern conveniences than the other. In the shop there is a large counter, a cupboard, and lots of shelves. There are two very large corn bins which when the shop sold groceries my grandma used to use. In the passage upstairs there is a wooden wall and about twelve feet up there is a very small latch which when you want to pull the starlings nests out of the attic you pull the latch and a section of the wall falls out. There are a lot of starlings nests in our attic and the latch is well hidden so that you cannot hardly see it against the wall. In our family there is my father, my mother, my brother and myself. We have a back yard and a garden which when the tide of the river is very high floods a small part of it. On one side of the garden is a rockery and a border is round the other three sides. On the boards there used to be a big flag pole but it fell down and so we broke it up. On the wall near the back yard is another rockery not as big as the first, and there is another even smaller one than that, that is nearly in the river. The house stands nearly into the river and is only about ten or so feet from it.

Saturday morning (17 November, 1953, age 9)

On Saturday mornings I wake up early about seven o'clock and get dressed. I go down stairs and wait for the postman to come. Usually he comes about a quarter past seven. I have to sort the letters very quickly for there are a lot of letters on a Saturday morning and I set off at half-past-seven. First I go to Anderton's office because they get at least forty letters on a Saturday. Sometimes if they get a lot of letters I have to go again to Mrs. Pilling which is quite near the office. Then I do the Square which is quite near our house. The next places I take letters to are New Row, Tutty Row and part of the new Airey houses. Then I go home and get some more letters for the other part of the new houses and the Council Houses. Then I work backwards past the telephone Kiosk and down Prospect Villa's, and go to Brantons for some sweets. When I get home it is usually about half past eight. Then I go and wake my brother up because he always sleeps late. Then at nine o'clock I have my breakfast which usually consist of ham, egg and sausages. After breakfast I feed my cats their names are Fluff who is nearly two years old and two small kittens who's names are Snowy and Dinky they are nearly six months old. By then it is about ten o'clock and I run a few errands and then if I want to, I go back to bed till eleven o'clock.

Hairy-willy band

'Why is it called hairy-willy band, mam?'
'I don't know, lad. I call it Post Office string myself. Ask your dad.'

'Dad, why does everybody but me mam call it hairy-willy band?'

'Well, band is string. Maybe it's hairier than ordinary string or binder twine. But I reckon your Uncle Arthur knows.'

'Uncle Arthur, why's this string called hairy-willy band?'

'Nay lad, tha' s'all ev ti wuk it oot for thysen.'

'But Uncle Arthur, I can see why it's called "hairy", but I can't work out the "willy".'

'Nay, lad, none of us can.'

Pigs

Half a century before, everyone who could afford to keep a pig kept one. In the late 1940's some people still kept a pig or two in a backyard sty. Minnie Rowbotham across the road kept a pig. Uncle George had five or six in a corrugated-iron-and-board pen in his orchard.

After a pig-killing you could go into some folks' houses and find lumps of pigmeat everywhere. Old Joby had a house with very high ceilings from which wicked metal hooks projected. After a pig-killing Old Joby's kitchen ceiling became an aerial butcher's shop. Large detached pieces of pig hung from every hook. It was a lesson in butchery. Whole legs and half-sides, red ribs showing, swayed gently in the draught. Joby and Edna sat at the table below supping tea. I didn't like Old Joby and would envision his doom as an enraged piece of pig unhooked itself and fell upon him.

Three doors up, opposite our Post Office, Minnie and Alf had a pig-killing every year at the same time. The pig was kept in a backyard sty, although he often got out and prevented anyone from approaching Minnie's back door. No one with any sense would approach an angry pig. Stories of the gaping holes carved in human flesh by pigteeth were all too common. Only Minnie or Alf could coax the animal back into its pen.

But all that smooth, violent pinkness was doomed when the pig-sticker arrived. He had another job, so the pig-killing always took place in the evening, and usually in the dark because it was approaching the 'back end'. The sticker set up some lights or flares, got out an old, stained board table, which had evidently seen much use, and had Minnie or Alf lead up the pig for sacrifice. Mother never let us see any more, but from across the road we waited in fearful expectation. Then the screams came. It was as if a nursery of babies was having its collective throat cut. You felt you could never face Minnie or Alf again. But country people are not sentimental about animals; sentimentality is an urban luxury indulged in by people who advertise to give kittens away instead of drowning them. Tomorrow there would be pig's scraps and soon chitterlings and black puddings. And a new pigling, small and squeaky clean, would be bought to fatten up for next year. Minnie's nephews always came for the pig's bladder, which they tied up and used as a football.

Uncle George, although well over six feet high and burly with it, had no stomach for pig-killing. He sent his pigs away to the bacon factory and received cold cash rather than warm hams and hocks. It was less exciting but easier on the nerves. You felt that Uncle George's pigs were not destined to die. So you could spend a pleasant hour with them, scratching their hairy backs, watching their deliberate rooting, absorbing that lovely smell, in blissful ignorance of their actual fate. Uncle George fed them the windfall apples and pears from his orchard, which they scrunched noisily with huge yellow teeth. It probably improved the flavour. Otherwise they were fed a hot steamy stew of vegetable scraps, potato peelings, and whole 'pig-taties'. The penetrating smell of pig-swill is something that lingers in the memory longer than in clothes and hair.

Drowning kittens

Fluff the cat came from Irene's across the street when a tiny kitten. She was a superb ratter and killed a fair number of Alf Peacock's racing pigeons before she was finally run out of lives and was poisoned (by Alf?) at about twelve years of age. Our river bank was alive with rodents which kept her busy all night, as did the local toms, in season. Few cats were ever neutered in our village, so Fluff produced a cupboardfull of kittens several times a year. Some were sired, incestuously, by her eldest son, one Snowball, a lovely kitten who became the ferocious one-eyed tom who deigned to sleep with us during the day.

Few people wanted kittens. The farm and Chemics were themselves overstocked. Supply greatly exceeded demand. Even if you gave a kitten away, you could never be sure that it would be well-treated. Faced with a large kitten surplus each year, villagers resorted to a frequent slaughter of the innocents, usually by drowning.

'They don't feel nothing.'

'They're only vermin at that age.'

'You have to do it before they've got their eyes open.'

'T'mother soon forgets 'em.'

'You'll have to give t'owd cat's titties a pull now and then, 'cos she's full o' milk.'

The worst part was getting the kittens away from their mother. Well-fed cats are especially loving and beautiful just after the birth. You could lose your hand in Fluff's milksoft bellyfur, only to be thrust away by four or five bullet heads searching for turgid teats. We would give Fluff a couple of day's contentment at least. The best ploy was to entice the mother away with some tidbit, then scoop up the kittens from the box where they lay groping blindly for their dam.

Problem: reduce kitten population.

Equipment: one sack, hessian; one short length of hairy-willy band; one brick.

Method: (1) Ascertain state of tide. If high tide, proceed. (2) Wrap brick in soft material; place brick in bottom of sack; add kittens. (3) Carry sack gently to jetty or river bank; tie top of sack; drop sack in river.

Result: kittens drowned.

Conclusion: Successful operation; kitten problem solved.

Recommendations: (1) Some use a bucket, but it is best to live near a river. (2) Never use a plastic bag (unless heavily perforated). (3) Have cat neutered (?). 'Taint natural'; 'They'll nivver get no pleasure, will they?'; 'Ten shillin'? Nay, lad, I s'all just keep on drownin' 'em.' 'D'ye hear yon? Ten bob just to cut t'owd cat's knackers off.' 'Sitha, get thi'sen one of them there 'lastic bands and fettle it wi' that.'

Caution: this operation may be damaging to the psyche.

A short walk with Tom and Harold

Coming home from bird's-nesting, just in time for Sunday dinner (1:30 p.m. or later, depending upon when the menfolk arrive home from the pub), you catch up with old Tommy Slater strolling bowlegged down the village street. Tommy wears a dark blue suit jacket, greyish-brown trousers that don't match, a collarless striped shirt, a muffler twisted around his lizard neck, a greasy flat cap. His creased and wrinkled tortoise face smiles into the noon sun. He walks a little lop-sided, cradling one jacket pocket with some care. You watch that pocket; you know his dinner's in there.

Outside Harold's house, fat Harold stands rigid on the doorstep, blinking at the sun, thumbs in braces, taking the air. Tommy decides to take Harold in hand, stir things up a bit. He stops, leans on the gate, looks at Harold's vegetables, cracks a yellow-toothed smile at the blinking Harold. After a couple of minutes of contemplation, Tommy says:

'Na' then, Harry'

'Na' then, Tom. Oo 'ist?'

'Only fair', says Tommy, 'only fair to middlin', lad; oo's thi'sen?'

'Nay, ah'm right champion', says Harold, who doesn't look it at all.

'Tha looks fair rigwelted t'me, stood theear like a gret mammal', says Tom.

'Ah'll mammal thee', says Harold. 'Ah've just gorrup tha'knows, off night-shift.'

'Aye', says Tommy, who never worked a night-shift in his life, being blacksmith before retirement.

'Ah'm just thinkin' whether t'dig garden', says Harold.

'Nay lad,' says Tommy, 'it's gone openin' time. It's aboot a-five-an-twenty to one by t'clock.'

'Are y'off to t'pub then, Tom?'

'Ah'm off noo, to see t'lads', says Tommy, 'we allus 'as us pint afore dinner, tha' knows.'

'Aye, but thoo's got no missus' moans Harold.

'Nay, an' ah'm not a ligabed, neither,' laughs Tommy, knowing what is coming next.

'Nay, nay, Tom,' says Harold, indecisive. Then, 'Ang thi'sen on, then, Tom, ah'll be wi' thee sharpish-like.'

Harold exits into the dark cavern of home. You and Tom laugh at Harold's mawky-looking veggies. The sounds of marital altercation ricochet through the open door. You and Tommy laugh again. Harold reappears in his Sunday gardening gear, an ancient three-piece suit, all matching, but with a collarless grey-white shirt. A shrill stream of imprecations, mostly about the inevitability of a spoiled Sunday dinner drying up in the oven, escorts Harold off the premises. You and Tommy cackle; you've heard it all before. Harold, as yet, is not amused:

'Bloody old woman's allus natterin'.'

'Aye, Ah hear tell,' says Tommy, winking at you.

'Allus bloodywell rattlin' and creatin' and damn well goin' on', continues Harold.

'Aye, Ah hear they're all t'same', condoles bachelor Tommy. 'But Ah nivver 'ed no hexperience wi' that theear.'

'Thoo 'ad right idea, then, Tom.'

'Why, Ah allus looks at it like this, "Arry. Y'ave ter pay fer y'pleasures".'

'Pleasures!' gasps Harold, aghast. 'Pleasures! What bloody pleasures?'

'Nay,' says Tommy, grinning lasciviously at you, and winking at the morose Harold, 'doo'ant tell me yo' nivver 'ed no pleasures since yo'were wed.'

'Aye, well,' muses Harold, 'if Ah cast mi' mind back a bit.'

'Thirty year,' laughs Tommy, winking again.

'Thirty bloody year. It's a life sentence. It's wuss. Nay, ah s'all 'ev more than a couple of pints this dinner.'

'Aye, an' then thy old lass'll play war wi' thee 'cos t'dinner's all bont up in t'oven ageean,' laughs Tommy, having achieved his goal.

'She'll bloody well 'av ter play 'ell, then,' grins Harold, happy to have been conned yet again. 'Yer can't win, can yer? In thirty bloody year she 'ent learnt not ter get dinner ready at openin' time.'

We reach the Club. As they enter, the doorway emits a warm rich savour, redolent of beer, cigarettes, and vomit; at least it makes you feel a bit sick. Is your dad in there, you wonder. But he's rarely late for dinner, and you've never seen him drunk.

You climb on the windowsill and peer through a crack in the frosted glass. Inside dark figures sit round tables, pints in hand, supping, laughing, smoking, swearing into the warm blue fug. It's a man's haven from the slings and arrows of, mostly, married misfortune.

Tommy buys Harold a pint. He has to, it's only fair. Harold opens his gullet and takes down three-quarters of the jar in one long draught, adam's apple escalating with vigour. Only then does he relax. After four or five more, he won't want Blanche's dried-up dinner.

Meanwhile, Tommy puts a wrinkled brown hand into his carefully cradled pocket, takes out an egg, breaks it open on the rim of his glass, and drops yolk and white into his pint of bitter. That's his Sunday dinner.

Envoi

Personal history and recollection, one hopes, serve to colour a scene and people it with live characters rich in idiosyncracies. This is intimate sensing rather than the geographer's more sophisticated but less authentic remote sensing of life and landscape via satellite imagery (Porteous 1987). Such intimate sensing may assist the reader towards an *understanding* of the village. For *knowledge*, see the next chapter.

7
The living village:
modernization 1930s–1960s

The only constant is change.
Aphorism

The problem is not change itself, but the tempo of change.
Alvin Toffler

Lest the preceding chapter be regarded as merely some form of elegy, giving the false impression of a static village stranded in time, the present chapter serves to provide its context. No community, in the Western industrial world at least, managed to remain unchanged during the period which commenced with the lessening of the impact of the Great Depression of the 1930s and ended with the acceleration of modernization in the 1960s. Had the impact of external forces, in the shape of industrial and cargo-handling firms (Chapter 8) never taken place, Howdendyke would inevitably have changed in character.

The change, however, would probably have been slower and less dramatic. It would also have been more easily adjusted to, on the part of the inhabitants, than the massive alterations of life, landscape, and livelihood which came about after the designation of the area as an industrial growth point in 1968, and which are described in detail in the following chapters. The present chapter, largely based on interviews and correspondence with current and former Howdendykers, describes the social life of the village in more intersubjective terms than in Chapter 6, and objectively investigates the slow process of modernization which took place in Howdendyke over the four decades from mid-1920s to mid-1960s.

Social life in Howdendyke, 1930s–1960s

In the 1950s Howdendyke attained its maximum size of over seventy households, for the last houses to be built in the village were completed in the 1948 and some of these were occupied by families from elsewhere. The 1950s, then, which is the era of the deeply subjective accounts of the previous chapter, was the village's twentieth-century high water mark in population terms, and also in terms of social life, before the joint operation of social modernization (via television and automobile) and industrialization began to alter the village forever.

Throughout the twentieth century there has been much intermarriage among Howdendykers, a characteristic persisting well into the 1960s. A strong feeling of 'insiders' versus 'outsiders' is still common. Assisted by a village informant of long residence, I attempted to discover by relationship analysis just how close-knit was the village in 1951. We quickly revealed, once marriage as well as blood ties were included, that Howdendyke's seventy or so discrete households readily coagulated into a small number of 'clans', of which four alone accounted for approximately one quarter of the total population. The major clan comprised ten families, and my own Mell clan included eight local households. Two-household dyadic clans, usually involving the separate household of a married child, were common, the ten cases accounting for a further quarter of all households.

Although this situation persisted in 1961, by 1981 the tightly woven pattern had become much looser, chiefly through death and out-migration. Few Mell connections remained, but two clans, each of five households, substantially dominated a village of only forty-six households. One of these clans, remarkably, consisted of an original parental household and the four, mainly adjacent, households of married children. Even in the 1980s, then, Howdendykers must gossip as carefully as of yore, for 'you're never sure who's related to who', and a slip of the tongue may be reported back to 'our Jack'. Mutual assistance and comfort, however, are the other side of the coin. I still recall my childhood surprise and warm feelings on being told, by Tommy Palmer, that 'I'm akin to thou'.

Intermarriage evidently proved prolific, for post-war Howdendyke had a full complement of children. To compare 1956 with 1986, when the village had less than a handful of children of school age, is to compare a village lively and noisy with children to a tomb. The rural child culture was very strong in the 1950s, with its accepted seasons of birds'-nesting, marbles, street cricket, conkers, Mischievous Night, Bonfire Night, Christmas, pond-skating and, always, dangerous ventures into river mud, into the Chemical Works, up river banks, along hedges and ditches, and, most foolhardy of all, daring games of 'follow my leader' (known as 'cappers', from 'I can cap thee') along the greasy mud-covered spars of river jetties. Children roamed fields and farm, were given school holidays to pick potatoes ('tatie-scrattin' holidays'), were encouraged to harvest rose-hips, helped with harvesting and threshing, dammed dykes, chased the farm carthorses, were chased by the bull, drank milk foaming from the cow, brought moorhen eggs home for tea, scrumped orchards, fell in ponds, caught tadpoles and sticklebacks, ate from the hedges.

According to my informants, the few remaining children in the Howdendyke of the 1980s perform far fewer of these activities, and with less enthusiasm.

Plate 13. Coronation 1953

Plate 14. Village women visit London

Mischievous Night (November 4) for example, is a long-established regional saturnalia which gives children one evening in the year to engage, without much adult retaliation, in mischievous tricks such as knocking on doors, tying terrace house door-knobs together, tapping on windows, removing garden gates, frightening adults with fire crackers, and suchlike pranks (Opie and Opie 1956). In full swing in the 1950s, this activity had dwindled to a merely perfunctory door-rapping by the 1980s.

Lack of a 'critical mass' of children in a depopulated village was chiefly to blame for this. By the late 1970s, moreover, many of the activities of the 1950s were impossible, for during the intervening period new agricultural practices ensured that many hedges were torn out, many trees cut down or uprooted, almost all ponds filled in, and even some field dykes culverted.

Adult social life, to some extent, meshed with that of the child culture. Mischievous Night was tolerated, and a few adults got their exercise by giving chase to the miscreants. The following evening, Bonfire Night, was a spectacle enjoyed by the whole village. Gangs of youths collected combustibles for over a month and the Bonfire was lit on the river bank outside the Jubilee Hall. The latter was extensively used for birthday parties, wedding receptions, whist drives, the annual children's Christmas Party (when every child in the village, not merely Anderton employees, received a gift from the Pillings) and the annual New Year's Dance, which was attended not only by adults but by children of all ages.

The Ouse Chemical Works Workingmen's Club and Institute (The 'Club') served as a retreat for adults, and not wholly men. Officially open to Anderton workers only, in practice the Club catered not only for Howdendyke villagers but also for regulars from other settlements, including some from the town of Howden. Club, Jubilee Hall and Post Office, all located in The Square at the junction of Howdendyke's two streets, were the joint social focus of the village. Their loss, threatened in 1986 (Chapter 10) would be an irretrievable blow to such a small community.

At the other end of the village lay a permanent pasture known as the Cricket Field (now a warehouse). Although Howdendyke's football teams died out with World War II, cricket was revived and throughout the 1950s the village team played the teams of adjacent settlements in a very minor league. The same field was used for sports on irregular occasions, the most spectacular being the Coronation sports of 1953, following a lengthy fancy-dress parade which wound its way throughout the village from its assembly point in The Square. These were the days before Howdendykers could afford personal televisions; those who wished to view the Coronation ceremony were provided with a giant screen in the Jubilee Hall.

Adults, naturally, spent much of their waking lives working, mostly in the Ouse Chemical Works, which employed a number of women in various capacities. Scarr's Shipyard provided job opportunities which fluctuated wildly with orders, from less than ten in poor years to about twenty in good. Correspondents reminded me of the importance of the shipyard as the provider of spectacles at irregular intervals, the chief and most momentous spectacle being the launch of a newly-built vessel. The word being out, crowds would line the river bank to witness the successful splash.

While women baked, knitted, and mended, men would spend many evenings and weekends gardening. A number of workmen, including my two local uncles, had large and flourishing orchards. Indeed, my Uncle Roland's orchard (Figure 15) was so large that it was let off to at least three others, including my father. People grew orchard fruits, bush fruits, and a wealth of vegetables, kept hens and even pigs, though not, strangely enough, in the area known as The Pigyard. During the 1950s at least seven distinct areas in the village were in orchard and allotment use and at Elm Tree and beyond market gardeners flourished.

Most of the housing, as well as the Chemical Works, was owned by the Pillings, who lived in the modest country home known as Kilpin Lodge, on the Kilpinpike edge of Howdendyke. Their rather benevolent control of much employment, most housing, and many social events was less in the nature of the corporate company town (Porteous 1971) than in the style of a benign rural squirearchy (Chapter 5).

Kilpin Lodge was a two-storey amalgamation of earlier cottages and outbuildings, based on a plan involving long corridors. Besides the usual offices and six bedrooms, the house boasted laundry room, billiard room, smoke room and school room, with outbuildings and walled grounds which included courtyards, stables, garages, tennis courts, saddle room, greenhouses, kitchen gardens and a paddock (with pet donkey and turkey). At the front of the house was a walled sunken Italian garden resplendent with roses; beyond the wall lay the river bank and a small wharf where the Pillings' modest motor yacht, *White Heather*, was anchored. Nearby, three cottages housed gardener, chauffeur and handyman. The house was immediately adjacent to the factory; indeed, one wall served as a party wall with the factory bag store.

The occupants, Mr and Mrs Pilling, frequently had young relatives to stay, but had no children of their own. Their social life involved their own far-flung families and other middle-class people in the Howden and Goole area, notably physicians, clergy and bankers. Theirs was a fairly modest establishment with a live-in staff of three before World War II, dwindling to fewer, and on a live-out basis, in the 1950s. Social relations between family and staff were the normal ones. As a former resident remarks: 'there wasn't a green baize door but [speaking of the kitchen area] that's virtually what it was'.

Three staff – cook, housemaid, and parlour maid – were required because of the Pilling lifestyle. Until World War II everyone dressed for 8 p.m. dinner, which was preceded by tea at four, lunch at one, and bountiful breakfasts.

Frequently 'They had big parties. Mr Pilling enjoyed shooting, and Mrs Pilling was involved in a lot of work, church work, WVS, meetings and political things, there was always a lot going on.' Failing, this, Mrs Pilling 'would suddenly have nothing to do one morning so she'd go and stir up the Works and see what was going on there.' And, when, on one occasion, sulphuric acid rain from a Chemical Works operation had burnt off 'practically everything green, the lawn, the trees, the vegetable gardens', 'Did Mrs Pilling have something to say! She couldn't get out of the car fast enough to get over to the Works to tell them what she thought about it.'

Relations with the workpeople were cordial but, naturally, somewhat distant. The Jubilee Hall was a common meeting place, for the Pillings sponsored sales of goods there made by the blind, whist and beetle drives in aid of a number of causes, as well as parties, dances, and musical evenings. Above all, remarked a Pilling niece,

> The thing about Howdendyke was that you knew everybody. People going to work every morning lived just down the road, could go straight into the works, home for their dinners [lunch] and things like that. And we often used to send round to see how Mrs so and so was and did she need anything ...

Howdendyke then, in the 1930s and even in the 1950s, retained many of the rural attributes which we associate with Flora Thompson's *Lark Rise*, set in the 1880s.

The characteristic most remarked upon by interview informants, in association with the frequent recall of parties, dances, football games, and methodist services in the Jubilee Hall, was a spirit of community. Neighbourly help in sickness was part of the normal fabric of life, people shopped locally, and generally 'there was a very good spirit in those days ... all the games the kids used to play and the mothers would be at the gate watching....'

Modernization 1930s–1960s

Despite the general feeling among interview and corresponding informants that Howdendyke was a pleasant, self-contained, living community in the 1930s–1960s period, many of them noted that changes had begun to occur as early as the 1920s. Until the 1960s, however, I have the impression that these changes did not significantly alter village life, but simply served to render the daily round a little easier, especially for women. The changes associated with the arrival of electricity, piped water, sewerage, and street lighting cannot, therefore, be compared in their impact with either the private acquisition of televisions and automobiles nor the external impacts of industrialism, both of which became major characteristics of the village in the late 1960s.

Until the 1920s Howdendyke was closely connected to the town of Goole, a few miles downriver. Howdendyke Ferry, an ancient institution, ran several times a day depending on the tides, from Bishop's Staith upstream from the Post Office to the village of Hook on the West Riding side of the Ouse. The ferryman occupied Ferry House on the staith, property of the Ecclesiastial Commissioners, successors to the Bishop of Durham (Chapter 2). Ferry Farm was also a public house, known as the Ferry Inn or Steam Packet. By means of the ferry an adult could reach Goole in not much more than an hour and a half, even on foot.

The ferry, however, was not always reliable. When a bridge at Boothferry was proposed in 1905, various witnesses testified that they had suffered delays or had been refused passage. All were from Howden, and the town of Howden also prepared a general petition stating that both Howdendyke and Booth ferries were primitive, reduced trade, caused delays in fair weather, and were a 'grave source of public danger in foggy and stormy weather'. In northerly and westerly gales, apparently, a rope had to be rigged across and the boat hauled hand-over-hand across the river, 'an exceedingly slow, uncomfortable and tedious process'. Both passengers and ferrymen had recently drowned and many cattle and sheep had jumped overboard. Traffic across Howdendyke ferry in the week July 16–22 1905 consisted of 553 foot passengers, 341 bicycles, 6 saddle horses, 6 wheeled vehicles, and 10 items of 'heavy traffic', totalling 916 items, compared with Boothferry's 1087 in the same period. Clearly, Howdendyke was one of the two major traffic routes between Howden and Goole at this time. Nothing was done about a bridge, however, for another quarter of a century.

In 1929 Boothferry Bridge, about two miles upstream, became the first road bridge to cross the Ouse below Selby, ten miles upstream from Howdendyke. Bus services between Howden and Goole began to operate, later extended (at weekends) to Howdendyke and adjacent villages. In consequence of lessening through traffic, Howdendyke public houses closed, but were replaced by the Club, and villagers gained more assured access to Goole.

But more assured access, undeterred by tides, is not necessarily more frequent or cheaper access. Via the new bridge, Goole was now actually further from Howdendyke. Via public transportation, it was more expensive than with the ferry. For workpeople with limited time and money, and especially those limited to foot or bicycle, it is likely that the village of Howdendyke became relatively more distant from the town of Goole in the 1930s. Certainly it became a relatively more remote place as through traffic to the ferry abruptly ceased.

Nevertheless, the 1930s saw the first of the major social changes which ameliorated the lives of Howdendykers in the modern era (Table 26). Extensive modernization of the Chemical Works, which involved one of the first uses in

Britain of the American Broadfield granulator, was matched by a thorough renovation of much Anderton housing property. This, in turn, was partly related to a programme of housing modernization and utility provision begun by Howden Rural District Council.

Unlike the rest of the village, Kilpin Lodge had running water and gas-lighting in the 1930s, the latter being replaced by a diesel power house which provided DC electricity before the general electrification of the village. As the Chemical Works was supplied with gas from the Howden gasworks and water from the Anderton windmill at Sunny Bank, these could readily be extended to the Lodge, and to a small number of nearby houses, for my earliest memories of the Post Office (mid-1940s) include gas lighting. The bulk of the village,

Table 26. The Modernization of Howdendyke, 1920s–1980s

Year or era	Event
1920s (late)	Ferry closed down (Boothferry Bridge opened), bus service begins, independent public houses close, Ouse Chemical Works Club opens.
1935	Schoolroom extended, refurbished, renamed 'Jubilee Hall'.
1935	Chemical Works modernized and extended; new granular plant.
1936	Demolition of eight houses in North St., north of Post Office.
1936	Eight council houses built on 'field side' of village.
1937	Rural District Council 'scavenging' system begun (for both refuse and emptying of lavatories).
1937	Extensive alterations and repairs to Anderton tied housing (relates to new water supplies and scavenging scheme).
1939	Water supplies laid on to most houses.
1948	Eight more council houses (Airey type) built on 'field side' of village, completing a continuous line of buildings on this side from Post Office to village's northern entrance.
1949	Electricity supplies laid on to most houses.
1950s (mid)	Gradual phase-out of mixed farming (horses, bull, threshing, milk delivery direct from farm).
1950s (late)	Acquisition of televisions becoming general.
(1959–60)	Deaths of the Pillings.
1960s (early)	Acquisition of automobiles becoming general.
1960s (mid)	Sewerage system and street lighting installed.
1968	Shipyard closes; Anderton-Richardson Ltd. acquired by Hargreaves Fertilizers Ltd.
1970s (early)	Closure of two of three shops, leaving only the Post Office.
1970s (mid)	Acquisition of telephones and other appliances becoming general.
1960s–80s	Farmers begin to plough up public footpaths, tear out hedges and trees.
1960s–80s	Growth of cargo-handling facilities on both sides of village with subsequent destruction of at least half of village's houses (see Chapters 8–10).

however, subsisted without piped water into the very late 1930s, without electricity until ten years later, and without sewerage into the 1960s.

The face of the village was radically changed when eight decrepit houses in North Street, north of the Post Office, were demolished and their tenants rehoused on the opposite, 'field side' of the village, in eight council houses of bright red brick (Figure 13). In the late 1930s these houses were a great improvement on the remainder of the housing stock, for all had bathrooms (adjacent to the kitchen, strangely enough, and therefore easy to fill with wood, if not coal) and piped running water.

The latter was the greatest change, especially from the woman's point of view. Older respondents vividly remember obtaining their water from a North Street standpipe; piped water to one's house proved a great boon, for water is very heavy. The water system did not emerge without controversy, however. Between 1935 and 1938 several meetings were held in the village hall in association with the deliberations of Kilpin Parish Council. The records of these meetings show that these were the best-attended parish council meetings since the council's inauguration in 1894. Attendance varied between thirty-five and forty, all males except for the invariable and last-listed Mrs Mell, my shop-owning grandmother. No issue was so thoroughly to exercise Howdendykers until the revelation of their village's impending destruction in the late 1970s (Chapters 9, 10).

The latter half of the 1930s, then, saw the introduction of basic services, the building of new housing, and the refurbishing of the old. No major changes were thereafter to occur until the very late 1940s when eight further council houses, of the pebble-dash 'Airey' type, completed the building line along the 'field side' of the village from river bank to the Howden road. Almost simultaneously, the village was given an electricity supply, although the use of paraffin lamps continued well into the 1950s (Chapter 6).

Electrification was to be a major stimulus for social change, although Howdendykers, never affluent, were generally unable to purchase televisions until the mid-or late 1950s. Growing affluence in the early 1960s promoted automobile purchase, which in turn led to greater access first to Goole and later to Leeds, Hull and York. As a result, the two village shops had closed by 1972 and the Post Office reduced its general store function considerably. As a former village shopkeeper expressed it:

> We were always tied to the place. We had to open from eight in the morning until ten at night. Then V.A.T. started and needed so much paperwork. It was alright while Howdendyke was a nice little community and people did things locally and shopped locally. But then they all got cars which got them out and then they all got televisions which kept them in. . . .

None of this, of course, is specific to Howdendyke. It is the common litany of decline in village services since the 1950s, whereby the poor and elderly become ever more relatively deprived, the usual planning solution being to remove them to larger 'key settlements' (Cloke 1977; Chapter 8).

Paradoxically, then, just as the village began to enjoy the full benefits of modernization in the form of electricity, street lighting, and a water-borne sewerage system, its inhabitants acquired the means to reorientate their shopping activities to other centres and their social activities to the fireside and glowing screen. There is no reason to believe, however, that the effects of these changes in community life would have been any more destructive than in any other small village. Indeed, there is evidence (Chapter 10) that Howdendyke would have received its complement of commuters had more houses been available for sale and rehabilitation in the 1970s.

Landscape change

Around the village, however, an inexorable process of landscape change took place in the 1960s and 1970s. A series of land use maps (Figures 16, 17, 18) at ten-year intervals summarize these developments. The chief motive force behind landscape change was agricultural modernization and rationalization, which began in the 1950s with the general move from mixed farming to specialized farming, and accelerated with the application of the EEC's Common Agricultural Policy in the 1960s.

During the 1940s shire horses were a common sight. Mr Ernest Austwick was ploughing his fields with horses into the 1950s. In the same era, my companions and I had to move the huge retired carthorses of Ferry Farm, Tom and Bonny, whenever we wished to play cricket. Farms were invariably mixed, and a wide variety of poultry, cattle, sheep, cereals, and related seasonal events were normal. This life-style remains intact in the 1980s on Hasholme Carr farm, about ten miles from Howdendyke.

From the late 1950s, however, the minutes of Kilpin Parish Council are filled with reports of farmers felling trees, rooting out hedges, filling in dykes and ditches, removing and infilling ponds, and ploughing up balks, headlands, public footpaths, and even unregistered common land. The great government-subsidized drive by local farmers, chiefly based in Kilpin village, to add to the unsalable mountains of agricultural produce stored by the EEC, resulted in remarkable changes in the landscape. It became much barer than before, less leafy, less able to support wildlife, and much more intervisible. Had the agrarian landscape not so changed, the visual intrusions, at least, of new industry at Howdendyke, would have had far less impact on the villagers of Kilpin and Skelton.

Rather more specialized than the land use maps are Figures 19 and 20 which

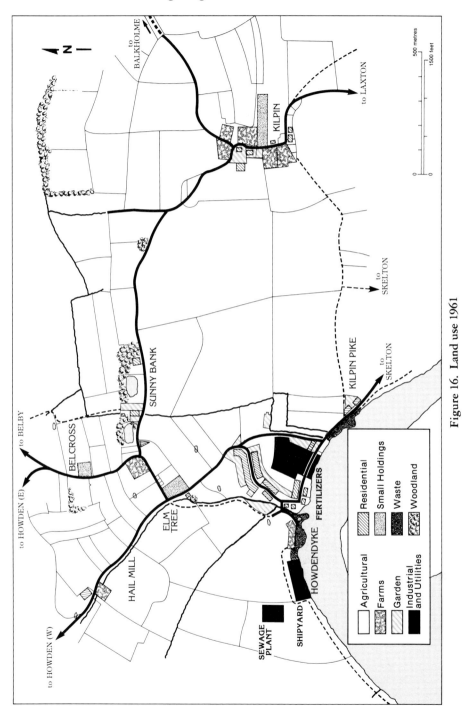

Figure 16. Land use 1961

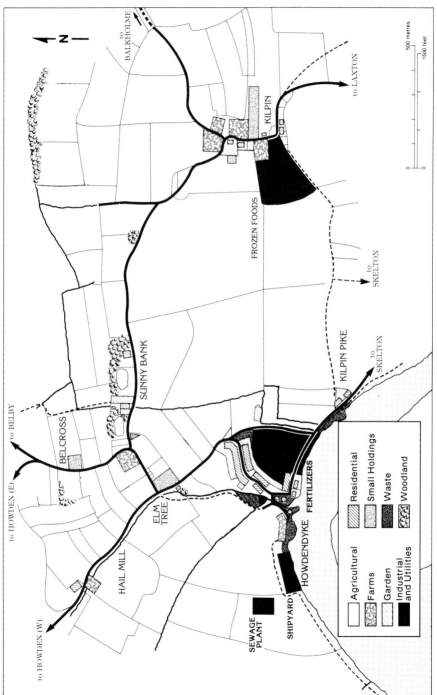

Figure 17. Land use 1971

The living village: modernization 1930s—1960s

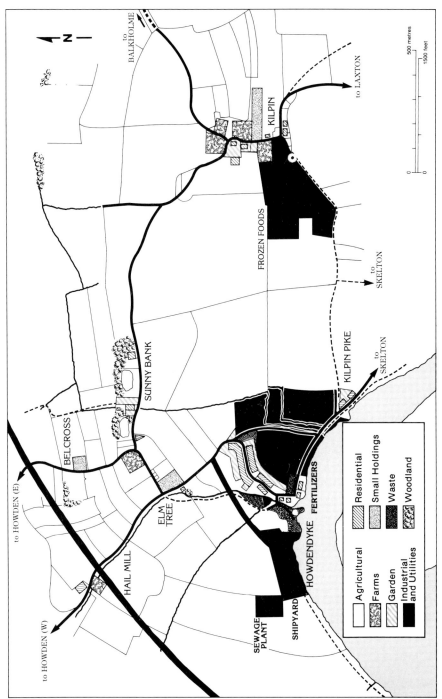

Figure 18. Land use 1981

Legend:
- Agricultural
- Residential
- Farms
- Small Holdings
- Garden
- Waste
- Industrial and Utilities
- Woodland

117

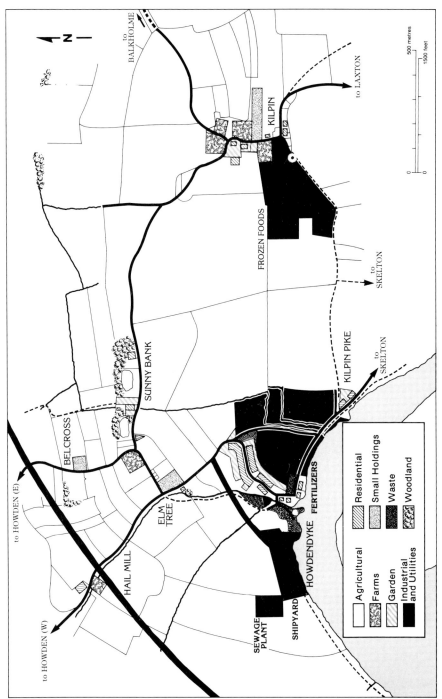

Figure 18. Land use 1981

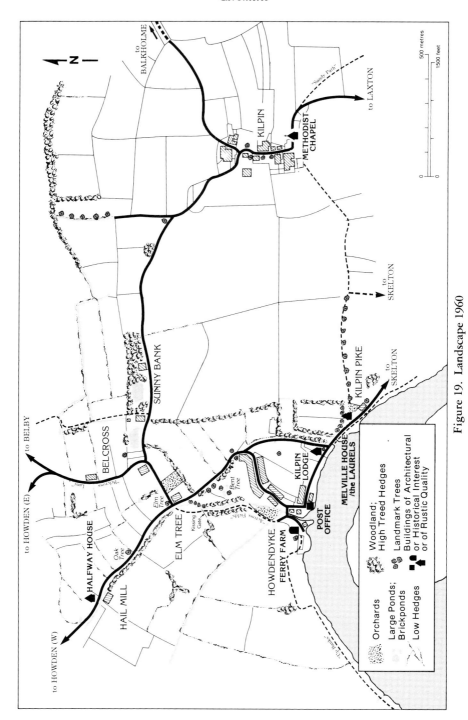

Figure 19. Landscape 1960

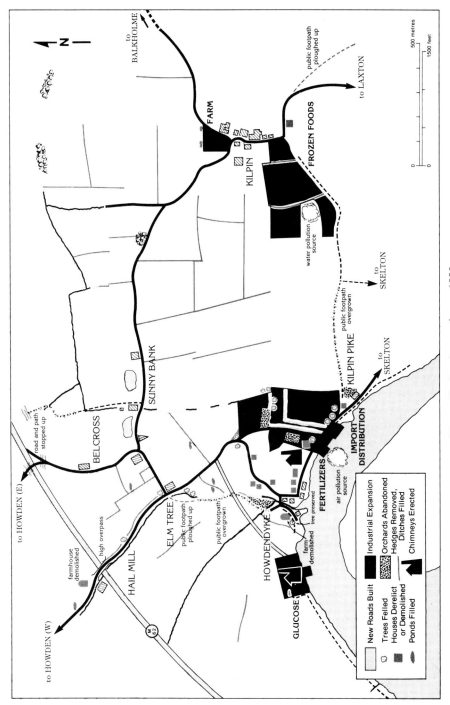

Figure 20. Landscape change 1980

summarize significant landscape transformations in the period 1960–80. It is possible to assess this in cost-benefit terms, but not quantitatively. The overwhelming transformation is clearly the immense growth of industrial sites, not only on both sides of Howdendyke but also in the hamlet of Kilpin. Before the closures of the glucose and frozen food factories in the early 1980s, these enterprises had added more than fifty new jobs, no mean feat in a basically rural area.

Offsetting this growth in employment opportunities, however, is a series of disbenefits, many of which cannot, like employment, be measured in quantitative terms. They can, however, be measured in terms of qualitative loss. Compared with the situation in 1960, the parish of Kilpin in 1980 was a much less interesting and a much more unpleasant place to live. The comments of a number of interview respondents, letters to the editor, and protests against planning proposals (Chapter 9) all confirm this.

It is no longer pleasant, in the mid-1980s, to walk the fields. Most hedgerows have been removed, most ponds have been infilled, many trees have been chopped down or wholly uprooted. All orchards and allotments have disappeared; common land has been ploughed up by farmers, as have some public footpaths. Others are so overgrown that progress is impossible should anyone even wish to walk in this prairie landscape. And one of the major reasons for such walks, the observation of wildlife, has been all but eliminated. Without hedges, trees, ditches, and ponds, wildlife habitats have been drastically reduced.

The most significant vegetation loss has been of landmark trees and high hedges. The latter, some several hundred of years old (pre-Enclosure) were composed of many different species, including both hawthorn and elderberry growing to approximately 20 feet in height, interspersed with mature examples of oak, ash, horse-chestnut, walnut, and elm. Although some of the landmark trees have been removed for safety reasons, particularly at the entrance to Howdendyke and at Elm Tree, most have been the victims of farm rationalization. By far the greatest culprit, however, in high hedge removal and ditch-filling has been the industrial enterprise which occupied the fields adjacent to Kilpin Lodge after 1968 (Figures 20 and 21). In this zone, high hedges, large trees, several interesting houses, orchards, and dykes have given way to open storage yards and large red warehouses.

Pollution is the inevitable result, and is chiefly dealt with in subsequent chapters. Suffice it to say that with the sudden arrival of several industrial enterprises in the late 1960s Kilpin parish began to suffer much increased levels of air, water, noise, traffic, soil, and visual pollution, the latter rendered far more damaging over a wide area by the coincident removal of hedges by farmers. And whereas the problems created by farmers dominated Kilpin Parish Council during the period 1958–67, the period following 1968 has been

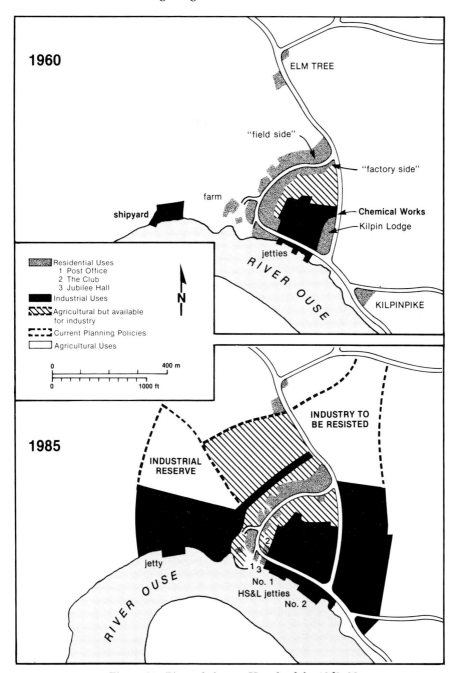

Figure 21. Planned change, Howdendyke 1960–85

121

overwhelmingly devoted to combatting, with little success, the pollutive consequences of the planning decision to turn Howdendyke into a minor industrial port zone (Chapters 8–11).

Demographic trends

The remarkable differences between the demographic structures of Howdendyke in the periods 1851–81 (Chapter 4) and 1951–81 are not specific to this village but accord with dominant secular trends during the past century towards fewer children per family, smaller households, greater availability of family housing, wider travel opportunities, and increased opportunities for female employment. It is notable, however, that the general trend towards embourgoisement has not occurred in Howdendyke. Rather, chiefly through the deaths of the Pillings and selective out-migration as daily travel

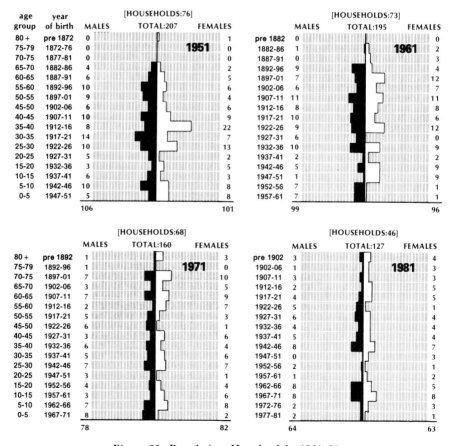

Figure 22. Population, Howdendyke 1951–81

opportunities improved, the relationship between white collar and blue collar workers, a ratio of approximately 1:9 in the late nineteenth century, had become 1:19 a century later. Howdendyke has clearly become a more thoroughly working-class village (Table 27).

As the overall census figures show (Table 4), the total population of Kilpin parish fell throughout the period. In the most recent intercensal period, 1971–81, the parish population fell by more than 20 per cent, the greatest fall of any parish in the new Borough of Boothferry. Most of this fall was accounted for by a rapid decline in Howdendyke's population after the mid-1960s. Although the census does not disaggregate settlements within parishes, my social reconstruction survey (Appendix) provided census-like material for Howdendyke (including Elm Tree and Kilpinpike) for 1951, 1961, 1971, and 1981 (Figure 22). The slight fall in the period 1951–61, involving 12 persons or under 6 per cent, is probably not significant. But the percentage fall between 1961 and 1971 was 18, and that in the following decade almost 21 per cent.

Such a catastrophic population decline, of almost 35 per cent over twenty years (1961–81), would be likely to cause consternation in any size of settlement. It becomes critical when the original population is only 200. And this already high rate of depopulation has risen in the 1980s. The forty-six households of 1981 had become a mere thirty-four by early 1986 (Chapter 9), a decline of over 26 per cent in only five years. The continuation of such a depopulation rate would see an entirely uninhabited village by the early twenty-first century.

The depopulation trend is, however, likely to be accelerated by the rapid ageing of the village population, chiefly caused by the unavailability of housing for couples of child-bearing age (Chapter 9). While the average number of persons per family remained stable at approximately 2.7 throughout the period 1951–81 (Table 28), the age structure of these persons changed dramatically (Figure 22, Table 29). After 1961, population pyramids become strongly etiolated, showing the absence of children and considerable population ageing. The modal age of household heads, 35–54 in 1951 and 1961, became 55 and over from 1971. By 1981, 98 per cent of household heads were over thirty-five, the most dramatic change being the fall in the percentage of household heads

Table 27. Head's socioeconomic class (%)

Class	1951	1961	1971	1981
1 (upper)	1	0	0	0
2	9	5	5	4
3	20	25	25	28
4	17	14	21	11
5 (lower)	53	56	49	57

Source: Social Reconstruction Survey.

Table 28. Persons per household (%)

Number per household	1951	1961	1971	1981
1	12	12	27	24
2	36	40	32	35
3–5	47	44	40	39
6–8	4	4	1	2
9+	1	0	0	0
(mean)	(2.8)	(2.7)	(2.6)	(2.7)

Source: Social Reconstruction Survey.

Table 29. Head's age and head's wife's age (%)

Head's age	1951	1961	1971	1981	Head's wife's age	1951	1961	1971	1981
under 35	26	12	20	2	under 35	35	15	39	13
35–54	44	51	25	44	35–54	49	56	26	57
55+	30	37	55	54	55+	16	29	35	30

Source: Social Reconstruction Survey.

Table 30. Number of head's children (%)

Number of children	1951	1961	1971	1981
0	47	55	57	57
1–2	46	38	32	28
3–5	6	7	9	15
6+	1	0	2	0
(mean)	(0.8)	(0.7)	(0.9)	(0.9)

Source: Social Reconstruction Survey.

Table 31. Household type (%)

Household headed by	1951	1961	1971	1981
Married male	86	82	68	65
Single male	3	3	3	13
Widowed male	1	3	3	2
Married female	0	0	0	0
Single female	1	1	1	2
Widowed female	9	11	25	17

Source: Social Reconstruction Survey.

under thirty-five from 20 to 2 in the single intercensal period 1971–81.

Clearly, after 1961 Howdendyke became not only significantly smaller, but also significantly older in population terms. For the families which remained, one to three children was the rule, conforming to national norms. But childless households increased throughout the period (Table 30), the drastic fall in

Table 32. Birthplaces (%)

Head's birthplace				Place	Head's wife's birthplace			
1951	1961	1971	1981		1951	1961	1971	1981
39	33	27	22	Howdendyke	48	36	35	33
3	4	1	0	Kilpin	2	0	0	0
20	20	16	11	Howden	8	7	9	3
8	11	8	9	Goole	6	5	7	7
13	12	19	24	Within 7 miles	9	15	22	30
1	3	8	11	Within 15 miles	0	8	4	0
4	7	9	6	From agricultural East Riding	8	10	13	17
3	4	5	9	From industrial West Riding	3	5	4	3
5	3	4	6	Rest of U.K.	11	12	4	7
4	3	3	2	Foreign	5	2	2	0

Source: Social Reconstruction Survey.

Table 33. Employment by industrial group (%)

Head's industrial group				Group	Head's wife's industrial group			
1951	1961	1971	1981		1951	1961	1971	1981
0	0	0	0	Professional				
7	5	6	2	Agriculture	0	0	30	57
10	10	3	7	Ship building	8	6	0	29
61	58	36	24	Chemical manufacture	50	44	20	0
4	3	9	15	Distribution	8	6	0	0
0	0	0	0	Shipping				
5	4	9	11	Services	34	44	50	14
0	0	0	0	Personal service				
13	20	37	41	Residual				

Source: Social Reconstruction Survey.

households headed by married males being matched by a rise in those headed by single males (never married or divorced) and, especially, widowed females (Table 31). In 1971, quite remarkably, a full one quarter of Howdendyke's population consisted of widows, most of them elderly.

A small village in which 57 per cent of the population have no children, and in which one third of the population live in single-person households, is likely to suffer rapid demographic decline unless in-migration occurs. Indeed, it is estimated that when the median age of a community reaches thirty-five, deaths begin to exceed births, and decline becomes a function of low birth rates as well as out-migration (Bertrand 1980). And in Howdendyke public policy (Chapters 8, 9) prevents in-migration and encourages emigration in a variety of ways (Chapter 9).

What Howdendykers call 'real Howdendykers', that is, those born in the village, suffered a dramatic decline in the 1960s, from over one-third of the population to little more than a fifth (Table 32); 'there aren't any Howdendykers here anymore', noted one of my interviewees. As late as 1981, however, two-thirds of the inhabitants had been born within seven miles of the village (81 per cent in 1951) and three quarters of all head's wives were born locally throughout the period.

This remarkable population decline after the 1960s has been matched by, and partly related to, an equally dramatic change in employment structure (Table 33). In 1951, the era of peak twentieth-century population in the village, nearly 80 per cent of household heads were employed in the three traditional Howdendyke occupational categories, chemical manufacture, shipbuilding, and agriculture. By 1981 this proportion had fallen to just under one third, and two fifths of the population were now retired or otherwise unemployed.

The most obvious decline is in persons employed in the Chemical Works. About 60 per cent of household heads and almost 50 per cent of their working wives were employed by Andertons in the 1940s and 1950s. By 1971 these proportions had fallen significantly, coincident with the change of ownership of the Chemical Works and the rationalization process introduced by new owners (Chapter 8). After 1968, when Scarr's small shipyard closed, shipyard workers had to commute to Goole. The rapid rise in number of women employed in agriculture from the late 1960s relates to the opening of a frozen-food factory in the village of Kilpin (Chapter 8).

Commentary

Howdendyke, a viable living community in the 1950s, had by the early 1980s become a mere shadow of its former self. Although social life inevitably changed with the purchase of television and automobiles, and landscape change wrought by farmers was considerable, these agencies cannot explain the marked population decline endured by the village after the late 1960s.

The frequent references to subsequent chapters in the above paragraphs indicates that the causes of those remarkable demographic changes will shortly be investigated in detail. What will emerge from this investigation is that Howdendyke appears to have been deliberately depopulated, without the consent of the villagers, by a combination of private enterprise and public policy.

III

Revelations

People of Earth, your attention please ...
This is Prostetnic Vogon Jeltz of the Galactic Hyperspace
Planning Council ...
As you will no doubt be aware, the plans for development of
the outlying regions of the Galaxy require the building of a
hyperspatial express route through your star system, and
regrettably your planet is one of those scheduled for
demolition. The process will take slightly less than two of your
Earth minutes. Thank you.
There's no point in acting surprised about it. All the planning
charts and demolition orders have been on display in your local
planning department in Alpha Centauri for fifty of your Earth
years, so you've had plenty of time to lodge any formal
complaint ...
What do you mean you've never been to Alpha Centauri? For
heaven's sake, mankind, it's only four light years away you
know. I'm sorry, but if you can't be bothered to take an interest
in local affairs that's your own lookout. Energize the
demolition beams!

Douglas Adams

Whether the metaphor of death can appropriately be applied
to communities is a question that sociologists and economists
may want to debate, but few archaeologists or historians will
have any reservations on this score.

William Adams

8
Action

Is then no nook of English ground secure
From rash assault?
                    William Wordsworth
        No such nook.
                    Gavin Porteous, aged 6

The processes which are leading to the slow destruction of the village of Howdendyke had their roots in fundamental changes which began in the late 1950s. The most important of these changes involved the relinquishing of direct control of the Anderton fertilizer company by the Pilling family.

G. H. Anderton Ltd. was a purely family concern until incorporation in the early twentieth century. Even thereafter it was very much under the control of Mrs Maude Mary Pilling, only scion of the Howdendyke Andertons, and her husband, Richard Norman Pilling. Postwar legislative changes induced the Pillings to consider means of reducing death duties, and directorships were accepted by a number of white-collar employees. Later, in 1958, G. H. Anderton Ltd. was amalgamated with Henry Richardson Ltd., a York wholesale seed merchant, the resulting company being registered as Anderton-Richardson Fertilizers Ltd.

This was a judicious move, for Mrs Pilling died in 1959, to be followed by her husband in the following year. The nearest relatives were cousins, nephews, and nieces; there were no children to take personal interest or control. The firm continued without significant change for some years, but was taken over in 1967 by Hargreaves Fertilizers Ltd., a company partly owned by the Imperial Chemical Industries conglomerate (ICI) and whose headquarters were housed in the former Richardson offices in York. At the time of writing the plant is owned by BritAg, a wholly-owned ICI subsidiary.

Rationalization by Hargreaves

The Ouse Chemical Works of Anderton-Richardson Ltd. underwent several expansions in the 1950s and early 1960s, including some 'rationalization' which involved the sale of barges and sundry company-owned houses in the town of Howden and elsewhere. But it was only with the take-over by Hargreaves in

Plate 15. Howdendyke *c.*1955

Plate 16. Howdendyke *c.*1970

1967 that major changes began to be felt in the village of Howdendyke.

Personal control wielded by the Pillings from Kilpin Lodge in the village itself was replaced by the control of an alien company exerted from a distance. The corporation's chief concern is cost-efficiency; to Hargreaves the Ouse Chemical Works was merely their Howden Division. The Hargreaves company had no interest in Howdendyke as a village, or the chemical works as other than a single unit in a larger web of operations. Hence the notions of a 'closed' community, dependent upon a paternalist family firm, of company-owned 'tied' housing, or of a self-sufficient industrial operation, were foreign to the new owners. Consequently, Hargreaves developed a policy of strict 'rationalization' and began in 1966–67 to divest themselves of all Howdendyke operations not directly connected with fertilizer production.

In particular, the following divestments of the late 1960s were to be of great consequence for the later destruction of Howdendyke.

(1) G. H. Anderton Ltd. had owned a small fleet of lorries and river barges. These were sold off and the new company's transport needs were contracted out to independent haulage and wharfage companies. This seemingly minor adjustment in day-to-day operations was to be of overwhelming importance, for it provided an opening in Howdendyke for the operations of an import-distribution company later to be known as Humberside Sea & Land Services Ltd. (HS & L).

(2) G. H. Anderton Ltd. had, since the mid-1950s, owned most of the privately-owned housing in Howdendyke (Figure 13). True, some of the peripheral houses remained in individual hands, but these included only a single dwelling at Elm Tree, Ferry House (Ecclesiastical Commissioners) and four dwellings at Kilpinpike (three owned by the Mell family). Within and around the triangle of roads which defined Howdendyke proper, however, Andertons controlled every unit of non-council housing except the Post Office (also in the Mell family). An internal company memorandum revealingly states that Anderton house purchases in the early 1950s would ensure their ownership of 'The whole Triangle'. This housing stock, numbering over forty dwellings in Howdendyke proper, was apparently an embarrassment to Hargreaves, and they attempted to sell the houses off to sitting tenants. Howdendykers, however, had a long tradition of renting, and in the 1966–68 sale period only twelve houses were sold to occupants. Half of these dwellings lay on the 'factory side' of Ferry Road, Howdendyke's main street.

(3) Further, G. H. Anderton Ltd. had run a more or less self-sufficient industrial unit, with its own bricklayers, blacksmiths, plumbers, electricians, and other time-served tradesmen. The works being part of a larger enterprise, these trades were not now needed, and as tradesmen retired they were not replaced. This policy had some consequences for the future of the thirty-one company-owned village houses which Hargreaves were unable to sell.

(4) Of much greater consequence was the change in ownership of several fields lying between Kilpin Lodge and Kilpinpike. G. H. Anderton Ltd. had for many years rented these fields, but Hargreaves terminated the rental agreement. The owner quickly sold the fields to East Coast River Services Ltd. (East Coast), the forerunner of HS & L.

(5) As if to match the loss of these waterfront fields (the 'downstream' site) to a new company, Hargreaves sold Andertons' 39-acre Ferry Farm (the 'upstream' site) to a former tenant in 1967. Within four years this farmer had sold most of the farm to industrial land development firms. Recession and retirement of the owner led to the closure of the very small shipyard, adjacent to the farm, in 1968. This area, and the farmhouse, were purchased by the sugar firm Tate & Lyle under the name of Howden Glucose Ltd.

By 1968, then, the village of Howdendyke was no longer surrounded by mere farmland, but by potential industrial sites. The two greenfield sites upriver and downriver to Howdendyke were each approximately equal in extent to the whole village as it existed in 1967 at the end of the Anderton-Richardson era. Together, the two tracts entirely surrounded the village.

The Planning context

Any use of these greenfield sites, however, was constrained by planning controls exerted at the county level.

In 1960, the year that R. N. Pilling died, the East Riding County Council issued its first County Development Plan. This plan designated 11 acres of Howdendyke as 'industrial land', largely consisting of the existing Ouse Chemical Works and only part of the field immediately adjacent to the plant and within the Triangle. All other non-residential land at Howdendyke remained as 'white land', essentially unallocated land not to be developed. According to the plan, which was expected to cover development up to 1971, all industrial expansion of a non-agricultural nature was expected to take place in urban areas, although some consideration would be given to rural river-related industry.

The house sales on the 'factory side' of Howdendyke village, which were later to become a thorn in the side of Hargeaves, suggest that the new owners of the Ouse Chemical Works had no firm long-term plans for expansion of the plant. Yet other evidence indicates that Hargreaves may have participated in plans for the general industrial expansion of Howdendyke as early as 1968. Given the sale of shipyard and farm, the divestment of former Anderton agricultural land on either side of Howdendyke, and some evidence of joint enterprise between Hargreaves and East Coast (later HS & L) in the matter of river jetties, all of these occurring in 1967–68, the following series of planning events does not seem likely to be merely coincidental.

In the first three months of 1968 Hargreaves applied for planning permission to build a large new river jetty opposite Kilpin Lodge, the former Pilling residence, which was to be demolished. A 'Howdendyke Wharf Company Ltd.' also applied to convert the former shipyard into a cargo-handling and import storage area. These proposals were enthusiastically welcomed by local politicians, for in April Howden Rural District Council, the local government authority, applied to the East Riding of Yorkshire County Council, the ultimate planning authority for the area, to have both upstream and downstream greenfield sites rezoned. Specifically, the Rural District requested that the 'white land' designation of these areas be altered so that the land could be redesignated as suitable for river-related industrial development. Hargreaves withdrew its jetty proposal in August, for it had been replaced in June by an almost-identical proposal for a 200 foot wharf (enormous in comparison with existing Anderton jetties) submitted in June by East Coast River Services. East Coast specifically stated that the jetty (later to be Wharf No. 1) was for the handling of fertilizer materials. This seemed reasonable, for Hargreaves, as has been seen, had rid themselves of company barge and lorry fleets and therefore had to contract out any transportation of materials.

The East Riding County Council Town Planning Committee discussed a number of issues at its October meeting. Some of these were referred to the Hull and East Riding Advisory Planning Committee for further discussion. Apparently, this was not necessary for the application to add twenty-four acres of 'unallocated' land at Howdendyke to the eleven acres of industrial land already designated on the County Development Plan.

Howdendyke's fate, therefore, was sealed in October 1968 by a group most of whose members had never seen the village. The East Riding County Council minutes (1968–69, pp. 156–8) state tersely: 'RESOLVED – That, subject to the concurrence of the Minister, the Committee see no objection to the 24 acres indicated by the County Planning Officer being used for industry making use of water-borne transport.' The villagers of Howdendyke, with no access to the corridors of power, had no knowledge of this resolution. Public participation in planning was not yet a major issue, and no official or businessman thought fit to enquire about the feelings of residents in 1968. When, a decade later, Howdendykers had become aware that their village was under threat of destruction, it was far too late, for the seeds planted in 1968 had already borne monstrous fruit.

Much of the initial development of Howdendyke in the post-Anderton era took place under the planning constraints of 1960 and 1968. Indeed, soon after 1968 Howdendyke found itself surrounded by developments both dangerous and noxious. A glucose factory appeared on the upstream site, while the downstream site became a cargo import and warehousing facility. With the failure of the glucose factory in 1980, both sites came into the hands of HS & L and its associates and both are now used for cargo-handling and warehousing.

By the time of the appearance of the Humberside Structure Plan in 1979, then, both 'industrial sites' could be regarded as pre-existing non-conforming land uses. The glucose factory had indeed conformed to the 1960/68 ruling that industry should be river-related. But the expansion of HS & L on the downstream site, although initially merely to provide service to the existing fertilizer plant, clearly involved not river-related industry but river-related import distribution of raw materials and processed goods, all of which could readily have been accommodated at existing Humber ports.

Permission to develop this non-conforming land use appears to have come about because of the local authority's obsession with industrial development and a very generous interpretation of the term 'industrial'. Local government reorganization in 1974 led to the replacement of Howden Rural District Council by Boothferry Borough Council. Unlike the Howden authority, whose headquarters were a little over one mile from Howdendyke and whose interests were mainly agricultural, Boothferry Borough consisted of an amalgamation of parts of the former East and West Ridings of Yorkshire with a portion of north-west Lincolnshire. Its interests were more inclined to the industrial and its headquarters lay in Goole, five miles from Howdendyke, across the river, and in a different former county.

In the larger Boothferry perspective of very active encouragement of industry, Howdendyke seemed ripe for designation as one of the five motorway-related industrial estates being developed in the jurisdiction. With the completion of an M62 motorway exit close to the deepwater channel at Howdendyke, the 35-acre industrially zoned area at that village seemed most suitable for industrial development based on river-borne raw materials.

The Humberside Structure Plan (1979) provided the context for the type of development to be expected at Howdendyke. With regard to industry, 'only industry which specifically requires deepwater frontage will be permitted to locate on riverside sites, and such industry will be allowed to develop specialized port facilities despite the plan's general prohibition of port developments outside the major ports', (paras. 8.19, 8.22). Cargo-handling services, however, were to continue to use existing ports such as Goole, only five miles away by road and less by water.

The Structure Plan also designated Howdendyke as a 'non-selected settlement'. Whereas in 'selected' settlements, or regional growth-poles, residential development would be encouraged, in the majority of villages 'only replacement of existing dwellings and the erection of new buildings on infilling sites will be permitted in non-selected settlements, all other planning matters being satisfied' (paras. 11.11, 11.16).

Given these planning parameters one would have predicted a fairly stable residential village, a continuing fertilizer factory (Hargreaves) within the village, and some river-related industrial growth on upstream and downstream sites surrounding the settlement. What one would not have predicted is precisely what had occurred by 1986, namely:

(1) the continuous expansion of apparently non-conforming cargo-handling operations on both former greenfield sites, working in direct competition with existing Humber ports;

(2) the running down of the fertilizer factory, so that, despite the designation of 24 further acres of industrial land in 1968, Howdendyke in 1986 had fewer jobs in manufacturing industry than in the 1960s;

(3) the demolition of over half the housing in the village of Howdendyke, with the prospect of further destruction to come.

Before the reasons for these 'developments' are considered, brief descriptions of the actual changes which have occurred on each site since 1967 would be useful.

Development in Howdendyke 1967–86

In 1966 the name Howdendyke referred to a compact residential village partly enclosing the Ouse Chemical Works, the whole surrounded by prime agricultural land. By 1968 Howdendyke comprised five separate non-agricultural sites: a downstream greenfield site; two upstream sites (formerly the Shipyard and Ferry Farm); the chemical works; and the residential village (Figures 13, 21).

The downstream site

Except for an abortive local authority plan to erect four council houses thereupon in 1964, the four fields adjoining Belby Clough drain, and fronting the Ouse between Kilpin Lodge and Kilpinpike, had been in agricultural use time out of mind. With the withdrawal of the early 1968 Hargreaves application for a new jetty, East Coast River Services Ltd. obtained planning permission for an almost identical 200 feet river wharf opposite the site of Kilpin Lodge, which was demolished in favour of warehousing. This new jetty, technically, was mainly on the Ouse Chemical works site, and was ostensibly built to supersede two of the three old Anderton jetties as an unloading point for raw materials destined for the fertilizer plant.

In 1969, however, East Coast began a series of applications for planning permission to build storage warehouses on the Belby Clough fields. Although the warehouses were clearly for the storage and distribution of goods imported via the new jetty, an activity which can hardly be termed 'industry', permission was not denied. East Coast made at least nine planning applications in the five years 1968–72 (Table 34). The results included a major wharf for cargo importing, extensive road widening at Kilpin Lodge corner, three large

Table 34. Planning applications, downstream site, 1968–85

Year	Applicant	Dimension	Use	Known objection	Status
1968(a)	ECRS[1]	–	jetty	yes	OK
1968(b)	ECRS[1]	–	warehouse and open storage	yes	withdrawn
1968(c)	ECRS[1]	–	road widening for jetty	no	OK
1969(a)	ECRS[1]	–	widening of jetty	yes	OK
1969(b)	ECRS[1]	–	further road widening	no	OK
1969(c)	ECRS[1]	32,850 sq.ft.	warehouse and office	yes	OK
1969(d)	ECRS[1]	10.5 acres	4 warehouses and open storage	yes	?
1971	ECRS[1]	30,000 sq.ft.	warehouse extension	no	OK
1972	ECRS[1]	30,000 sq.ft.	warehouse	no	OK
1973(a)	ECRS[1]	–	new jetty	yes	withdrawn
1973(b)	ECRS[1]	2,250 sq.ft.	rock salt mill	no	OK
1973(c)	ECRS[1]	636 sq.ft.	amenity block	no	OK
1974	ECRS[1]	–	messroom	no	OK
1978(a)	HS&L[2]	–	road realignment	no	OK
1978(b)	HS&L[2]	288 sq.ft.	office extension	no	OK
1978(c)	HS&L[2]	–	jetty extension	yes	withdrawn
1979(a)	HS&L[2]	200 feet	jetty extension	yes	OK
1979(b)	HS&L[2]	14 sq.m.	jetty office	no	OK
1979(c)	HS&L[2]	–	meal screening plant	yes	OK
1981(a)	HS&L[2]	–	powder off-loading system	yes	OK
1981(b)	HS&L[2]	–	convert dwellings into offices	no	OK
1983	HS&L[2]	–	extend jetty	yes	OK
1984	HS&L[2]	–	canteen block	no	OK
1985(a)	HS&L[2]	–	convert dwelling into offices	no	OK
1985(b)	HS&L[2]	–	demolish dwelling, replace with office	no	OK

Notes: [1] ECRS: East Coast River Services Ltd.
[2] HS&L: Humberside Sea & Land Services Ltd.

Sources: Boothferry Planning Office; local newspapers.

warehouses each covering about 30,000 square feet, and an extensive area of open storage for imported materials. The whole complex occupies a site of about 15 acres in the riverside fields between Howdendyke proper and Kilpinpike.

There were only minor objections to this development. Howdendykers, long part of a rather patriarchal system under the Anderton-Pilling regime, were not notable as objectors. Further, the developments meant new and varied job opportunities for the area. And no one had any idea of what this first flush of development would eventually mean in terms of quality of life and village viability.

By 1973, however, residents had sufficient exposure to the operation of the East Coast wharf to make strenuous objections to a grandiose proposal for a very large second jetty (Figure 23). This plan would have involved a wharf stretching from the site of Kilpin Lodge to Kilpinpike (Figures 13, 21). Besides residents' objections, the Yorkshire River Authority pointed out that such a wharf would likely hinder the outflow of the land drainage channel known as Belby Clough Drain. Finally, the Mell family, owners of the foreshore, refused to sell all of it to East Coast, being anxious because of family associations to retain ownership at least of Kilpinpike Staith.

East Coast lay low for a time, but the jetty plan resurfaced in 1978 as a more modest proposal to extend one of the remaining Anderton jetties by 200 feet, which was granted. A reapplication in the 1980s, which resulted in a rebuilding of this jetty as a second major wharf (Wharf No. 2) on Hargreaves land within Howdendyke village, is dealt with later in some detail.

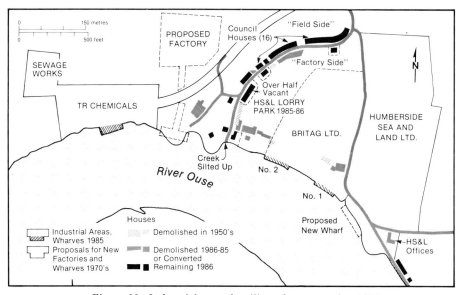

Figure 23. Industrial growth: village deconstruction 1985

One local observer suggests that the ploy of making a grandiose proposal, allowing protesters to become exhausted, withdrawing the proposal, and then replacing it with something more modest, whereupon the protestors feel relatively relieved, has been used to develop the downstream greenfield site and its waterfront. In the period 1968–85 East Coast and its successor, HS&L, made twenty-five planning applications, scoring twenty-one successes and three or four withdrawals. Three of these withdrawals re-emerged later as successful applications.

The net result of this activity by 1986 consists of two major wharves, 155,000 square feet of covered storage involving four large warehouses painted hideous shades of grey and red, sundry mechanical plant units for metal screening, powder off-loading, and the like, canteens, amenity blocks, and the conversion of all four dwellings at Kilpinpike into an office block. The operation of this complex has generated severe and continuous complaint from nearby residents, and has materially assisted in the partial evacuation of Howdendyke residents, as will be explained in Chapter 10.

The upstream (former Shipyard) site

The Howdendyke Wharf Company's application of early 1968 to convert the former shipyard into a cargo handling and storage area came to nothing; perhaps the immediate need was satisfied by the Hargreaves/East Coast operations on the downstream site. In 1973–74, however, Tate & Lyle Refineries Ltd. obtained permission to erect, on the shipyard site, a plant to manufacture glucose from imported potato starch.

This factory covered almost 60,000 square feet, involved a wharf and seven buildings, and required diversion of the riverbank public footpath as well as a new road cutting across the fields of the upstream (Ferry Farm) site. This road was said to be 'temporary', as direct access to the M62 could not be made until that motorway was opened in 1975; no direct access has yet been made, apparently because of Ministry of Transport discouragement. The company offered to landscape the factory to reduce its visual impact for motorists travelling along the M62. Little consideration seems to have been given to the impact of the factory's great bulk and height upon the visual amenity of the adjacent village of Howdendyke. And the shifting of the public footpath was seen merely as a fait accompli, as 'construction of the plant was already underway'. The explosive nature of potato starch (farina) was discounted by the company, which stated that not only would explosions be unlikely, but 'the area of effect would be relatively small'.

As with the East Coast/Hargreaves demolition of Kilpin Lodge, Tate & Lyle's operations at the shipyard site resulted in the loss of a second attractive building. The company purchased part of the Ferry Farm site in order to build their new road, and this purchase included the two dwellings comprising the building known as Ferry Farm. This structure was praised for its architectural quality and extensive river views by a Boothferry Health & Housing inspector, and Tate & Lyle's subsidiary, Howden Glucose Ltd., considered converting it to offices. After reconsideration, however, they demolished the building.

Howden Glucose continued operations for only a short while following this demolition; its whole operating life was less than seven years. Shortly after a congratulatory visit in 1980 by Prime Minister Margaret Thatcher, who praised 'this showpiece of British technology,' the plant was closed down by Tate & Lyle as a cost-cutting measure.

The Howden Glucose plant had clearly conformed to the 'river-related industry' planning rubric. This was soon to change. Between 1981 and 1984 a series of planning proposals from HS & L, TR International (Chemicals) Ltd., and Tinoverman Ltd., an HS & L subsidiary, (Table 35) were considered and mostly accepted, leading to the reopening of the site for import cargo handling, warehousing and storage, mainly of chemicals. Only permission for the open storage of imported materials was refused. The site is now jointly owned by HS & L and TR Chemicals, and all wharfage operations are performed by HS & L's Tinoverman subsidiary.

In effect, the upstream (shipyard) site was quickly converted after 1980 from a short-lived manufacturing use to a facility with very much the same operations as HS & L's downstream site. By 1981, then, the peripheral 'industrial' areas of Howdendyke, as designated in 1968, had ceased industrial activity in favour of port work in non-conformity with the Structure Plan. The planning rationale given for this anomaly was the existence of the plant and wharf and the need to retain employment opportunities in the area.

The upstream (Ferry Farm) site

With the development of the downstream (HS & L) and upstream (Shipyard) sites, only the Ferry Farm site remained of the area designated for industrial use in 1968. Largely zoned industrial, 27 acres of agricultural land were jointly purchased from the farmer of Ferry Farm in 1973 by Silver Street Nominees (Hull) and Helnita Ltd. A firm known as Wykeland Ltd. was then formed to promote the area as land ripe for industrial development within the Howdendyke industrial estate.

The large site is broken into two parts by the Howden Glucose road, and has a narrow waterfront between the glucose factory and Howdendyke village. Part of this waterfront, comprising both staiths and Ferry House, was purchased from the Ecclesiastical Commissioner by J. Wharton Shipping, a river Trent wharfage company. Perceiving the possibility of constructing a wharf on this waterfront, a number of firms made applications to build factories on the Ferry Farm site (Figure 23). In 1974–75 Helnita Ltd. applied, withdrew, and was then refused a second application to build a wharf and access road to their proposed

Table 35. Planning applications, upstream (shipyard) site, 1968–85

Year	Applicant	Dimensions	Use	Known objections	Status
1968(a)	Howdendyke Wharf Co. Ltd.	–	change of use from shipyard to cargo handling with storage	no	?
1968(b)	Howdendyke Wharf Co. Ltd.	–	small jetties to be replaced by major wharf	no	?
1973	Tate & Lyle Refineries	18,600 sq.ft.	glucose factory (7 buildings)	yes	OK
1974(a)	Tate & Lyle Refineries	38,180 sq.ft.	glucose plant extension and access road	no	OK
1974(b)	Tate & Lyle Refineries	–	landscaping and public footpath diversion	no	OK
1975	Howden Glucose Co. Ltd.	–	standby generator house	no	OK
1976(a)	Tate & Lyle Refineries	–	convert Ferry Farm to two dwellings	no	OK
1976(b)	Tate & Lyle Refineries	–	extend effluent treatment plant	no	OK
1977	Tate & Lyle Refineries	–	convert Ferry Farm to offices	no	OK
1981(a)	Humberside Sea & Land Services Ltd. & TR Chemicals Ltd.	–	convert part of former glucose factory to storage and distribution facility	yes	OK
1981(b)	S. Banner Ltd.	–	use of former factory for vegetable oil refinery	?	?
1983(a)	TR Chemicals Ltd.	–	change part of warehouse to office	no	OK
1983(b)	Tinoverman Ltd.	–	erect 4 fuel oil storage tanks	no	OK
1983(c)	Tinoverman Ltd.	–	adjacent open storage	no	refused
1983(d)	TR Chemicals Ltd.	–	2 loading tanks	no	OK
1984(a)	TR Chemicals Ltd.	–	new warehouse and amenities block	no	OK
1984(b)	Tinoverman Ltd.	–	extend jetty, install bulk transfer system and amenity building	yes	OK

Sources: Boothferry Planning Office; local newspapers.

'industrial estate'. In 1978–79 Humber Kitchens Ltd. similarly applied, withdrew, and were then refused their second application for a wharf, access road, and modular kitchen factory on the site.

There were strong local objections to these schemes, and a major intervention on the part of the Department of Agriculture, now sufficiently aroused to defend first-class agricultural land in the area. The chief problem with all the applications for use of the Ferry Farm site, however, was that they were either for import-distribution wharves only, or for factories, such as a modular kitchen assembly plant, which could not be said to be directly dependent upon riverborne transport. Whereas local planners and politicians appear to have overridden their official rubric in favour of HS & L and shipyard/glucose site operations, they have consistently applied it in the case of the Ferry Farm site and, as will be seen below, with regard to the chemical works.

The Ouse Chemical Works site

G. H. Anderton Ltd.'s Ouse Chemical Works underwent major expansion in the mid-1950s, and a new gas scrubbing system (whereby an ugly, tall plastic chimney replaced an elegant brick one) was installed in 1965. More significant and expensive anti-pollutive changes occurred during the Hargreaves era (Table 36) for ICI found the Anderton factory to be rather 'foul and filthy' in comparison with the corporation's other plants.

In 1982, however, after takeover by BritAg Ltd., application was made to change the use of the plant from the manufacture of chemical fertilizer to general importing, warehousing, and distribution, including ironically the 'possible import of finished fertilizers'. This suggests that BritAg wished to cease local manufacture of fertilizers, which belies the assurances of industrial expansion given over the years by Hargreaves, and which were in part responsible for the destruction of many dwellings, as detailed in Chapter 10. It is significant that the map accompanying this application included almost the whole Triangle, thus asserting an intention to be rid of most of the housing on the 'factory side' of Howdendyke village.

The proposed loss of Howdendyke's only remaining manufacturing industry, so soon after the demise of Howden Glucose, and the consequent conversion of the whole of the Howdendyke industrial estate into a series of wharves and warehouses handling general cargo, was grossly in contravention of Structure Plan guidelines. The application for change of use was refused. The grounds for refusal are worth detailing, especially as they apply, theoretically, also to HS & L operations and to the successors of Howden Glucose. Outlined in 1983, the refusal stated that storage and distribution facilities should more appropriately be located at major ports, and that the limited riverside space at places such as Howdendyke should be devoted to manufacturing industry directly dependent upon access to the river.

Table 36. Planning applications, Ouse Chemical Works, 1948–82

Year	Applicant	Dimensions	Use	Known objections	Status
1948	G. H. Anderton	4,200 sq.ft.	shed extension	no	OK
1951	G. H. Anderton	4,532 sq.ft.	granulating plant	no	OK
1953	G. H. Anderton	2,592 sq.ft.	storage shed	no	OK
1954	G. H. Anderton	20,000 sq.ft.	storage shed and new access	no	OK
1960	Anderton-Richardson Fertilizers Ltd.	–	vehicular access improvement	no	OK
1963	Anderton-Richardson Fertilizers Ltd.	28,000 sq.ft.	storage shed	no	OK
1965	Anderton-Richardson Fertilizers Ltd.	150 ft. chimney	gas scrubbing system	no	OK
1968(a)	Hargreaves Fertilizers Ltd.	–	jetty (No. 1)	yes	withdrawn
1968(b)	Hargreaves Fertilizers Ltd.	–	storage shed	no	withdrawn
1968(c)	Hargreaves Fertilizers Ltd.	15,960 sq.ft.	storage shed	no	OK
1971	Hargreaves Fertilizers Ltd.	1,525 sq.ft.	amenity block	no	OK
1972	Hargreaves Fertilizers Ltd.	500 sq.ft.	office extension	no	OK
1979	Hargreaves Fertilizers Ltd.	–	scrubbing system replacement	no	OK
1982	BritAg Ltd.	–	change of use from factory to general warehousing and distribution	yes	refused
1985	BritAg Ltd.	–	lorry turning area	yes	OK

Sources: Boothferry Planning Office; local newspapers.

Three years later, despite constant assurances on the part of Hargreaves that the plant had been viable and might even expand, BritAg decided to reduce operations at the works and make over half the fifty-four workers redundant. Somewhat later in 1985 HS & L also proposed a large lorry park and turning area on the site of former BritAg houses in The Square, in conjunction with Wharf No. 2, which would make life unbearable for residents of BritAg's remaining houses on the 'factory' side of the village.

Howdendyke village

Given the almost complete encirclement of Howdendyke village by dangerous, noisy, dusty, and rather ugly cargo handling sites, it seems ironic rather than amusing that the Lower Ouse Drainage Board should be refused permission to use a railway waggon for a toolshed on the grounds of 'loss of visual amenity' (Table 37).

Table 37. Planning refusals, Howdendyke and Kilpinpike, 1967–75

Year	Applicant	Use required	Reason for refusal
1967	a resident	new dwelling	'white land', to remain undisturbed
1972	Lower Ouse Board Drainage	railway waggon for use as implement store	detrimental to visual amenity
1973	a resident	convert dwelling to shop/dwelling	'white land', to remain undisturbed
1974	residents	new dwellings	'white land', to remain undisturbed

Source: Boothferry Planning Office.

In contrast to the rapid development of nearby agricultural land, Howdendyke village has generally been refused permission for housing improvement since 1968, although improvements have been made to all the council houses and some others on the 'field side' of the village. This issue is most appropriately considered in the following chapter. It is sufficient to state here that the expansion of cargo handling facilities on the outskirts of Howdendyke has been matched by widespred house closures, evacuations, and demolitions within the village itself, and that the two processes are not unrelated.

Non-resident protest

Non-residents were quicker than residents to protest the changes which began to occur in Howdendyke after 1968. Two major groups of non-residents are evident, those chiefly opposing the development of Howdendyke as an alternative to established Humber ports, and those residents of nearby villages offended by increasing levels of traffic and pollution.

Objections to port development

Serious and sustained objections to Howdendyke's recent development as a private port have been made since HS & L's original jetty proposals of 1968. Bursts of protest have accompanied each of HS & L's subsequent major proposals, most notably those for a second jetty (1973), a jetty extension (1978), and the rebuilding of jetty No. 2, formerly a small Hargreaves installation (1983), together with Hargreave's proposal to convert their fertilizer factory into a general warehousing and distribution facility (1982–83) and a joint HS & L-TR Chemicals proposal to convert the former glucose factory into a similar warehouse zone (1981–83). It is noteworthy that all these proposals were eventually approved except the fertilizer factory conversion. Nevertheless, the use by HS & L of the whole of Hargreaves' waterfront in the shape of their wharves No. 1 and No. 2, and their interest in the upstream site, ensured that by 1986 almost the whole of the waterfront of Howdendyke had been given over to import wharfage, largely controlled by HS & L.

Assuming no significant increases in Humber river traffic, the development of small private wharves is likely to reduce traffic to and from existing Humber ports, and especially the Humberhead port of Goole. By 1985 it was estimated that at least thirty private wharves had come into existence on the Humber river system, many of them having little or no connection with river-related industry, and thus contravening the guidelines of the Humberside Structure Plan. This development is only part of a recent massive investment in private ports along the South and East coasts, apparently encouraged by central government, and which is resulting in the collapse of trade in traditional registered ports.

It is not surprising, therefore, that the chief objectors to Howdendyke's revival as a river port have been groups representing established ports, particularly Goole, which is a mere five miles from Howdendyke. Protesting agencies include the British Transport Docks Board (BTDB), the Goole Docks Labour Board, the Goole and District Docks Committee, and the Transport and General Workers Union (TGWU). Their chief objections throughout the whole period 1968–86 have been that, first, the Port of Goole is perfectly adequate for the river trade, and second, that the growth of private wharves such as the HS & L enterprise at Howdendyke will seriously damage the profitability of public enterprises such as Goole docks.

During the jetty extension fight in 1978 about 100 dockers converged on Howdendyke to protest the HS & L application. They were joined by representatives of Goole area stevedoring and road haulage firms, and made some attempt to join forces with Howdendyke residents. A number of residents, however, felt unable to do so, and it was decided that the two groups should work separately as they were 'fighting on two separate issues' (*Howdenshire Gazette*, 24 November 1978).

Failure to make this operational connection was not to Howdendyke residents' advantage. For during the extensive protests of 1981–85, dockers' statements and actions received much more coverage in local newspapers than did those of Howdendykers. Lacking organizational ability themselves,

Howdendyke residents could perhaps have benefited from the cohesive power of the docks group.

During the successful proposal to convert the glucose factory site to cargo handling, and the unsuccessful plan to convert the fertilizer factory to similar use (1981–83), the docks group made reasoned appeals supporting their point of view. They charged that such use changes would divert traffic from Goole and reduce efficiency at that port, which would result in increased dock charges, which in turn would produce 'a down-trade spiral' (*Howdenshire Gazette*, 16 October 1981, 12 November 1982). The end result of increasing job opportunities at Howdendyke would be dock lay-offs in Goole.

Objectors further noted that the growth of Howdendyke as a port might encourage firms already using Goole docks for imports, such as Humber Kitchens, to try to move their trade to Howdendyke. It was also suggested that unregistered wharves such as Howdendyke creamed off the most profitable traffic, whereas established docks must take profitable and less profitable traffic alike. The Goole branch of TGWU noted that the number of registered dock workers at Goole had fallen from 480 to 230 in the five years to 1983, while the BTDB pointed out that 300,000 square feet of covered storage alone existed at Goole, and that this capacity was 'considerably underused'. The Chief Planning Officer advised Boothferry Council that both proposals called for the conversion of river-related industrial premises to mere cargo handling facilities and that as such changes contravened the Structure Plan, they should be refused and other, industrial, use encouraged (*Howdenshire Gazette*, 7 January 1983).

It is interesting to compare Boothferry Council's responses to these two very similar applications. With regard to the glucose factory conversion, approval was given on the grounds that the site and plant would continue in some form of use, that the applicants were already 'represented' at Howdendyke, and that no job-creating scheme could be refused in times of severe unemployment (*Howdenshire Gazette*, 17 December 1982). As the planning department noted, it was a case for 'political judgement' (*Yorkshire and North Humberside Times*, 4 September 1981). The majority of Council appears to have made this judgement along the lines recommended by Councillor Bray: 'I want to see people back at work again. If we keep messing about and deferring they [HS & L and TR Chemicals] could clear off elsewhere' (*Howdenshire Gazette*, 9 October 1981).

In contrast, Council refused Hargreaves permission to convert the fertilizer plant, but only, apparently, because of a strong recommendation from Humberside County Council that they do so (*Howdenshire Gazette*, 6 May 1983). The reason given for refusal was contravention of the Structure Plan. Council was deeply divided on this issue, ranging from Councillor Crowther, who suggested, surely erroneously, that the BTDB had already had to close major ports, possibly because of private wharf development, to Councillor

Wise, who declared, 'We shouldn't act as a protection society for the port of Goole. This is not Goole Borough Council any more, it is Boothferry Borough Council (*Howdenshire Gazette*, 7 January 1983). This unwise remark elicited considerable negative response from the residents of Goole, the only major town (c.20,000 population) in the Borough.

Subsequent HS & L plans to increase their jetty No. 2 wharfage area four-fold in 1983 were also vigorously opposed by all the dock groups, as well as by Humberside County Council and by Boothferry Planning Department, both of the latter citing Structure Plan contravention. Goole Chamber of Commerce, however, despite the urging of Councillor Park, refused to express disapproval (*Howdenshire Gazette*, 16 September 1983). Humberside County Council, taking the broad view in favour of both their Structure Plan and protecting Goole jobs, clearly had a greater concern for the Port of Goole than had its own business people.

The general feeling among all these groups was that such developments, if unrestricted, could 'kill off the Port of Goole' (*Howdenshire Gazette*, 9 September 1983). In a joint meeting with Boothferry Council, the County Council made four objections to the wharf proposal: that it would route 30,000–40,000 additional tons of general cargo through Howdendyke when such cargo could better be handled by Goole; that increased traffic would cause excessive wear and tear on rural roads; that, having refused Hargreaves permission to convert their factory to cargo handling, some consistency in planning decisions was clearly necessary; and that approval would encourage similar proposals elsewhere, which could adversely affect Boothferry District as a whole (*Howdenshire Gazette*, 4 November 1983). The latter prophecy came true as early as 1986 with proposals for extensive dock development at Flixborough on the Trent just outside Boothferry's boundaries (*Howdenshire Gazette* 19, 26 June, 24 July 1986).

Nevertheless, Boothferry Council chose to disregard this advice and approved the plan in late 1983. Prominent among the supporters of HS & L, as usual, was Councillor Bray who observed that no one could guarantee that trade lost to Howdendyke would be re-routed through Goole. He went on to praise HS & L and stated that he did not care 'a tinker's cuss' about the objections from TGWU and the BTDB (*Howdenshire Gazette*, 9 September 1983). Councillor Reed made the perhaps prescient remark that 'some rural councillors want to cut Goole down to size' (*Howdenshire Gazette*, 30 September 1983) while Councillor Mant assessed Goole's regional multiplier factor and observed: 'Goole is a port in the centre of Boothferry. If you kill off the centre then the whole area will die' (*Howdenshire Gazette*, 4 November 1983).

Approval of jetty No. 2, of course, directly paved the way for HS & L's application of 1985 to provide an adjacent lorry park and turning area, which would involved six acres of Howdendyke village, demolition of the Club, the village social centre, and further loss of village environmental quality. This issue is discussed in Chapter 10.

It is more pertinent to note here that by 1985 it was estimated that at least two road hauliers had gone out of business in Goole, and another reduced from six to one employee (*Howdenshire Gazette*, 14 November 1985). And in the same year Goole Docks was compelled to ask for a reduction of twenty registered dock workers' jobs because of lack of work (*Howdenshire Gazette*, 14 November, 26 December 1985). As Goole dock manager Hugh Whitehead remarked: 'The whole thing is beyond comprehension. In a place like Goole where the port is in such a close relationship with the council, the council seems unable to prevent the proliferation of private wharves. It's going to be economic suicide' (*Howdenshire Gazette*, 5 December 1985). It is extremely unfortunate, noted one respondent, that Boothferry Borough Council is dominated by a majority of Conservative rural councillors, often ignorant of urban affairs, dock facilities, and economic theory, yet who are able to decide the fate of Boothferry's only major town, which happens to have been a traditional Labour stronghold before the jurisdictional reorganization of 1974.

Objections to environmental degradation

Whereas the dock groups are solely concerned with issues of port trade, a number of residents of Kilpin parish, as well as Kilpin Parish Council (KPC), have more local concerns. Residents of Kilpin and Skelton, Howdendyke's sister villages in Kilpin parish, have repeatedly objected against development in Howdendyke since 1968.

Many of the objections to increasing land, water, air, visual, and noise pollution are similar to those of Howdendyke residents, which are treated in Chapters 9 and 10. Briefly, both Kilpin and Skelton residents were concerned about the high levels of noise and smell emanating from HS & L and Hargreaves operations, as well as the frequency of clouds of dust from the jetties. Clearly, HS & L's Howdendyke facility has pollutive effects which extend over much of Kilpin parish.

More pertinent in this context are the objections by non-Howdendykers to the increasing lorry traffic volumes generated by Howdendyke, and the extension of Howdendyke warehousing operations into the farming hamlet of Kilpin. Residents of Kilpin were especially sensitive to these issues because of the development of the Garden King frozen food factory in the village in 1968, the same year HS & L appeared at Howdendyke. The factory had been approved despite being a departure from the County Plan, the Chief Planning Officer stating that it was not a major departure from the plan and that the whole neighbourhood would not be effected. Unfortunately, the pollution of dykes and the release of intolerable smells was characteristic of Garden King until it ceased operation. Refusing an extension proposal in 1974, Howden

Rural District Council noted the firm's 'well-documented history of blatant disregard for the local people and the environment'.

By the early 1980s both the Garden King factory and other agricultural buildings in Kilpin were vacant. In 1983–84 applications were made to establish a road haulage business in Kilpin and also to permit the storage of fertilizers, cement, and animal feedstuffs for HS & L. As one respondent comments, 'All we could see with the haulage application was Kilpin going the same way as Howdendyke. Life seemed a constant battle to keep one step ahead … Humberside Sea and Land seem to get everything through [the planning process] on the nod regardless of written objections by residents or the parish council.' In this case, however, Humberside County Council opposed HS & L's proposals to extend their operations to Kilpin and the plan was refused. It is interesting to note, in view of his promotion of industry at Howdendyke (Chapter 9) that Councillor Bray supported refusal of permission, stating that Kilpin villagers had suffered from industrial encroachment 'long enough'! (*Howdenshire Gazette*, 5 October 1984).

Nevertheless, heavy traffic throughout Kilpin parish continues to cause problems. In the 1950s Anderton's Fertilizers Ltd. had four lorries, for which the narrow unclassified rural lanes of Kilpin parish were adequate. By the 1980s developments in Kilpin, Skelton, and especially Howdendyke had generated traffic amounting to several hundred lorry-trips per day, including Sundays, early mornings and late evenings. A petition of '24 ratepayers' in 1973 complained that 'Howdendyke Road is already subjected to far more heavy traffic than it can take. The noise, pollution, and road hazards are already far in excess of anything that local residents can be expected to suffer in silence.' A year later complaints were still being made, but now citing the rash of accidents which had recently occurred in and near Howdendyke (*Howdenshire Gazette*, 11 March 1983). By 1986 the area had become known locally as an 'accident blackspot' (*Howdenshire Gazette*, 12 June 1986).

In the mid-1970s a compulsory purchase order was necessary for road realignment at Elm Tree, after residents of this Howdendyke peripheral zone had declared that 'our priceless stretch of land is not for sale. We bought it with the intention of living here in comparative peace and comfort in our old age, and we have suffered more than enough increasing heavy traffic upsetting the whole of what was a most peaceful and quiet village known as Howdendyke'. The realignment of the Howdendyke Road at Elm Tree, and its widening to 24 feet, chiefly to accommodate an M62 overpass and increased lorry traffic, did little to ameliorate what a contemporary meeting of residents expressed as 'the most destructive traffic we have ever known'. A traffic count made on Friday, 31 October 1975 recorded a flow of 1,264 vehicles between 6 a.m. and 10 p.m., of which 260, or approximately 20 per cent, were heavy goods vehicles. Significantly, heavy goods traffic was well established by 6 a.m. and did not cease until about 8 p.m.

The history of Howdendyke's traffic problem throughout the 1970s and early 1980s is one of frequent protests on the part of residents, other Kilpin parish villagers, and KPC, most of which have simply been ignored by the local authorities. The problem was brought to a head in early 1986 when a lorry carrying steel girders tore the roof from a small car passing the HS & L depot in Howdendyke, killing the car's driver. The lorry driver was later charged with a whole array of offences, including having an unattended rear load, an unmarked projecting rear load, defective tyres, defective brakes, and unmaintained stop lamps, marker lamps and indicators. Other lorries are in similar condition (*Goole and Howden Chronicle*, 31 July 1986). HS & L are not responsible for the condition of independent vehicles which use their yards.

KPC expressed sympathy, pointing out that 'we have, for many years, endeavoured to make the road through Howdendyke less hazardous to use' (*Howdenshire Gazette*, 10 April 1986). While Councillor Bray lamented the passing of 'a good farmer, a well-respected lad', Howden Town Councillor Bob Lewis drew attention to traffic problems arising from 'Boothferry Borough Council's rapacious policy of continuous and extensive industrial development of Howdendyke, and the area surveyor's rejection of requests for remedial action' (*Howdenshire Gazette*, 17 April 1986).

Both KPC, Howdendykers, and nearby non-residents have been demanding a direct access road from Howdendyke to the M62 for a number of years. Such an access road would considerably reduce dangerous traffic on local roads, improve quality of life in what remains of Howdendyke, and radically improve the life of one elderly Skelton lady who has cycled local roads for many years. 'I daren't bike along these roads any more' she explained, 'it's too dangerous. I can't drive a car. How am I to get about?'

Commentary

During the decade following industrial rezoning in 1968, Howdendyke trebled in size. This was entirely because of the rapid expansion of 'industry' on both upstream and downstream greenfield sites. By the early 1980s the old village of Howdendyke was almost wholly surrounded by new wharves and warehouses devoted to the handling of imported materials brought upriver by seagoing vessels.

Yet this overwhelming emphasis on cargo handling appears to contravene the planning constraints which permit river-related industry at places such as Howdendyke but relegate cargo handling to existing ports. Boothferry planners and politicians were clearly correct in their refusal to permit cargo handling facilities on the upriver (Ferry Farm) site and the change of use of the Ouse Chemical Works from manufacturing to import-distribution. Had such a refusal been given to East Coast River Services Ltd. in 1968, the destruction of

Howdendyke village may have been averted. By adhering to the Structure Plan in 1983, but condoning the far more serious loss of 'white land' to East Coast after 1968, local officials did little to redress the fate of a village whose doom was sealed by the faulty judgement of their counterparts of fifteen years before.

Boothferry planners and politicians inherited, in 1974, the plans and judgements of Howden Rural District Council. They have shown little consistency in applying planning regulations, have done little to alleviate the problems caused by the faulty judgements of their predecessors, and, as in the case of the Drainage Board railway waggon, have demonstrated their ability to strain at a gnat and swallow a camel.

On the business side, it appears that Hargreaves/BritAg and HS & L share more than a jetty. The jetty application of 1968 and the subsequent operations suggest some degree of co-operation between two firms whose operations are adjacent and who share physical plant. Overall, the process which triggered the fundamental changes which occurred in Howdendyke after 1967 seems to have begun with the devolution of power from a paternalist resident industrial family to a more distant corporation.

The first decade of major change, 1966–75, was marked by the rapid expansion of physical plant and the rather ineffective protests of residents. As detailed in the following chapter, the second decade, 1976–86, saw the consolidation of earlier growth in the 'industrial areas', the destruction of half the dwellings in the village, and an outburst of protest on the part of residents.

9
Reaction

The central conflict of the 20th century [is] the efforts of individuals, families, and communities to preserve their freedom against the overwhelming power of the modern techno-industrial superstate.

Edward Abbey

In 1960 Howdendyke, with its environs, was a thriving community of 75 households. By 1986 the number of households had been reduced by more than half. The theme of the second decade of change, 1976–86, is one of industrial consolidation and village destruction.

The twenty-five years following the 1961 Census, when Howdendyke, Kilpinpike and Elm Tree together had seventy-five households, has seen dramatic and devastating changes wrought in both landscape and community (Figure 21). Instead of a modest 11 acres of occupied industrial land, an area more than treble that size is now devoted to so-called 'industrial' use, much of it already covered by wharves, warehouses, and open storage areas. In contrast to the seventy-two houses in Howdendyke and Kilpinpike occupied in 1961, by 1986 twenty-nine had been demolished, four had been converted into offices, and a further eight were standing empty because of closure orders (Figures 13, 23, Table 38). A threefold increase in 'industrial' space, therefore, has been complemented by a loss of usable housing units of well over 50 per cent (Table 39). The consequences of trebling the industrial activity and halving the housing of a small village are likely to be devastating to community identity, activity, and morale. The process of destruction and its consequences is described below. First, however, a description of the actors involved is necessary.

The actors

The chief actors involved in any planning situation are: the private applicant for planning permission, who initiates the process, in this case HS & L Ltd., Hargreaves Ltd. and BritAg Ltd.; the planning officials who assess the application's merits according to existing planning guidelines, in this case Boothferry Planning Department; the district politicians, who take the

Table 38. Housing loss, Howdendyke, 1960–86

Area (Fig. 15)	Dwellings demolished	Dwellings converted to other uses	Dwellings condemned and vacant	Dwellings occupied 1986	Total dwellings
Howdendyke proper (factory side)					(40)
Kilpin Lodge	1				1
The Square	12		1		13
New Row			6	3	9
Ferry Road Cottages				2	2
Prospect Villas/ The Cottage	12				12
Kilham Cottage/ The Bungalow	1			1	2
Post Office				1	1
Howdendyke proper (field side)					(28)
Creek House/Ferry House area			1	3	4
Ferry Farm	2				2
Tutty Row/Woodbine Cottage	1			4	5
Ouse Cottage				1	1
1936 Council Houses				8	8
1948 Council Houses				8	8
Kilpinpike		4			(4)
Elm Tree				3	(3)
Totals	29	4	8	34	(75)

Table 39. Percentage housing loss, Howdendyke, 1960–86

Area (see Fig. 15)	Dwellings occupied 1960	Dwellings occupied 1986	Loss 1960–86	Percentage loss
Howdendyke proper	68	31	37	54.4%
Howdendyke/Kilpinpike	72	31	41	57.0%
Howdendyke, Kilpinpike, and Elm Tree	75	34	41	54.7%

planning officials' recommendations into consideration when voting for or against the application; and the public, who may be ignored or may become involved via public hearings, if held, via protest, or via the protestations of their local parish council, in this case Kilpin Parish Council.

Private enterprise

The chief agent in actual village demolition has been Hargreaves Fertilizers Ltd. and its successor, BritAg Ltd. Neither HS & L nor its sister firms, successors to the Howden Glucose site, own dwellings, for Howden Glucose demolished Ferry Farm (two dwellings) and HS & L demolished Kilpin Lodge and converted all the housing at Kilpinpike into offices (five dwellings in total).

In contrast, Hargreaves in 1967 found itself the owner of most of Howdendyke village. With the erection of eight council houses in 1948 all new house-building ceased in Howdendyke. In a vigorous campaign throughout the 1940s and early 1950s G. H. Anderton Ltd. succeeded in purchasing almost every available house property in the village proper. Whether the intention was personal aggrandizement on the part of the Pillings or a shrewd move to gain control of all available land in case of industrial expansion, or both, cannot now be ascertained. A pencil-written memorandum in the Anderton files only attests to a desire to 'own the whole Triangle'.

ICI executives were appalled at Howdendyke's housing conditions, and, according to a company spokesman, made plans to renovate, only to be told by the local authority that most village houses had a very limited life. To the Hargeaves company, therefore, these houses were a nuisance to administer, brought in little rent, were expensive to repair, and stood in the way of any possible expansion of the chemical works within the Triangle. After selling off twelve of these houses in the late 1960s, nothing more was done except the installation of indoor taps in housing lacking this facility. Corporate reorganization in the late 1970s may have provided the impetus for a decision at that time to remove as much Hargreaves-owned housing as possible.

Planning Department

The role of district planners, such as Boothferry Planning Department, is to receive the planning proposals initiated by private enterprise or individuals, assess their appropriateness with regard to existing guidelines, and make recommendations to the local decision-taking authority. Site notices may be displayed at the site of the proposed development so that nearby residents are informed of the situation. The planner can only advise council; he has no executive authority. In very controversial cases, an issue may be referred to the county planning office, in this case the Humberside County Planning Office at Beverley. If a case is deemed problematic, Council's Planning Committee may decide on a site meeting, where the site is visited and local objectors perhaps met in person. When permission is given, certain conditions (e.g. for landscaping) may be laid down by Council.

In general, Boothferry Planning Office has been guided by the County Plan of 1960, superseded by the Structure Plan of 1979. Whereas County plans were rather rigid documents on the lines of the now-discredited 'master-plan', structure plans were developed in the 1970s as flexible tools which emphasized not a rigidly-defined mosaic of planning areas depicted on a master plan but rather a set of general guidelines to be applied in individual instances. On the other hand, districts such as Boothferry can, with the assistance of their planning offices, develop Local Plans for specific settlements, thus providing a kind of mini-masterplan for the town or village concerned. Such a Local Plan was developed for Goole/Hook, the central settlement in Boothferry district, and this evoked a great deal of public debate.

Finally, according to the Humberside Structure Plan, planners should wherever possible involve the public in the planning process.

Health and Housing Department

Although this department has played the least active role of the four actors outlined here, its role is very significant in that it is responsible for 'condemning' houses, that is, recommending that Council place closing and demolition orders upon them.

Boothferry Health and Housing Department operates under the Housing Act 1957 (5 and 6 Eliz. 2 Ch. 56). According to this Act, a house may be deemed 'unfit for human habitation' if it is found defective in any one or more of eight fitness standards, which relate to: state of repair; structural stability; freedom from dampness; quality of natural lighting; quality of ventilation; water supply adequacy; drainage and sanitary conveniences; and food preparation and disposal facilities. If unfit houses are discovered, a 'time and place' notice is served on the owner who is asked to submit repair plans. If no undertaking to repair is made within twenty-one days, a demolition order is served. Should demolition be temporarily impossible, for example where it would negatively affect an adjoining house, as in a terrace, a 'closing' order is served instead.

The most important issue with respect to Howdendyke is by what means Housing personnel are led to make an inspection of a house. According to Boothferry's Housing Department, inspection most frequently comes about in a 'roundabout way'. There is no evidence that Hargreaves ever asked to have its property inspected. Most usually a tenant, unable to get repairs done or wishing to be placed in a better-built council dwelling, will approach Health and Housing rather than complain to the landlord. To obtain the desired council house the tenant must prove 'hardship', which involves a Housing inspector's assessment of the tenant's current housing conditions. Once a negative assessment is made, the department must follow the 'time and place' notice procedure.

Uninspected houses can become extremely deteriorated because tenants may be fearful to complain to or of their landlords, because rents may be very low, thus further inhibiting complaint, and because many local councils have become reluctant to force landlords to make repairs to older housing stock because of the 'unreasonable' cost of making such repairs.

All these conditions appear to apply in the case of Howdendyke, were 'time and place' notices began to be served at an increasing rate from early 1977. In the three years 1977–79 alone, at least sixteen closing and demolition orders covered all eleven houses in Prospect Villas, two in New Row, one in the Square, and the two dwellings at Ferry Farm. Typical inspector's reports for Prospect Villas and New Row provide an indication of an outsider's objective view of a dwelling:

(a) *No. 7 Prospect Villas* (two bedrooms, living room, kitchen, outside wc and coal store): ceiling cracks, rising damp to 2 ft. 6 in., illfitting sashes and doors, front door not weatherproof, uneven floors. Steep, narrow stairs, treads loose, no handrail. Rear door illfitting. Cracked plasterwork, floorboards loose, perished and open-jointed brickwork in walls and chimney stack, skirting boards decayed. Dilapidated outbuildings.

(b) *No. 6 New Row* (two bedrooms, living room, kitchen, outside wc and coal store): cracked plasterwork, illfitting doors, open-jointed ridge and pantiles, rising damp throughout, wc in outbuildings. No bath, wash-hand basin or hot water supplies, only a cold water tap over the kitchen sink. Bad internal arrangement – inadequate space outside bedrooms, stairs open directly into kitchen.

Insider's views, of similar, but better-kept dwellings as loved homes, are presented in Chapter 10. Meanwhile it is sufficient to ask why these properties were allowed, by their owner, to deteriorate to such levels.

Politicians

In Boothferry Borough, as elsewhere, district politicians are elected by wards, each ward consisting of a number of parishes. Boothferry Council is unusual in that its members come from three pre-1974 counties and retain strong loyalties to these areas. It is also likely that any individual member will have little knowledge of settlements in another former jurisdiction. In such a situation it seems incumbent upon elected ward councillors to support the desires of residents of their own wards.

Boothferry is a largely rural area with high unemployment, and Council was quick to inaugurate an Industrial Development sub-committee whose goal is to 'offer every possible encouragement to both established industry and to new developers seeking sites or premises within the Borough' (*Howdenshire Gazette*, 12 June 1981). The same report notes Council's general approval of then Industry Minister Norman Tebbit's demand for the removal of 'obstacles' in the way of 'hard work and enterprise', especially via 'cutting controls'. Councillor Bob Park's suggestion that the goal of attracting industry should not be at the expense of a 'balanced environment' thus probably fell on deaf ears.

Boothferry Borough's latest brochure, *Opportunities for Development* (1986), boosts the area's potential for new industry, notes that Howdendyke lies in a 'Rural Development Area' and development there may therefore attract grants, and notes, without irony, that 'The Council has an impressive record in dealing with *planning applications* for industrial and commercial use – over 89% were approved in the 10 years up to 1984. In 1985 the record touched 95%'. Again without irony, the brochure goes on to laud the district's 'picturesque small towns and villages where passing the time of day is still a way of life'.

In the late 1970s and early 1980s Boothferry Council's overriding aim, then, has been to follow national policy promoting industrial development and cutting planning controls which might hamper such development. Hence Council was hostile to a suggestion by Boothferry's Chief Planning Officer (CPO), that village local plans be created for non-selected settlements. According to the CPO, the fifty or so non-selected settlements vary so much in size and character that it had proved impossible to apply 'broad development policies', and it would be better to have a map for each village designating the boundaries of housing development. In view of the fate of Howdendyke, where the bulldozers were even then at work, such an exercise would have been interesting and perhaps even helpful.

Councillors were not impressed by this suggestion (*Howdenshire Gazette*, 26 June 1981) and rejected it by a twelve to seven vote. Their arguments seem rather contradictory in view of the CPO's suggestion of fifty or so local plans: 'local needs' are more important than district needs; each planning application should be judged on its merits; such a scheme would be too inflexible, especially in view of the recent call of the Department of the Environment for more 'flexibility' in planning. According to Councillor Pantry, no such scheme was necessary because 'every planning application goes to the appropriate parish council whose members are asked for comments', a statement whose value we shall probe later. Councillor Hill seems to have captured the mood of the majority: 'Let's have a little more freedom on the planning side. Let's have flexibility within the guidelines, but without ... the rigid diktat coming from the planning office of 'thou shalt not'. This sickens a lot of people'. (*Howdenshire Gazette*, 26 June 1981). Mr Hill, unlikely to have Howdendyke in mind, went on to say that 'it was people and not buildings who mattered'.

The public

The public at large are rarely consulted by private enterprise, planners, or politicians. Very few public meetings are held in Boothferry regarding planning issues. Theoretically, the general public's opinions of any planning proposal are ascertained by the local parish council and forwarded to the planners or directly to the district council. In practice, most parish councils meet infrequently, may be overworked, are underfunded, have no means of consulting their constituents on a regular basis, and have no significant powers. Hence their recommendations are often ignored by planners and politicians at the district level.

In the case of Howdendyke, the village is represented by Kilpin Parish Council which in recent years has rarely included more than one Howdendyker in its membership. As will be seen below, lack of consultation or consideration led Kilpin Parish Council (KPC), as well as Howdendyke residents, into various forms of protest against too-rapid change in the village.

The decision for village destruction

By the mid-1970s conditions in Howdendyke had become intolerable. Cargo handling facilities had become a major source of noise and air pollution. Ships and their crews harassed villagers by means of noise and lights at night and actual molestation. The Hargreaves Company failed to perform anything more than absolutely essential renovation work on its tenanted houses, and the general appearance of the village had become much deteriorated. Villagers noted that once vacated by tenants, houses were not re-let, but were closed up and even demolished. Worst of all, villagers had begun to feel very insecure and had no idea of what kind of future lay in store for their community.

A petition addressing these issues was drawn up by villagers and sent to Hargreaves in 1977. The company promptly approached Boothferry Planning for 'advice', stating that: company houses were largely substandard; the company had no intention of renovating them; and that, although there were no plans for factory extension in the next five years or so, expansion was likely in the long term.

The planners' response was that, given the extent of new development since 1968, and notwithstanding the fact that much of this development did not conform to Structure Plan guidelines, Howdendyke was an 'exception' and therefore industry should have precedence over housing. In particular, no permission would be given for new housing or dwelling extensions if these were likely to inhibit or limit industrial expansion. As any expansion of the Ouse Chemical Works would naturally take place within the Triangle, this decision did not bode well for the future of the 'factory side' of Howdendyke, which originally had forty houses, compared with twenty-eight on the opposite, 'field side' (Table 38, Figures 13, 21, 23).

Accordingly, Boothferry Planning advised Hargreaves to: buy back any houses already sold off; demolish houses rather than renovate them; and, by taking over former house sites as industrial land, complete their effective control over the Triangle. Hargreaves naturally agreed with this seemingly made-to-measure policy.

In effect, this Hargreaves-Boothferry Planning policy sanctioned the demolition of at least twenty-four of the twenty-eight houses which remained within the Triangle on the 'factory side' of Howdendyke. The policy, then, whether explicitly stated or not, clearly envisioned a future Howdendyke

Plate 17. Ferry House, 1987

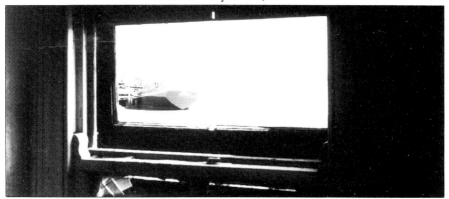

Plate 18. Through a Ferry House Window, 1987

Plate 19. Site of Ferry Farm, 1987

Plate 20. Ferry House, Chemical Works, and HS & L docks, 1987

Plate 21. Village Focus: Club, Jubilee Hall, Post Office, 1987

Plate 22. The village: field side (left) and factory side, 1987

Plate 23. Site of The Square, 1987

Plate 24. Jubilee Hall (left) and Club, 1987

Plate 25. Abandoned housing,
New Row, 1987

Plate 26. Site of Kilpin Lodge
and Kilpinpike fields, 1987

consisting of a maximum of twenty-eight houses, sixteen of them owned by Boothferry Borough and only four of them on the 'factory side' of the village.

Apparently, this plan to reduce the community by more than half (from sixty-eight households in 1971 to about twenty-eight in the late 1980s) was not communicated to the villagers. Indeed, it was not even submitted to their local representatives, Kilpin Parish Council (KPC) for comment. The policy may have remained submerged for years had not one Mr Stephen Spivey decided to renovate a house known as 'The Cottage'.

'The Cottage' stood at the north end of the terrace known as Prospect Villas on the 'factory side' of Howdendyke. An attractive small building, it was once a shop in the hands of Charles Mell Snr., my great-great-uncle. In 1979 Mr Spivey made application to Boothferry Health and Housing Department for a grant towards the improvement of the cottage. Simultaneously, he applied to Boothferry Planning for permission to make extensions to the dwelling. Health and Housing approved the proposal and awarded Mr Spivey a £2500 improvement grant; their counterparts in the Planning Department refused permission to improve.

Only in such ways do the hidden agendas of private enterprise, planners, and politicians come to the attention of the public. This cack-handed bureaucratic response to Mr Spivey's application was soon known throughout the village, brought to light the Hargreaves-Boothferry planning policy, and revealed to the startled inhabitants the vision of a future Howdendyke largely devoid of residents.

Many appeals for further information followed, not least from the planners' colleagues in Health and Housing. The Planning Department was asked to outline its Howdendyke policy to Boothferry Borough Council in September 1980.

KPC was astounded to learn of the Hargreaves-Boothferry Planning policy from a newspaper account of the Boothferry Council meeting. Responsible for three villages, KPC was annoyed at being totally ignored in the formulation of policy which was likely to result in the destruction of at least half of one of them, comprising perhaps a third of the parish's population. KPC remonstrated with Boothferry Planning, asserting that: Howdendyke was a viable community; there was no reason why industry and housing should not continue to co-exist there; no consideration had been given by the company to visual amenity in the village; no consideration had been given by Boothferry Planning toward making new industry compatible with the village's character; and, finally, that industrial expansion would inevitably destroy Grade I agricultural land. The KPC put most forcefully their feeling that some restrictions must be placed on industrial development, and that no plan should call for the loss of Howdendyke's identity as a village.

These points were vigorously restated when KPC representatives met with

Boothferry Council's Planning Committee in December 1980. In addition, KPC noted that Boothferry's own bureaucracy was in conflict over the Spivey affair and that parish council views were being blatantly disregarded. Reiterating their belief that industry and housing had long co-existed in Howdendyke and could continue to do so, KPC called on Hargreaves to maintain the village's housing stock and on Boothferry Council to cease creating conditions which would lead to the eventual disappearance of the village.

Boothferry's Chief Planning Officer spoke for the committee to the effect that his department could not compel Hargreaves to renovate property (strictly true, although Council could do so via Health & Housing) and was 'duty-bound' to promote industrial development. Howdendyke was one of only four riverside places in Boothferry District with good access roads, and was therefore an essential site for industrial expansion. Permitting houses to remain on the 'factory side' of the village would prevent future factory growth, as Boothferry Health and Housing would feel obliged to oppose industrial expansion towards existing houses on the grounds of nuisance. The planning officer did not feel that it was right to make it more difficult to attract industry to the site.

Boothferry councillors felt that it was ridiculous to allow housing 'expansion' when this could lead to a factory shutting down because of complaints of nuisance; that it was in the power of their Industrial Development Committee to bring industry to the village; and that about 90 per cent of the village was owned by Hargreaves Ltd. who could not be dictated to by Boothferry Council regarding the use of their own land. As usual, Boothferry Council failed to address the issue, asserted its power, and, in light of remarks about housing 'expansion' and inability to influence Hargreaves, clearly misunderstood the Howdendyke situation.

Appealing to Structure Plan guidelines, KPC compelled Boothferry Council to ask its Chief Planning Officer for advice regarding possible contraventions of the Structure Plan at Howdendyke. The CPO replied to the effect that the Structure Plan was 'very flexible' and that 'there are different ways of interpreting the Structure Plan in different circumstances'. Given this rather equivocal answer, KPC's final question to Boothferry Council was: 'Do we (a) get rid of the people, (b) get rid of the factories, or (c) develop both?'

Politicians and planners clearly cannot cope with such direct questions, and no answer was given. While KPC was clearly in favour of proposal (c), a reasonable compromise, it seemed clear to them that both Boothferry politicians and bureaucrats were strongly in favour of proposal (a). When Hargreaves was appealed to, the company handily passed the buck by replying that they had been 'requested' to demolish their housing property and had no wish to act against the desires of Boothferry Council. Faced with these evasions, and realising that the company, the politicians, and the planners were united against them, KPC and Howdendyke residents began to appreciate that their village was doomed.

Not yet in despair, KPC made a further attempt in early 1981 to influence Boothferry Council in favour of Howdendyke residents. Their chief point was that there was no assurance of the expansion of Ouse Chemical Works, and that 'although members appreciate the importance of industry, they consider it quite another thing to induce the sacrifice of existing houses to nebulous long-term development'. A neat point. But the CPO reiterated that the Hargreaves company had insisted that the Howdendyke factory 'had a long-term future' and that even if Boothferry Council agreed with KPC, neither group had the power to compel the company to improve already-empty houses (for Hargreaves were not standing still during this discussion, and Howdendyke houses were being condemned by Boothferry Health and Housing, evacuated, and boarded up or demolished at a rapid rate).

Two statements by influential Boothferry Council members appear to have carried the day against KPC (*Howdenshire Gazette*, 1981). Councillor Bill Bray, the member for the ward containing Howdendyke, an inhabitant of the attractive rural village of Laxton but a keen proponent of industrial expansion at Howdendyke, declared that the demolition of all houses within the Triangle was 'the only sensible way to tidy up the boundaries and make a proper building line. The houses in Prospect Villas are unrepairable and need demolishing'. He went on to say that Boothferry Council was 'at the mercy' of Hargreaves, and that 'I hope we can retain good relations and get them to tidy up'.

Councillor Bob Park, the member for Howden ward, adjacent to Howdendyke, clinched the matter by informing his colleagues categorically, although wholly erroneously, that 'It might be difficult to accept for the people of Howdendyke, but this village has been running itself down for the last thirteen years to my certain knowledge.' He went on to say that he felt Hargreaves had been 'sincere' in their recent meetings with Council representatives and that 'if we allow housing development it will hinder [Hargreaves]'.

Note the emphasis on tidyness, an ancient shibboleth, the emphasis on badly-built Prospect Villas (eleven houses) rather than well-built New Row (nine houses) although both were equally doomed by the new policy, the desire to promote industry and appease individual firms, the introduction of the spurious notion of housing 'development', and the equally spurious declaration that Howdendyke was disappearing by its own volition. It is notable also that neither Councillor Bray nor Councillor Park, nor indeed any member of Boothferry Council, resided in or near Howdendyke village.

Nevertheless, councillors Bray and Park were spokesmen for the Howdendyke area. On the basis of their dubious arguments, it seems, Boothferry Council agreed to accept the Hargreaves-Boothferry Planning policy for 'the industrial development of Howdendyke'. KPC's single victory was Boothferry's approval of its recommendation that Hargreaves should be asked to carry out landscaping to improve the twin eyesores of industrial plant and the rubble-strewn sites of already-demolished houses.

Shortly after this defeat of local desires by the combined forces of industry, bureaucracy, and politics, the following notice was placed by KPC in Howdendyke Post Office, the unofficial hub of the three villages in Kilpin parish. It is worth quoting in full.

POLICY OF KILPIN PARISH COUNCIL IN RELATION TO HOWDENDYKE
1. To preserve the housing and amenities which residents already have and to preserve the character of the village.
2. That the Industrial Concerns operating in Howdendyke should be expected to fulfil their obligations to the environment and to the public as promised, by conforming to conditions imposed, in the interests of the visual amenities of the locality.

POLICY OF BOOTHFERRY BOROUGH COUNCIL IN RELATION TO HOWDENDYKE DATED 2 April 1981. THE ONLY DIFFERENCE BETWEEN THIS AND THE ORIGINAL PROPOSAL IS THE ADDITION OF THE FINAL PART OF PARAGRAPH 3.
1. That the Council considers the area adjoining the existing fertiliser factory at Howdendyke and bounded by the existing road system on three sides to be suitable in the long-term for industrial development.
2. That the erection of new dwellinghouses within the above area should be refused and the extension or renovation of existing dwellinghouses, where the Council has jurisdiction, should not be permitted.
3. That Hargreaves Fertilisers Ltd. should be encouraged to pursue the above policy in conjunction with the Local Authority and to carry out landscaping and other remedial measures to improve the environment of the locality.

At first sight, the KPC policy calling for the preservation of existing housing seems to be at odds with Boothferry's insistence merely that new house erection should not be permitted. What Boothferry's explicit policy fails to make explicit is the fact that, even as the policy was being enunciated, Howdendyke was undergoing not a rash of house construction, but an orgy of house demolition. Most of the dwellings listed as demolished or condemned in Table 38 were evacuated and bulldozed in the late 1970s and early 1980s.

Coping with place annihilation
Residents reacted in a wide variety of ways to the news that at least half their village was being planned to death. A few expressed indifference. Some did not wholly believe that 'they' could do such a thing. The most complacent, a very small number, were residents of council houses on the relatively safe, 'field side' of the village. Most owner-occupiers, who totalled no more than a dozen, feared

a drastic fall in house values and made strenuous attempts to sell their properties in 1981. Local newspapers of the time contain a number of advertisements of such sales. In general, however, outsiders had become well aware of Howdendyke's problems. In particular, the only buyer on the 'factory side' of the village was none other than Hargreaves Fertilizers Ltd.

Despite knowledge of the Hargreaves-Boothferry policy, a number of residents still felt, in 1981, that an appeal to reason would help save their community. Some letters to the editor of the local newspaper appeared. The reasonableness of their tone is evinced by a single example:

> Letter to the Editor, *Howdenshire Gazette*, 3 July 1981, from C. Standring [owner-occupier, 'factory side'].
> ... Boothferry Council has put a cloud over our long-established community ... Howdendyke. You know, the semi-rural and semi-industrial village in the parish of Kilpin. It is where the council appears to want to demolish 21 houses, that is, half of the total village, so that possible industry may be given priority.
> These [house] properties would have potential if their occupiers were allowed planning permission and grants for improvements. You have only to look around you to see how old properties have been preserved.
> So come on, Boothferry Council and Hargreaves, by all means tidy up the village, but don't exterminate it. Is there really any need to spoil our village with speculative planning?

Unfortunately for Mr Standring's point about possible improvements, most of the houses were owned not by their occupiers, but by Hargreaves, who had no intention of improving their house property. Individual house-owners were refused planning permission to improve, and thus had no option but to sell to Hargreaves with the knowledge that such a sale meant immediate closure and eventual demolition (as indeed occurred in the celebrated case of 'The Cottage').

Howdendykers are prone to grumble at the assaults of 'them', but have little knowledge of planning procedures or the organizational skills necessary for opposing bureaucracy. Some were already demoralized by 1982 and expressed feelings of helplessness during interviews.

On behalf of worried villagers, KPC made strenuous efforts to bring its point of view to the attention of a wider public. During 1981 the parish council sent a number of letters to Boothferry Health and Housing Department, drawing attention to complaints of residents about 'lack of consideration by nearby industry'. Some of these complaints were from Kilpinpike residents suffering from noise and air pollution generated by the HS & L (downstream) site (*Howdenshire Gazette*, 3 July 1981).

No replies being received, KPC took its case to the Humberside Association of Parish and Town Councils (HAPTC), asserting that 'Boothferry Council had been unco-operative with the parish council as far as industry was concerned'.

This appeal came to nothing. KPC did not send a representative to the June 1981 meeting of the HAPTC Boothferry branch; Boothferry Planning did. The Chief Planning Officer assured HAPTC that KPC's allegations of 'planning blight' were untrue, that the house demolition policy at Howdendyke applied to 'only a small part of the village where there were houses which were relatively close to industry', and that Howdendyke would not thereby be reduced to a village of sixteen council houses only, for 'there are other dwellings which would remain within the village' (*Howdenshire Gazette*, 26 June 1981). These 'other dwellings' actual total about ten, but HAPTC was clearly either convinced by the CPO, uncertain of the facts, or unable to help KPC.

The latter then delegated its sole member resident in Howdendyke (actually at Elm Tree, on the Howdendyke periphery) to survey the villagers' opinions, in the hope of presenting evidence of a collective will to resist place annihilation. A survey conducted in June 1981 was able to contact thirty-five of the forty households remaining at that time. The respondents represented fifty-nine adults and thirty-five children, more than 80 per cent of the village population. Of the thirty-five respondents, twenty-five were tenants and ten owner-occupiers. Six worked for HS & L, seven for Hargreaves, three were self-employed, nine gave no occupational details, and ten were retired. Two respondents indicated degrees of uncertainty, but the other thirty-three signified that they wished to continue to reside in Howdendyke, and affixed their signatures to that effect.

This desire to 'continue to live in the village' was the major issue for Howdendykers. Yet as homes were demolished, the total housing stock in Howdendyke diminished; for according to the Hargreaves-Boothferry Policy no new housing could be built on the 'factory side' of the village. Further, vacant land on the 'field side' of the village was zoned industrial and wholly owned by industrial or speculative entrepreneurs who had no intention of selling land for housing. And no private individual would consider having a house built in a village so obviously being squeezed by industrial growth on all sides. Consequently, many residents of houses on which a closing order was made by Boothferry Health and Housing (the preparatory step to demolition by Hargreaves) had little choice but to leave the village. Younger couples purchased houses in other villages, but elderly persons were invariably found council flats in the nearby town of Howden.

Clearly, Howdendykers had expressed a wish to stay, if not in their existing houses, then in new houses erected, by Boothferry Council perhaps, in Howdendyke village (alas for this possibility, Boothferry Council had long had a Conservative majority, more active in selling council houses than building them).

KPC forwarded the results of their survey to the area's MP, the Conservative Sir Paul Bryan, who replied that he would 'do all he could to help retain

Howdendyke as a living village' (*Howdenshire Gazette*, 31 July 1981). The MP wrote to Boothferry Council and replied to KPC, but his letter was of no help, being 'merely a resume of some of the facts' (*Howdenshire Gazette*, 2 October 1981). In a letter to me (21 October 1981) Sir Paul regretted his ineffectiveness in 'saving this village' but felt that nothing could be done unless the Borough Council appeared to be acting unconstitutionally or unlawfully, whereas its actions were clearly well within its constitutional powers.

Meanwhile, Boothferry Health and Housing had finally replied to KPC complaints about industrial nuisance by stating that no action could be taken unless residents could 'make a log of the date, time, duration, and nature of the nuisance'. This, of course, is the classic fob-off, as few people have the time, means, inclination, or ability to take up such a suggestion. KPC's capacity to fight for Howdendyke then received another blow in the form of the death of its only Howdendyke member. By the end of 1981 the only concession obtained by KPC was a promise on the part of Hargreaves that the company would try to eliminate rats and tidy up some areas of rubble left after recent house demolitions.

Given the general atmosphere of uncertainty and an overwhelming feeling of powerlessness in the face of Boothferry's plans, the three owner-occupiers in Prospect Villas and New Row sold their houses back to Hargreaves. Soon afterwards, Boothferry Health and Housing issued closing orders on those houses in Prospect Villas not already condemned, and a demolition order for the whole row of twelve houses (including 'The Cottage'). Hargreaves' bulldozers then knocked down the whole terrace and levelled off the area. In one blow a quarter of Howdendyke's remaining housing was annihilated and its residents dispersed.

1985–86

Anthony Burgess' novel *1985* (1978), unlike Orwell's *1984* (1948), depicts the excesses and injustices of a Britain run by trade unions. For Howdendyke, 1985 was the year in which the full reality of being run down by private enterprise made itself apparent to village residents.

According to the 1981 Census, Kilpin parish recorded a 26 per cent fall in population during the period 1971–81, the largest such decline in the whole of Boothferry Borough (*Howdenshire Gazette*, 4 March 1983; Table 4). Almost the whole of this decline was due to house closures, evacuations, and demolitions in Howdendyke.

By 1982 both KPC and Howdendyke residents seem to have accepted the inevitability of their village being deliberately reduced to half its former size. The destruction of the twelve houses in Prospect Villas was a fait accompli, and most of the thirteen houses in The Square were gone, as well as Ferry Farm (Table 38). By late 1986 Howdendyke village consisted of: (1) on the 'field side':

sixteen council houses; seven privately-owned houses; and one BritAg-owned dwelling housing a retired worker; (2) on the 'factory side': the privately-owned Post Office; three privately-owned houses in Ferry Road; and New Row, a Hargreaves-owned terrace comprising three tenants, and six vacant, boarded-up houses. In the second half of the 1980s then, there remained a total of thirty-one households in a village which a decade before had held twice that number.

In the 1950s Howdendyke/Kilpinpike had two shops, a Post Office, the Workingman's Club (which was, in effect, the village pub), and a village hall known as the Jubilee Hall. By the 1980s both stores had closed, largely because of increasing car-ownership in the village, but the triad of Post Office, Jubilee Hall, and Club remained in The Square as the nucleus of village social life and activity. The Post Office had long been privately-owned (by three generations of the Mell family 1918–72), but both the Club and the Jubilee Hall were owned by BritAg. Whereas the latter was used only on occasion for children's parties and the like, before its abandonment in 1985, the Club was in use every night on a regular basis not only by Howdendykers but by a substantial non-local membership.

Early in 1985 HS & L announced plans for a six-acre lorry park and turning area on BritAg land, and which appeared to involve the demolition of both the Club and the hall. As if on cue, Boothferry Health and Housing Department carried out a public health inspection of the Club and asked for certain repairs to be undertaken. The 130 members, quite reasonably, refused to commit themselves to the expense of these repairs unless they received some assurance from BritAg that the Club would not soon be demolished (*Howdenshire Gazette*, 11 April 1985). This was refused, and the health authorities then threatened to order the Club to cease operating pending the carrying out of repairs. Catch-22.

Established in 1922, the Club is the village social centre. Loss of both pub and village hall would be a devastating blow to what remains of Howdendyke's sense of community. Residents, by this time, were fully apprised of the hidden agendas, now largely revealed, of BritAg, HS & L, and Boothferry planners and politicians. And whereas in 1981 letters to the editor of the *Howdenshire Gazette* had been headlined 'The village that will not die', by 1985 the typical byline had become: 'Another nail in the village's coffin?'

Incensed at the threatened closure of the Club, KPC complained bitterly about the refusal of Boothferry Council to listen to Howdendyke residents or their grass-roots representatives, pointed out the total lack of public participation in formulating Boothferry's policy for Howdendyke, and demanded 'a well-thought-out, overall, long-term plan for the whole of Howdendyke with due consideration given to the residents' (*Howdenshire Gazette*, 18 April 1985).

A perceptive resident of a nearby village opined that 'Howdendyke is a classic example of planning blight. It is NOT dying. It is slowly being killed off by piecemeal development ...' and pointed out the slow, stealthy way in which Howdendyke village had been dismantled bit by bit, in favour of 'industrial' growth, since the 1960s. 'I say "stealthy" because the closure [of the Club] is not accidental or indeed inevitable, but is the product of business interests working against the community to acquire land for their use ... Whatever the industries say, they are apparently only interested in the demolition of the whole village' (*Howdenshire Gazette*, 18 April 1985). The fate of the Club is reviewed in the following chapter.

Commentary

The twenty-five years following the 1961 Census, when Howdendyke had over seventy inhabited houses, have seen dramatic and devastating changes wrought in both landscape and community. Instead of a modest 11 acres of industrial land, by 1986 an area more than treble that size was devoted less to river-related industry than to cargo handling involving large wharves, silos, warehouses, and unsightly open storage areas. An attempt has even been made to convert the fertilizer factory into a cargo handling facility.

In stark contrast, of the seventy-two Howdendyke/Kilpinpike dwellings of 1961, by 1986 twenty-nine had been demolished and four converted into offices. A further eight stood empty because of closure orders but could not be demolished because of their location in still partly inhabited terraces. A three-fold increase in 'industrial' space, therefore, has been complemented by a loss of housing, and hence residents, of the order of 57 per cent.

According to county planners, Howdendyke is a 'planning anomaly'. This anomaly has developed because of the deliberate actions of private enterprise, politicians, and local authority bureaucrats. These actions can be summarized as follows:

(1) Since 1968, most 'industrial' planning applications for development at Howdendyke have been approved. These include use changes, extensions, new plant, new wharves, and the conversion of dwellings to offices.

(2) During the same period, and with only minor exceptions, all applications for house renovations or extensions in Howdendyke and Kilpinpike, and for new houses in the latter, have been refused.

(3) Further, not only has permission for housing expansion been denied, but Boothferry Health and Housing Department, under the provisions of the 1957 Housing Act, has issued closure and demolition orders on approximately one half of Howdendyke's dwellings since 1977.

Since 1980 an uneven battle to save the village has been in progress. On the one hand are the remaining residents, Kilpin parish council, and some outside interests, none of whom have significant powers. On the other are arrayed the big guns: Boothferry Planning; Boothferry Health and Housing; two large industrial concerns whose subsidiaries operate at Howdendyke as BritAg and HS & L; and the ultimate decision-taking authority, Boothferry Borough Council.

According to Kilpin parish council, the alternatives for Howdendyke are the co-existence of industry and village, 'no industry', or 'no village'. Whereas KPC clearly favours the former, 'no village', or less than half a village, seems to be preferred by the powerful. And at least one member of Boothferry Council apparently believes that Howdendyke is disappearing of its own volition, rather than as a result of industrialists' 'cost-efficiency', planners' 'flexibility', and politicians' pursuit of 'development' and 'jobs' at almost any cost.

10
Creation

It is the writer's duty to hate injustice, to defy the powerful, and to speak for the voiceless. ...

Edward Abbey

In Yorkshire dialect, 'to create' means to make a fuss, to complain, to discourse at some length about a problem or injury (hence: 'he's creating summat awful about his tea not being ready'). In standard English, creation concerns the act of producing. By conflating these meanings, I believe that my interviews with Howdendyke residents and evacuees have resulted in a creative object, the collective interpretation of the injuries and complaints of many individuals concerning the impending death of Howdendyke.

On dying

For Howdendyke is dying. It is remarkable that, without forcing the material, many of the remarks made by interviewees fall into categories which bear a strong resemblance to well-recognized stages in an individual's dying process (Kubler-Ross 1969) or the coming to terms with bereavement (Marris, 1974). But one of the most important stages of the dying process – denial – was not common among Howdendykers. Few felt that the village would survive in anything like the form in which he or she had previously experienced it. Common categories, then, in the interview material include: a lament for the past; an assignment of blame; and an acceptance of loss.

Lament for the past

Most statements referring to a better recent quality of life and environment were quiet, modest, rather downplayed. Overt sentiment is not commonly expressed in this subculture. Nevertheless, there is a wealth of feeling in statements such as:

- It used to be a happy little village, did Howdendyke (John Asselby).
- Howdendyke was just a nice, ordinary village, a nice place to live in (Mary Knedlington).
- It was a lovely place to live, all that river and fields ... (Ann Partridge).
- It used to be a lovely little village. It's awful now that it's gone. It doesn't look like

170

Howdendyke now, does it? (Joan Ayre)
- It were a marvellous village (Tom Ayre).
- Everything seems to have gone, that used to be (Mavis Westoby).

Note the use of the past tense in all these statements, three of which were made by persons still resident in Howdendyke at the time of interview (1982).

The general impression is that Howdendyke was not loved for its architectural gems or splendid landscape features, for these are lacking. Rather, it was a quiet, ordinary, fairly peaceful village, 'nice' in the best sense of the word, where parents could raise their children amid fields and by the river. The river's beauty, indeed, was mentioned by a number of interviewees. In short, to these respondents, Howdendyke was a well-loved place, and it was home.

Nostalgia and regret for the quite recent past frequently took the form of a mild adulation of the Anderton regime which terminated with the deaths of the Pillings in 1959–60. A number of respondents reported the efforts of Mrs Pilling, formerly Miss Anderton, towards the general upkeep of the village. There were several variants of the following:

- If there was nowt much to do in t'Chemics, Mrs Pilling would send men round the village to sweep it up and keep it tidy (John Asselby).

The conclusion one draws is that management since 1960 has expressed little concern for the village environment.

There were dissenters of course, and a fragment of my family history suggests that some residents, at least, may have felt the disadvantages of paternalism:

- Richard Norman Pilling (surveying Howdendyke from the river bank, its sole vantage point): 'I own all this'.
- Cecil Roland Mell (my uncle, labourer, orchard owner and house owner): 'No you don't'.

Nevertheless, even the remnant Mells tend to agree with the general opinion of Howdendykers that a process of irreversible decline began in the 1960s, accelerated in the 1970s, and could lead to the destruction of the community by the 1990s.

Assignment of blame

The deaths of the Pillings in 1959–60 is the joint event which was most clearly seen by interviewees as a major break in historical continuity and as the beginning of the end of their village. Had the Pilling regime continued, it was felt, then the annihilation process would never have occurred:

- This would never have happened if Pillings were alive (Herbert Snaith).
- After Pilling died the whole bloody place went to rack and ruin (Alf Saltmarsh).

The Pillings' lack of children, of course, rendered any continuation of their paternalist control impossible.

A number of residents attempted to visualize the effect upon the Pillings, and in particular Mrs Pilling, could they see the condition of their village in the 1980s:

- If Mr and Mrs Pilling could see what's going on here, they'd turn over in their graves (Emily Aire).
- If Mrs Pilling could lift her head up and see Howdendyke like it is now, she'd go straight back (Annie Oxtoby).

The Pilling family were clearly respected. Nearly a quarter of a century after their deaths their probable opinions are regarded as important and legitimate commentary.

Direct assignment of blame for Howdendyke's condition was not as common as expressions of loss regarding the Pilling regime. In particular, interviewees were guarded about making blame statements when being tape recorded. Nevertheless, in casual conversation, without being led, a few residents explicitly blamed one particular firm:

- East Coast, it's East Coast [now HS & L] that's done it (Gwen Smith).
- Well, I blame Humber Sea and Land (Albert Eastrington).
- They seem to be able to do just as they want to do with the village (Bill Oxtoby).
- Aye, but not what anybody else wants (Annie Oxtoby).

My general impression was that respondents felt that HS & L was the motive force behind change, and that Hargreaves/BritAg were, in large part, responding to and supporting HS & L initiatives.

Acceptance of death

By 1982 the general mood in Howdendyke was one of resignation, even acceptance. Some tenants had attempted to resist change for several years, but eventually the difficulties of old age in deteriorating housing and the loss of shopping facilities drove them to council housing in Howden. The ban on house building and extensions, of course, means that the declining population of Howdendyke cannot be renewed through the in-migration of young families or even the retention of some existing families.

The following quotations are examples of the most typical responses to questions about Howdendyke's future in the remainder of the twentieth century:

- There's nothing happening; Howdendyke's just fading away (Bill Oxmardyke).
- It's shrinking. There's only three children under school-leaving age (Esme Cottness).
- It's getting smaller every day (Arthur Snell).

And many respondents used the same expression concerning any possibility of reversing the process:

- Howdendyke's had it, Doug.

Given this general air of resignation, despite recent petitions and the efforts of the KPC, it seemed in 1982 that little could be done to avert the death of the community. At this point it is appropriate to ask by what means the death of the village was being managed by entrepreneurs and local authorities.

The annihilation process

How is a place annihilated, and how do the residents of a place undergoing destruction interpret the process? Two concepts from American urbanology, 'red-lining' and 'blockbusting' are of assistance here.

Red-lining occurs in the poorer, inner areas of large American cities when insurance companies and other agencies decide that property in a particular district is no longer of value. Although the inhabitants of the area may consider theirs to be adequate, loved homes, distant authorities decide that their houses will no longer be deemed suitable for insurance or other purposes. Without insurance, of course, mortgage loans and other forms of housing support are impossible to obtain. The immediate result is fear and uncertainty among house-owners; the end result is rapid decay of structures, abandonment, or forced sales to development companies or speculators. Redevelopment then takes place in the form of much more profitable structures such as office towers or high-rent housing.

It is quite obvious that Howdendyke has undergone a form of red-lining by Boothferry planners and politicians who have decreed that no new housing development, extensions, or improvements shall occur on the 'factory side' of the village. I can attest to the demoralizing effect of this policy on some of the owner-occupiers of Howdendyke, especially those on the 'field side' who lack even the option to sell out to Hargreaves/BritAg. Once effectively red-lined, house values fall, and Howdendyke can be left to be destroyed piecemeal at a tempo decided by the village's industrial enterprises.

Once a district has been red-lined, speculators and developers are faced with the problem of accelerating the evacuation of the area by its residents. Here the process known as *blockbusting* comes into play; the term essentially means the process by which residents are deliberately made to feel so uncomfortable, both physically and mentally, that they 'voluntarily' leave their homes. More specifically, blockbusting originally referred to the process whereby speculators circulate rumours that undesirable minorities will soon overwhelm a neighbourhood, thus precipitating panic sales, a drop in prices, and a buyer's market (Abrams 1971). In Britain the processs 'of driving out tenants by harrassment', notorious in the 1960s, has been termed 'Rachmanism' (Abrams 1971).

In the case of Howdendyke there is no evidence that blockbusting has been deliberately engaged in with the goal of forcing tenants and owner-occupiers to leave the village. Nevertheless, the normal business practices of both Hargreaves/BritAg and HS & L have effectively acted upon Howdendyke in a manner which has had a blockbusting effect, whether deliberate or not. In Howdendyke, during the late 1970s and early 1980s, blockbusting has taken the form of overwhelming environmental degradation. This has occurred mainly in two forms: (i) air, noise, water, and visual pollution, by HS & L, along the Ouse waterfront; and (ii) deliberate neglect of housing repairs, with the creation of an atmosphere of uncertainty, by Hargreaves/BritAg, in the village as a whole. Houses in the now-demolished Square suffered on both counts.

From a large body of interview material, two accounts have been selected to demonstrate these twin processes of blockbusting at both macro- and micro-scales. The first deals with the severe environmental degradation that effects the whole village, but especially the waterfront. The interviewee was an owner-occupier. The second is a micro-study of passive blockbusting which effects most of the houses occupied by Hargreaves tenants, now mostly in the interior of the village. Both interviews date from 1982.

Blockbusting the waterfront

Joe Apthorpe bought a house (once my grandfather's) in Kilpinpike, two fields away from Howdendyke proper, in the early 1970s. Both he and his wife had white-collar jobs in nearby towns, but wished to live in the countryside for the 'peace and quiet' and the relaxed rural way of life. This is a common English middle-class ideal.

Joe's rural retreat included a house largely surrounded by fields and an uninterrupted view of the River Ouse. Unfortunately the fields comprised what I have previously termed the 'downstream site' for industrial development, while the view's middle ground was rapidly occupied by HS & L's 200 feet river wharf. Joe and his three neighbours in Kilpinpike were, throughout the 1970s and early 1980s, subjected to high levels of noise and air pollution, besides unpleasant visual intrusions and danger from increasingly heavy lorry traffic on narrow country roads.

Noise pollution was clearly the greatest evil emanating from the HS & L operation:

Humberside Sea & Land's jetty creates a lot of noise. First, ships coming upriver turn round by dropping anchor and swinging round on their anchor-chains, all to instructions on a loud-hailer. Then they draw back their metal hatches with a clatter. Ships have to come up with the tide, so these intolerable noises often go on in the middle of the night. Sleep is impossible.

The jetty cranes produce noise from their heavy engines and the rattling of unloading cargo. Some cargo goes into the warehouse yard, which is another source of noise. This comes from mechanical shovels arranging bulk cargo, from lorries, and from the foul language of lorry drivers. The drivers have to shout to make themselves heard. You can only appreciate the sound of metal ingots being dropped into a metal lorry if you've heard it for yourself. And the jetty works a seven-day week, so there's no rest from the noise even on Sundays.

Although noise pollution seems to be the major evil, many other irritations led to Joe's decision to leave:

The road's so narrow and there's an endless stream of lorries to and from the jetty. They can't pass properly so they destroy the footpaths, and they often park on the road, making it even narrower. The road's unsafe for pedestrians, especially children and pensioners going down to the Post Office. And the ships and the jetty leave their spotlights on all night. The light comes right through our curtains and makes sleeping difficult. And the lights dazzle motorists and make the road even more unsafe.

Air pollution is a third hazard:

These ships unload a lot of bulk powder cargoes. The dust covers on the grabs just aren't effective. On windy days you can see the dust blowing and coating the roads, the verges, the hedges, windows, even gardens. Fruit is unfit to eat, and vegetables. We don't know whether the dust is toxic. All the windows and paintwork need cleaning much more often than normal. And lorry drivers don't sheet their loads, so the dust streams off the backs of the lorries. There's sometimes so much dust in the air you can actually taste it.

This is a far cry from the previous rapid unloading directly into the fertilizer factory. Under the Anderton regime, cargoes, only some of which were in powder form, were unloaded less frequently, in lesser quantity, and perhaps with more care. The Ouse Chemical Works itself has always generated dust pollution in Howdendyke village, but rarely to the extent experienced after the arrival of HS & L. According to Joe Apthorpe 'Any surface inside the house is no sooner clean than, within an hour, there's a tangible coating of dust.' The operations of HS & L have clearly made Howdendyke a hell for the house-proud.

Corroboration of this comes from an incident related by Annie Oxtoby. Annie's daughter lived in an old Hargreaves-owned dwelling in the Square.

One day Annie went to visit her daughter only to find her in tears:

> They'd been unloadening those ships and you know what sort of a mess it was when they were landing that white powder stuff. She said to me, 'Mother, you can't see through my windows.' And it was blowing hard and powder was all over the roads. The poor little bugger was ill and she was crying, so I went to see the manager [of HS & L] and said 'just look at all that mess; people have to live here'. And he said he was sorry but it was the wind and so nothing could be done about it. And my lass said 'It's all right for you but we have to live here. It's all over the windows and all up the back of the house as well.' So he went and got a window cleaner to clean it all up, all the windows in the village. And then they got some big sheets and pinned them all up to great big posts to try to stop it.

The problem was finally solved for this resident by the demolition of the house in the early 1980s.

Little, generally, was said about visual pollution, although Joe Apthorpe and a number of correspondents of the *Howdenshire Gazette* noted that HS & L had repeatedly ignored visual amenity conditions imposed upon them as part of previous planning permissions. For example, a belt of trees around the warehouse and open storage sites, which would at least screen their ugliness, had not materialized. Indeed, the removal of hedges and trees by Kilpin area farmers served to heighten the intrusive visual effect of the three red warehouses built by HS & L. In this flat landscape the villages of Kilpin and Howdendyke, although less than two miles apart, were not intervisible in the early 1960s. Local farmers, therefore, have exacerbated the problem of visual pollution in the area.

Less concerned with visual amenity, waterfront residents complained most frequently of noise and dust. Other complaints concerned the influx of foreign sailors who manned the vessels delivering cargoes to upstream and downstream sites. Widows living alone were not the only interviewees to complain of harrassment by drunken sailors. Some spoke of continual nervous stress.

By the mid-1980s this waterside problem has been 'solved' by the removal of both the inhabitants and their dwellings. Of twenty-two inhabited riverside houses in 1960, only three remained inhabited in 1986. Tenants were rehoused in vacant council houses or, more often, moved to Howden or elsewhere. Owner-occupiers, naturally, experienced greater difficulties. Joe Apthorpe recalls the problem of trying to sell his house at Kilpinpike in the late 1970s:

> I felt bitter. I had my house on the market for years. The stumbling block was always Humberside Sea and Land's jetty and storage yard. One lady came to see the house but backed off when she heard the noise. Another said 'I couldn't live with that noise.' Another sale was almost clinched when the buyers heard that

Humberside Sea & Land were asking for an extension to the jetty. Even a group of county planners were disgusted by the noise. ...

Blockbusting terraced housing

Along the village street leading from the waterfront, blockbusting has so far been largely restricted to the 'factory side' of the village, and has taken a more passive form. For an understanding of this process, we turn to the testimony of Mavis Westoby.

Twenty years a widow, Mavis is proud that she has lived in the same house for forty-one years. The house has rich meaning for her as her established married home and as the chief repository of memories of her dead husband. 'I'd never want to move', says Mavis; 'this is where we were happy.'

Mavis' rented house is one of a row of nine. At the time of the interview (late 1982) five of these were empty, including those on either side of Mavis' home. The houses do not contain all modern conveniences, but Mavis accepts the absence of facilities deemed essential by middle-class persons, including planners and housing officials: 'As you see there are only four rooms, but they're four lovely big rooms and the only thing wrong is we haven't bathrooms and we haven't hot water. Well, I don't miss either because I haven't had it, so what you've never had you don't miss.'

Nevertheless, despite the lack of amenities (which could be remedied by local authority grants if the landlord – Hargreaves – would apply) the houses can readily be made into pleasant homes. A parish councillor, on a 'fact-finding' visit, expressed her surprise at the quality of Mavis' home: 'She said: "They're beautiful and comfortable and to think that they want to pull something down like this where a person's living comfortably. Has no one been to see your home?"' But the powerful interests who will be responsible for the eventual destruction of Mavis' home have rarely been to inspect a tenant's home, preferring to leave that chore to the Health inspectorate preparatory to a closing order. It is more convenient, at arm's length, to speaks of 'hovels' (a company director) or 'slums', or 'unfit housing' (Boothferry Council). Yet the demand for this particular housing is strong:

> They [Hargreaves] won't sell them, they won't let people rent them, yet there's lots of people wanting to rent them and lots of people wanting to buy them. They've knocked at my door, a considerable number of people, [asking] 'who did they belong to' and 'who should we see', and 'how long had they been empty', and 'what is the reason for them being left empty?' ... It seemed to be every weekend people were coming.

Such visitors had ceased coming by the mid-1980s, for the Hargreaves-Boothferry policy had by then become widely known.

The houses were, of course, being left empty as a staging process towards the time when, the whole terrace being empty, it could be demolished. Further, empty houses in a still partially-occupied terrace make for an easy type of blockbusting, the passive blockbusting of neglect. Such passive blockbusting goes on via: failure to thwart vandalism; increasing living costs for tenants; increasing nuisance for tenants; failure to make repairs; poor quality repairs; deteriorating physical quality of buildings and of the tenant's personal quality of life; and, overall, a feeling of impotence in the face of the landlord's deliberate policy of non-information regarding the future of the buildings.

One of the results of the partial evacuation of terraced housing is the imposition of higher costs on those tenants who remain. As Mavis notes: 'There's one empty on this side and three empty on that, and hence I'm spending a mint of money in fuel to keep it all aired and warm because naturally when you are between empty ones on either side you're not getting their warmth ...' At the same time, empty houses whose windows and doors are broken by vandals, and have been poorly boarded-up, create other problems:

> so of course you get the weather blowing in, raining ... it all goes in next door and everything is dreadfully damp. All the wallpaper's hanging off next door. The damp comes through the wall and I've consequently to have constant fires. If I go away for the weekend I can't have fires going so the house is dreadfully cold and a musty smell comes through from next door. It's not very pleasant.

As the occupied houses steadily deteriorate, the company's failure to make repairs becomes critical: 'Not that they ever refuse ... not actually refuse. But you ask for things and nothing happens, and it goes on and on and on until you think they've forgotten. So you've asked several times and you just come to the conclusion that nobody wants to know and you try and help yourself.' Mavis is cheerful, not a complainer, so she tries to make her own repairs. But elderly widows may find that doing their own repairs to the landlord's property can be hazardous:

> They won't do anything much. So rather than have the property look like the derelict ones either side, you try to help yourself. I do my painting outside. A couple of years ago I borrowed a big ladder to go up and do the bedroom windows outside and I got a good three parts of the way up and I daren't go any further. Only about four or five steps to go, but I just hadn't the courage. You try to help yourself, but when you have no husband it comes to a point where it's a man's work and you can't do it yourself and no one's willing to help [meaning the company], well, it just has to go.

Only in the direst emergency, apparently, is the company willing to fulfil its duties as landlord. One terrible winter, water pipes burst in the house next door. Company workmen then managed to break Mavis' stop tap, so that she had no control over her domestic water system for three weeks. In the end, she contacted the local water authority: 'just to ask a bit of advice, because I didn't seem to be getting any results from the people who owned the property, and I was even willing to pay for something to be done because winter was still going on ...' Only with the stimulus of 'someone with a little bit more push than I had' did the company return to make the repair, and even then 'it's a botch job'.

Mavis is not unaware that her predicament is due to a deliberate policy of running down the village of Howdendyke: 'As far as Hargreaves are concerned, they haven't any property.' Houses are emptied of residents whenever possible, but no information, either positive or negative, regarding the future of their tenancy is given to the remaining tenants:

> It's the indecision of everything. You feel so frustrated and you feel people are used and unkindly used. Why should they be allowed to play ducks and drakes with peoples' livelihood and where they're living? Granted they can't turn people out without suitable [alternative] accommodation. I understand that. But it's the indecision, not knowing when and how. If only they would come and talk to us.

But 'they' don't, and when tenants ask questions they receive only evasions couched in unsympathetic language. On which Mavis comments, 'And I hate being talked down to.'

The end result of such multiple frustrations is that tenants finally give up the struggle and especially if elderly, accept council housing in the nearby town of Howden. According to Mavis, the company, 'Wait for people to go out, and the people go out five times out of ten through frustration, because they're so sick and tired of the indecision and trouble.' She envisages the future of her terrace to be that of a number of nearby houses recently demolished by the company, 'You see these houses flattened and then for years brick rubble and the land left desolate and nothing done. It's a wicked shame, especially when people want to stay.'

Mavis is more eloquent than most. Nevertheless, almost every item in her testimony can be matched in the transcripts of other interviewees. Perhaps the most common complaint is that repairs have been difficult to obtain and have often necessitated work and expense on the part of the tenant. And according to Ellen Broomfleet, one of the last to leave The Square after many protestations, 'these houses haven't had a lick of paint on or a nail put in since Mr Pilling died. We have to live like gypsies now, Doug, just like gypsies.' Over twenty years without significant repainting hardly suggests an ideal landlord-tenant relationship.

Right of reply

It is only fair that decision-takers should have the right of reply to the above charges. In April 1986 I sent a condensed version of the first draft of Chapters 8–11 of this book to the chief participants in the Howdendyke drama (see Appendix). Although all the ordinary citizens whose addresses were still known (three of five) responded immediately, no effective replies were received from politicians, planners, or private enterprise. Accordingly, I travelled to England and interviewed five of the six targeted individuals in late July 1986. Their responses follow.

Private enterprise

A director of BritAg Ltd. explained the difficult problems of his firm in the face of the world glut of fertilizers which emerged in the 1970s. Rationalization was imperative, and of four Hargreaves plants, two were closed, Howdendyke being retained for its water-related site. When BritAg emerged in 1983 as a result of a merger with Allbright & Wilson, two further plants were involved. Only the closure of the older section of the Barton-on-Humber plant enabled BritAg to keep the Howdendyke factory alive. And it could only be kept going by a radical restructuring towards the production of domestic and horticultural fertilizers, and the shedding of thirty-four of the fifty-four jobs. Seven further jobs may emerge, along with some seasonal positions, when Scottish Agricultural Industries (another ICI subsidiary) gets into its stride in the Ouse Chemical Works.

Given this background, said the spokesman, it is easier to see that statements made in 1977 regarding expansion at Howdendyke were related to the closure of other plants and expected economies of scale; and that the proposal in 1982 to turn the works into a storage facility was an attempt to expand company options in rapidly-changing circumstances. The sale or lease of land and jetties to HS & L is a rational use of resources, given the extreme improbability of chemical factory expansion. With the growth of cheap North African imports, the current oversupply, increased competition from producers such as Norsk Hydro (formerly Fison's), and a likely decrease in demand for fertilizers when EEC agricultural policy comes to its senses, British fertilizer manufacturers face a bleak future.

The BritAg spokesman agreed that the initial sale of tied housing at Howdendyke was an error, and admitted, to some extent, that the company had been insensitive to local wishes; he noted, however, that 'progress means that someone always gets hurt'. Further, he explained that, in trying to keep the Howdendyke plant viable, Tunisian raw materials had to be imported. These, being very dusty, caused pollution and complaints. In trying to combat pollution, the plant entered the down-spiral of decreasing cost-effectiveness and increasing likelihood of closure. This was yet a further argument for the separation of people from industry, especially as people's desired environmental standards have risen drastically since the 1950s.

The spokesman discounted any notion of an agreement with HS & L to get rid of Howdendyke village; events and circumstances change too quickly for the formulation of such a strategy. In terms of this account, then, the destruction of Howdendyke appears to be a logical inevitability, the sad outcome of a tragic unfolding, but of no great importance in the general scheme of things.

A director of Humberside Sea & Land Services Ltd. agreed that BritAg did not have a close relationship with his firm: 'we are just tenants who pay a royalty for every ton we carry over their land'. There is a much stronger link with TR Chemicals (on the former Glucose site), for the site is jointly owned by HS & L, and Tinoverman Ltd., which does the shipping work for TR Chemicals, is an HS & L 'shell company'. HS & L, indeed, is a large firm with sixteen 'trading arms' in Humberside.

It was formed in the 1960s as a reaction to the 'endless delays and labour disputes at registered ports'. And despite the fact that HS & L workers at Howdendyke are unionized, 'there has been never a day's stoppage here'. This is attributed to good pay, considerable 'identity' between workers and management, and a 'small, intimate, family atmosphere', which has even extended to taking on certain Anderton-like traditions, such as sending Christmas hampers to Howdendyke pensioners.

The spokesman agreed that this paternalist stance did not offset the nuisance and noise caused by HS & L in the village, and admitted that one of HS & L's own workers, an owner-occupier in Howdendyke, was suing the company for loss of amenity and potential loss of housing value. The director expected that, at the very least, the company would be asked to either buy out some properties close to its operations or to double-glaze the windows of some of the village houses.

Attention was then drawn to the positive achievement of providing about 200 jobs (56 'outside workers', 21 office staff, and 40 workers at TR Chemicals), not to mention scores of independent lorry drivers and haulage firms. Allowing for BritAg's decline and the demise of shipyard, farm, etc., this means that HS & L and its associates have more than doubled the employment available at Howdendyke since the 1960s.

Nor was this achieved by taking trade from the port of Goole, for the low-value high-bulk cargoes handled by Howdendyke were unsuited to the slow turn-round of registered docks, and if trade were to be diverted from Howdendyke it would to to private wharves on the Trent. No expansion of HS & L was envisaged after 1986, for the plant was currently operating at only 75 per cent capacity, but should trade ever increase, Howdendyke was capable of doubling its current four-berth capacity, and the next most likely site for a wharf would be Bishop's Staith.

This interview took place in the HS & L offices at Kilpinpike, in what had once been my Aunt Everilda's front bedroom. One must give HS & L some credit for the retention of these buildings, although their facades have been renovated in poor taste.

Planners

Boothferry *Health & Housing* was represented by its director, the Chief Housing and Environmental Services Officer. He affirmed that in condemning Howdendyke houses he was merely performing his statutory duty, housing deterioration 'having become evident' or 'been brought to our attention', though not, apparently, by Hargreaves/BritAg. The synchronicity of a Health & Housing inspection of Howdendyke Club and HS & L's application to place a lorry park on its site elicited the reply: 'It is unfair to talk of anything but coincidence in this case: life is full of coincidences.'

When asked about the possibility of rehousing people from condemned houses in new housing in Howdendyke, a scheme perfectly permissible under Structure Plan guidelines, the director replied that first, Council were no longer building council houses except for old people, and second, that old people require services, which are not available at Howdendyke. He also expressed astonishment that his department had placed closing orders on 'thirty-odd' houses in Howdendyke.

The Chief Planning Officer (CPO) of Boothferry *Planning Department* was appointed only in 1974 and thus was able to say little about the policies of Howden Rural District Council. With regard to the fatal decision to industrialize Howdendyke made in 1968, he suggested that the East Riding County Council prepared a policy report recommending port-related industry at Howdendyke, even though it may have been against the County Plan, that a petition was received from local people, and that the Secretary of State was referred to, but did not intervene. When I asked for the names of the chief local architects of this plan, I was told that they were either dead or had moved away. The CPO then offered to send me a copy of the 1968 report; I have not received it.

The CPO also denied that Howdendyke was abnormal in having the greatest population decline in Boothferry Borough in the period 1971–81, for all Howdenshire riverside parishes had declined. He affirmed that all major planning applications for Howdendyke had been advertized in the local press, and that 'even neighbour notification may have taken place'. He confirmed that he had the discretion to hold public meetings, but stated that 'it was not usual to hold public meetings unless creating a Local Plan'. Given manpower problems, Howdendyke does not qualify for a Local Plan, for these are being generated only to cope with the pressing problems of expanding 'key settlements'. Finally, given the obvious need for private wharves in Boothferry, Howdendyke is the most suitable place in terms of river frontage and road access.

The CPO stressed that all planning recommendations and political decisions in Boothferry have been legal and procedurally correct. Howdendyke has been long considered a 'special case' exempt from Structure Plan guidelines. He agreed with the BritAg spokesman that it is ridiculous to replace houses which are at the end of their structural life, which do not qualify for local authority grants, and which are close to noxious industry.

Politicians

Of three politicians approached, one was unavailable and another, Councillor Bill Bray, whose ward includes Howdendyke, refused to speak with me ('I've nowt to say'). In a brief telephone conversation, however, Councillor Bray said: that Howdendyke is an industrial area, with roads suitable for this purpose, whereas Kilpin village has poor roads and should remain agricultural; that Howdendyke's houses were 'in a bad state' and rightly condemned; that there have been no complaints from anyone moved to Howden; and that 'what I want for this area is jobs, and more jobs'.

Councillor Bob Park, Mayor of Boothferry for 1986–87, spoke with me at length. He commended HS & L's provision of jobs at Howdendyke, spoke strongly in favour of further industrial expansion, asserted that Hargreaves' expectations of expansion in 1977 were made in good faith, confirmed that there was no need for a special plan for a non-selected settlement of low planning priority, and noted that failure to place closing orders on manifestly unfit housing could have led to charges of neglect of duty.

He stressed the 'ridiculousness' of renovating houses so close to industry, and noted that Howdendykers had a 'mentality' that led them to refuse offers of good housing in Howden. When I spoke of place loyalty, he agreed that Council could not 'compensate for sentiment'. Finally, Mayor Park stressed that job-generation was of great importance, that Council had always proceeded legally and according to due procedure, that all decisions were made democratically, that the development of Howdendyke did conform with the provisions of the revised (1985) Structure Plan, and that there can be no progress without some discomfort.

From the above interviews it would appear that Howdendyke, as a residential village, has been written off. The common emphasis on 'due procedure', however, does suggest that a degree of uneasiness lurks behind assurances that a wider vision of progress and betterment demands the sacrifice of a small place and its people's place loyalties. Little sympathy was expressed for the plight of Howdendykers.

When asked directly what were their visions of Howdendyke's future, inter-viewees made fairly consistent replies. BritAg saw little hope for the expansion of its factory and wished to terminate, when possible, the tenancies of its four remaining tied houses. HS & L felt the residential village, ultimately, had no future. While Health & Housing 'couldn't imagine' that the whole village would disappear, I was asked to remember that the majority of houses there was now Council-owned, and that half of these were built in 1936, and the other half were 'Airey houses' which elsewhere had developed structural problems too expensive to repair. The CPO would not express an opinion, but reiterated the theme that 'the location of the village was poor in terms of living conditions' because of the proximity to industry. This statement, common to several of the interviewees, is at best ahistorical.

Only Mayor Park bluntly spoke his mind, as is the privilege of the politician. 'I would like to see the whole village go' he said, 'and become an industrial area. I'd like to clear it and compensate house-owners and rehouse tenants elsewhere.' Clearly, in the eyes of planners, politicians, and private enterprise, the village of Howdendyke, in a striking reversal of normal roles, has become a 'nuisance' which interferes with the development of industry.

Clearing the village in one quick operation would at least be merciful. What is more likely to happen, however, is more of the slow, piecemeal attrition that has gone on since 1968. This attrition will occur with renewed force in late 1986 as HS & L begins to develop its new lorry park.

The future

Perhaps one of the most insidious features of the planned demise of Howdendyke has been the failure of private enterprise, planners, and politicians not merely to consult with village residents, but even to inform them of decisions taken which might affect their future lives. The most pervasive feeling in the village in the early 1980s was one of deep uncertainty and concern for the future, overwhelmingly emphasized by the sheer lack of information available to residents.

As Mavis Westoby remarks, with some heat:

> It's a wicked shame. No matter how you talk it just goes back to the point where you started. You seem to bang your head against a brick wall at every turn and no one comes to see you to discuss anything with you. The first thing that you see that's of interest to you regarding your future is what you read in the paper. Well, to me, that's not right. The people concerned should be spoken to before the journalists. It only seems to me to be the correct thing to do, the right thing.

Clearly, consultation before planning, which Mavis very reasonably regards as good manners and natural ethics, has been a very low priority with local enterprise and Boothferry Council.

The chief answer received by residents to questions about the village's future appears to be 'don't know'. In such an atmosphere of uncertainty rumours naturally abound. And it is not surprising that these rumours go as far to as visualize the complete razing of Howdendyke village in favour of port-related installations. One such rumour is reported as follows:

> He said 'I don't know what you're grumbling about because you'll all be out of the village in two years. You'll all be on Derwent Estate' [council housing in the town of Howden]. And there's even talk of pulling [Howdendyke's 16] council houses down, because he told me that the council would sell them all to East Coast (Annie Oxtoby).

As a former resident remarks, 'I think it's absolutely wicked that they left all these houses literally just to fall to pieces and not put anybody else in them. And I don't know whether they're even going to keep the council houses.' Speculation in 1982, rather prophetically, included the possible demolition of the already decrepit Jubilee Hall, The Club (both Hargreaves-owned) and even of the privately-owned Post Office, strategically valuable because of its waterfront location.

By the early 1980s residents clearly understood that forces were at work to rid some or all of the village of its residents. Such forces, typically, were referred to as 'they', but, when pressed, respondents would specify HS & L, Hargreaves, or 'the council', meaning Boothferry Borough Council and its Planning Department. Despite the general air of resignation noted earlier, a number of respondents made statements of resistance in 1982, avowing determination to remain in their home or at least in the village: 'A lot have left and gone to live in flats in Howden. They want us to go. It's going to be an industrial area. But I shan't go. I came here over fifty years ago. Howdendyke is home' (Ellen Broomfleet). Mavis Westoby gave more specific reasons for her wish to stay:

> There's never any words but you're drawing your own conclusions through the property being run down and what you've read in the paper that they're not repairing anything ... that they want us all to leave. Well, we're all of the same opinion, we don't want to go.... I've lived here forty-one years. I love my little village. I love my home; all my happy memories are here. This is what keeps me going from day to day, all these little thoughts of what it was when we were together [Mavis is a widow], it gives me courage to carry on. They're not morbid thoughts, they're happy thoughts. I don't want to lose what I've got and I don't want to start again. I'm not old, that's not the reason, the sole reason is I don't want to go because I've been happy here.

The quiet resistance of Mavis contrasts in style with Annie Oxtoby's hearty outburst:

> Myself, I think the village has had it, Doug. They're trying to make an industrial place out of it. They've even got [planning] permission to put sheds in the field at the bottom of our garden. But they aren't shoving me out. I were born and bred in this village and in this village I'm stopping. I'm stuck in here and they can't make

me go if I don't want to go. I'm staying here and they can't put me out. I'm staying where I am.

As of 1986 both Mavis and Annie remain in Howdendyke, on the 'factory side' and 'field side' respectively. But Ellen Broomfleet, in her eighties, has reluctantly moved to a flat in Howden and her former home is rubble.

An atmosphere of uncertainty, coupled with a steady leakage of population and only brief sparks of individual resistance, was common to the village in the early 1980s. Thus HS & L's 1982 plan for a new wharf replacing an existing jetty on Hargreaves' waterfront met more resistance from external groups than from Howdendyke villagers (Chapter 8). In 1985, however, villagers were shaken from their apathy by a direct threat to the Club, as predicted by some residents several years before.

As noted in Chapter 9, although Hargreaves/BritAg were refused permission in 1982 to change the Chemical Works into yet another general warehousing and distributing facility, HS & L simultaneously received the go-ahead to convert a small Hargreaves jetty into a large wharf (HS & L wharf No. 2) to match in size their initial 1968 wharf at Kilpin Lodge corner (HS & L wharf No. 1). Wharf No. 1 had soon demanded lorry turning space and other ancillary facilities. It was no surprise, then, to find HS & L requesting planning permission for a large loading and storage area adjacent to jetty No. 2 (Figure 21).

The Club, as has been shown (Chapter 9) was already under threat of closure because of Boothferry Health and Housing's demands for repairs and BritAg's refusal to guarantee the future of the building to the Club's members. The latter quickly generated a 76-name petition against the Club's demolition, which was matched by a 51-name petition against the whole plan. As the 6-acre loading and storage area would be only 50 feet from houses on the 'field side', would increase the threat to New Row and remaining 'factory side' houses, would probably cause structural damage to remaining houses because of noise and vibration, would further reduce the already heavily deteriorated quality of environment in the village, and would destroy the Club, the village's social centre, villagers banded together once again to save what was left of their village.

Boothferry Council's Planning Committee heard these objections in early 1986 (*Howdenshire Gazette*, 9 January; 6, 13 February 1986) including letters of protest claiming that HS & L was 'driving occupants out of their houses' and asserting that villagers were being 'squeezed out'. The local Environmental Health Officer noted that the Club and the Jubilee Hall provided the only real noise barrier between HS & L wharves and the remainder of the village. He concluded: 'The noise levels there are as high as they can reasonably be and we would want to see a reduction'. In contrast, Boothferry's Chief Planning Officer reiterated the by now entrenched Hargreaves/Boothferry Planning policy that the land was designated industrial and no permission would ever be given for housing improvement. This position effectively undermined his apparently reasonable opening statement that Howdendyke's was a 'classic case of weighing the balance of industry against residential environment'.

A number of committee members were clearly moved by the petitions, but the majority were not. When told by Councillor Knapton that the ratepayers' point of view should be considered, Councillor Engall responded for the majority by noting that 'Humber Sea and Land (sic) are also ratepayers'. When HS & L agreed to screen the site with trees (a promise which has had pathetic results, at best, around their 'downstream' site) and to provide 'alternative social facilities in the village', councillors moved that despite the need to see detailed plans of layout and landscape they were 'mindful of approving the application'. At this point the Club petition was withdrawn (although the 51-name petition objecting to the plan in principle remained standing). At which Goole Town Councillor Crowther remarked, 'The [former] objectors don't know what they are letting themselves in for. I'm still convinced there will be a lot of noise and nuisance for the villagers' (*Howdenshire Gazette*, 6 February 1986).

The approved plan calls for the 'formation of a hardcored vehicle reception and cargo holding area, and erection of a new community centre ...' The 6-acre site will finally fill, completely, the remaining open space within the Triangle (Figures 13, 21, 23). HS & L has purchased the waterfront land formerly comprising The Square, including the derelict Club and Jubilee Hall, and has leased the remainder from BritAg.

What remains of the village is to be protected by a high, treed embankment along the 'factory side' of Howdendyke's main street, an embankment whose curves will exclude the few remaining houses on the 'factory side' from the industrial area. On this side also, and outside the embankment, a new community centre is to be built by HS & L. In this way the focus of the village will shift radically from the waterfront, leaving the Post Office isolated and immediately juxtaposed with cargo yards and lorry turning area, an intolerable position.

The conditions imposed on the new development illustrate the problems which have been faced by Howdendyke residents since 1968:

- nothing to be stored other than what is generated by HS & L wharves;
- no cargo unloading between 7 pm and 7 am, Monday to Saturday;
- no cargo unloading on Sundays or Bank Holidays;
- gates to be provided to 'prevent the trafficking of Tutty Row by heavy goods vehicles';
- the community centre to be completed within one year;
- landscaping to be begun within six months.

The reasons given for these regulations include, ironically, 'the interest of the amenities of the nearby residents', 'the interest of highway safety', and, in relation to the storage only of wharf-related cargo, 'the location of the site in an area where general storage would not normally be permitted'. Although the County Planning Office opposed the development, Boothferry Council asserted:

- first, that the development was quite in accordance with the new Structure Plan of 1985, whose paragraph E6 (ii) permits new estuarial port developments in the case of 'Special terminals ... which are required in the national interest, or which have stringent locational requirements that cannot be satisfied by alternative sites';
- and second, that Boothferry Borough Council had long adopted a policy (23 March 1981) 'That the Council considers the area ... bounded by the existing road system on three sides be suitable in the long-term for industrial development.'

Very laconically, the planning report notes that 'five letters of objection and two petitions of objection were also received'. These latter have already been mentioned; it is sufficient to note here that one of them was signed by persons representing 93 per cent of the village population. The letters are more eloquent:

- 'It seems that certain people in high places are doing their utmost to drive us out ...',
- 'the company [HS & L] seems to have little interest in what happens to the village and its residents',
- 'for the last two years the two major companies in Howdendyke have been bent on the virtual destruction of the remains of this tiny village',
- 'our postmistress has wonderful views of giant ships moored just outside her bedroom window',
- 'the village was here before the factories. We wish to stay here, not be hounded out by the industries around us.'
- 'we feel we are being squashed out of existence from the place we have lived in all our lives',
- 'Please help us'.

No help was offered. When a resident complained to the Tory MP for the area, Sir Paul Bryan, Boothferry Council responded by informing the parliamentarian, in the usual way, that all Boothferry Council decisions were made legally and democractically.

The new site, theoretically, will be screened from the village by a bosky embankment. Given HS & L's history of inept tree-planting and site screening, however, one may question the ability of such a construction to mitigate the effects of lorry movement and cargo-handling mere yards from most of Howdendyke's remaining front windows. Double-glazing of these windows will effectively make residents prisoners within their own houses. For the noise nuisance is likely to be enormous.

In objecting to the plan, the Chief Port Health Inspector for the region declared that: 'Development of this magnitude is bringing Howdendyke out of the realms of a normal wharf operation into the category of a large-scale dockland operation ... the potential for noise and dust nuisance is very great ...' The Chief Housing and Environmental Services Officer for Boothferry was in strong agreement, stating:

> noise monitoring ... done at the site ... suggests that daytime noise levels at domestic properties in Howdendyke are already higher than at virtually any other domestic property in the Boothferry area ... and are already at the maximum that we could consider acceptable. [Yet] the whole of the dockland is effectively being moved even closer to the doorsteps of domestic properties in Howdendyke, some of which will be virtually surrounded by the very active dockland development ... The proposals ... are almost certain to increase the existing disturbance to local residents ... [even to those] who previously were well removed from the wharf activities.

This plea came to little beyond the agreement to erect noise mounds. Unfortunately, politicians, planners, and directors of private enterprise are not yet required, by law, to live for at least six months with the nuisances they have generated before taking decisions to augment those nuisances.

Commentary

By the early 1980s the remaining residents of Howdendyke appeared to have reached the stage of acceptance of the dying process. Half their village was already gone and, according to rumour, some or all of the remainder was threatened. Laments for the past, seen as idyllic as late as the 1950s, were matched by a belief that Howdendyke was, sooner or later, doomed to extinction.

The general process of annihilation was not apparent to all, for most residents had no clear understanding of the planning process and the effective relationship between private enterprise, local politicians, planners, and the health and housing inspectorate. And no attempt was made by any of these groups to provide information to residents. Without adequate data or understanding of the planning process, resistance is not likely to be successful. Whereas individuals clearly understood the processes by which they personally were induced to move (Joe Apthorpe) or made uncomfortable (Mavis Westoby), no resident was able to explain to me how it was that 'they' were legally able to continue their slow but inexorable destruction of the village.

11
Epitaph

I'm not suggesting any sort of plot,
Everyone knows there's not,
But you unborn millions might like to be warned
That if you don't want to be buried alive by slagheaps,
Pitfalls and damp walls and rat-traps and dead streets,
Arrange to be democratically born
The son of a company director
Or a judge's fine and private daughter.

> Buttons will be pressed,
> Rules will be broken,
> Strings will be pulled
> And magic words spoken.
> Invisible fingers will mould
> Palaces of gold.

Leon Rosselson

During the last two decades the village of Howdendyke has endured two separate but related phases of rapid change, both connected with the building of HS & L wharves. The first phase, which began in the late 1960s and continued into the early 1970s, saw a rash of ownership changes, closures of old establishments, and the inauguration of new ones. During the two years 1967–68 the shipyard closed, Hargreaves took over the Anderton-Richardson Chemical Works, twenty-four acres of agricultural land were dedicated to industry, and HS & L built their first wharf on Hargreaves land. Shortly afterwards, cargo handling and industrial establishments sprang up on greenfield sites on both sides of the village.

The second phase began in the late 1970s, after a period of relative quiescence in the mid 1970s, and still continues. The major events in this period include: the conversion of the upstream site, formerly a factory, to cargo handling for companies related to HS & L; the conversion of Hargreaves into BritAg, the simultaneous attempt to convert the fertilizer factory into a cargo handling facility, and, this failing, BritAg's layoff of many workers at the plant; and the building of a large wharf (No. 2) by HS & L on Hargreaves/BritAg land within the village, with subsequent plans to turn much of the village's remaining waterfront (formerly a neighbourhood known as The Square) and the remainder of the vacant Triangle into a 6-acre lorry park and storage area.

The main casualty of the second phase of activity has been Howdendyke village itself. As explained in Chapter 9, the Hargreaves/Boothferry policy has been to demolish at least half of Howdendyke's houses; the net result of their actions has been a loss of housing by 1986 (compared with 1960) of the order of 57 per cent. Should this process continue, and the attitudes of private enterprise, politicians, and planners suggest that it will, even optimistic scenarios (Table 40) point to a housing loss over the period 1960–1999 of between two-thirds and three-quarters of all housing. No once-vibrant community can survive such losses and live.

Table 40 Housing loss scenarios 1960–1999, Howdendyke/Kilpinpike

Scenario	Houses occupied 1960	Houses occupied 1986	Houses occupied 1999
1 (probable)	72	31 (57% loss)	25 (65% loss)
2 (likely)	72	31 (57% loss)	21 (70% loss)
3 (possible)	72	31 (57% loss)	5 (93% loss)
4 (pessimistic)	72	31 (57% loss)	0 (100% loss)

Scenario 1: loss of six remaining units on 'factory side' of village.
Scenario 2: further loss of four remaining waterfront units.
Scenario 3: demolition of sixteen council houses; tenants relocated.

In spatial terms, by 1986 HS & L and related companies had succeeded in gaining control of much of the waterfront from Kilpinpike to the former shipyard site (Figures 21, 23). Within the residential village, most of the waterfront had been cleared of residents except for the four riverside houses upstream of, and including, the Post Office. Further, by 1986 the entire neighbourhood known as the Square had disappeared, along with almost all of the houses on the 'factory side' of the village. And even on the 'field side' several houses had been demolished and the remainder had come to feel uncomfortably 'squeezed' between Hargreaves/HS & L on the 'factory side' and threats of industry expanding into the remaining fields on the 'field side'.

But the effects of development were not restricted to Howdendyke village alone. Of Howdendyke's two peripheral sections, the four houses at Kilpinpike were converted to HS & L offices, and the three houses at Elm Tree subjected to road realignments and dangerously heavy traffic. Kilpinpike abuts on the village of Skelton, and residents of both Skelton and Kilpin have suffered greatly from the heavy traffic and the noise, air, and visual pollution generated by HS & L and its enterprising neighbours in Howdendyke. And there is some evidence that the growth of Howdendyke as a cargo handling port may be having deleterious effects on the viability of Boothferry Borough's chief town, the port of Goole.

These are the facts. It is now time to turn to a more difficult issue, that of the analysis of the goals, motives, and policies of the chief actors in the tragedy of Howdendyke, namely private enterprise, planners, politicians, and the public.

Private enterprise

One of the more dramatic problems of the modern age involves the eminently geographical dimensions of scale and distance. Modern corporate bodies, whether private or government organizations, tend to develop to a scale incomprehensible to the ordinary citizen, the eternal outsider. Further, the decision-taking bodies controlling these large corporations grow even more distant from the average citizen, both physically, socially, and psychically. In extreme cases, one's life may be severely influenced by a large corporate body whose decision-takers reside on another continent. If he tries to confront such an organization, the citizen quickly becomes lost in the toils of those seas of obfuscation and misery known as public relations and corporate law.

Large organizations influence the citizen in many ways. Whether we consider state enterprise in centrally-controlled economies (e.g. nuclear power plants in the USSR) or in basically capitalist societies (the Windscale-Sellafield nuclear reactor in Britain), or even corporations such as universities (the effects of the expansion of Harvard and MIT on the city of Cambridge, Massachusetts), the common denominator is the power of major enterprises to alter people's lives. The concern of this book, however, is wholly with the effects of private enterprise, in a capitalist society, on citizens and their homes.

The chief goal of private enterprise, in a capitalist society, is profit, although power (usually via growth) is also of major importance. This is not the place to argue the merits of capitalism; I accept, for this argument, the validity of the profit motive. It is notable, however, that since the nineteenth century all major capitalist nations have seen fit, through the actions of democratically elected governments, to place curbs on the actions of private enterprise. Even in Reaganite America and Thatcherite Britain, where deregulation of industry is being pursued and the Victorian cry of 'free enterprise' has been revived, private enterprise must still work within a complex framework of regulatory controls. The case of Howdendyke demonstrates how poorly these controls work.

In this analysis the minor characters in the Howdendyke tragedy, Howden Glucose (Tate & Lyle) and the like, can be ignored. The protagonist is clearly Humberside Sea & Land Services Ltd., a company jointly owned by Interdom Holdings Ltd., a Humberside firm, and the national conglomerate Powell Duffryn Ltd. The major supporting role is taken by Hargreaves, alias BritAg, a company controlled by Imperial Chemical Industries Ltd.

As the Ouse Chemical Works became a relatively smaller and smaller unit in a growing conglomerate, and yet within a generally depressed economy, questions as to its viability were asked. Clearly, Hargreaves/BritAg had no use for the low quality housing inherited from Anderton-Richardson, and it seemed natural to divest themselves of this encumbrance. The move from Anderton control to Hargreaves control was a move from private enterprise tempered by social paternalism, administered locally, to private enterprise administered by absentee owners whose chief concern, quite properly, was the profitability of their whole corporate system.

The indictment against Hargreaves/BritAg, then, is chiefly one of lack of sensitivity and compassion. Some of their houses were unrepairable, but they neglected repairs to those considered by both occupants and potential purchasers as amenable to improvement. The continued neglect of repairs led to the houses falling into the category of 'unfit', and to their demolition. Further, Hargreaves/BritAg can be charged with failing, over a period of more than a decade, to provide residents with clear information as to the future of both the village and of individual dwellings. Kept in the dark about their future, it is little wonder that many residents despaired, gave credit to rumour, and left.

There is no evidence that this long-term process of neglect and lack of information was a covert company policy of malign neglect and disinformation. But its continuance for such a long period, despite the frequent pleas of residents for both repairs to their houses and some indication of the village's future, suggests, at the very least, that the process was accepted by Hargreaves/BritAg as contributing to their overall goals.

Similarly, there is no evidence of anti-village collaboration between Hargreaves/BritAg and HS & L, but the circumstantial evidence is strong. HS & L's Wharf No. 1 was built on Hargreaves' waterfront; its initial storage and lorry turning area occupied the site of the former Anderton residence, Kilpin Lodge; the importing company's chief warehouse and storage complex was built on agricultural land previously rented by Andertons and recently given up by Hargreaves. Further, during the period 1982–85 Hargreaves desired the conversion of their fertilizer factory to warehouse storage, presumably for the use of HS & L; the latter's Wharf No. 2 was built on the site of a former Hargreaves jetty; and the subsequent demand of HS & L for an adjacent 6-acre lorry park and turning area envisaged the use of land previously cleared of Hargreaves-owned housing and the demolition of two of the three village social centres, the Hargreaves-owned Jubilee Hall and Club.

Hargreaves' preferred role seems to be that of eliminating much of the village and then withdrawing in favour of HS & L, the protagonist of the tragedy. Unlike Hargreaves/BritAg, HS & L had no legacy of interest in Howdendyke as a village. Its vision, whether originally conceived in 1968 or developed ad hoc as it grew and prospered, seems to involve control of the whole village and its environs. As noted above, the company controls almost the whole waterfront except for a wedge of four houses (one of them Hargreaves-owned) along the creek north of, but including the Post Office, and the three remaining staiths. It is unlikely that the owner of the Post Office, the village's last social focus, will be able to sell to anyone but HS & L. Behind the waterfront HS & L owns, or seeks to control, large tracts of land for warehousing, open storage, lorry parks, and traffic turning areas. These areas envelop the residential village and also penetrate its core, leaving at best a thin string of housing on the former 'field side' of the village, although these dwellings could readily be removed by Council fiat, for most of them are council houses. Further, by converting the houses of Kilpinpike into offices, HS & L has begun to penetrate the village of Skelton, and seeks also to involve the hamlet of Kilpin in its quest for warehouse space.

Like Hargreaves/BritAg, HS & L can readily be accused of being a bad corporate citizen, regarded by Howdendykers as a single-minded profit-oriented enterprise displaying little concern for the havoc it has wreaked on the local landscape and the lives of its neighbours. There is evidence, for example, that despite landscaping constraints placed on HS & L's various planning permissions, the company has been extremely slow to comply. Complaints by residents are ignored, evaded, or dealt with in a rather half-hearted manner. During the various overlapping planning controversies of 1978–86, the contribution of HS & L's Howdendyke manager to reporters' requests for information has invariably been 'no comment'. When I approached the manager for the first time in 1980, merely for historical information regarding title deeds to the former fields now occupied by HS & L warehouses, he was most unhelpful.

If HS & L's vision is control of the whole area and its conversion into a private port, then the chief characteristic of the company's campaign towards this goal is the relentless barrage of planning applications which crosses the desk of Boothferry Planning and must be dealt with by Boothferry Council. This application bombardment, together with seemingly related applications by Hargreaves and other concerns, must be both tiring and tiresome to planners and politicians alike.

On analyzing these applications, one detects a rather interesting process. I have noted earlier a respondent's claim that HS & L indulges in a deliberate tactic to defuse protest: the generation of a grandiose planning application; apparent submission to the subsequent storm of public protest by withdrawing the application; resubmission of a smaller, but still radical proposal, with the effect that former protestors give up further objection either through exhaustion or relief. HS & L has also made a number of promises and compromises, not all of which have been fully carried out.

But these are tactics. The overall strategy of the period 1968–86 appears to be a masterpiece of manipulation. In 1968 HS & L built a Wharf (No. 1) ostensibly to take over Hargreaves' raw material importing functions. The adjacent storage rapidly proved too small for the jetty's capacity, so HS & L applied for, and received, permission to erect warehouses on a site which, almost simultaneously, was designated industrial land by county politicians. During the 1970s HS & L made a number of applications for planning permission to extend Wharf No. 1, build a second wharf downstream towards Kilpinpike, and use and rebuild a Hargreaves jetty (later Wharf No. 2). Some of the arguments used in favour of these plans included the need to accommodate larger vessels, the need to berth two large vessels at once, so that vessels can avoid the demurage charges levied by shipowners, and the fear that without these changes traffic would flow to other private wharves (not, note, to Goole).

But the most interesting claim made by HS & L in the 1970s was that a second wharf was necessary because their warehouse capacity was far greater than a single jetty could handle, so that trade had to be turned away. Thus warehouses created to accommodate the spare capacity of Wharf No. 1 were then overbuilt to provide a rationale for constructing Wharf No. 2. This ploy continued in the 1980s. The erection of a large Wharf No. 2 in turn demanded the conversion of the Ouse Chemical Works into storage; when this was denied, the logical outcome was demands for storage in nearby villages and for a large lorry parking and turning area close to the new wharf. Should excess storage capacity somehow emerge in the Howdendyke area, no doubt the demand for yet another wharf will arise, and so on. When his attention was drawn to this process, a spokesman for HS & L agreed that such had been the case, stating that 'it is the nature of businesses to grow'.

The planners

Since the 1960s there has emerged a moderately large literature which can only be described as a literature of 'planner-bashing' (Porteous 1977). There is a tendency to believe that urban and regional planning is the root cause of many contemporary woes, from the evils of inner city urban renewal to the devastation of the countryside. What seems so often to be forgotten is that local planners operate within a framework of rules, often not of their own making. Second, planners can only advise; politicians make the final decisions. Third, bureaucratic planners are not the only ones who plan; in fact, these planners spend most of their time responding to the plans submitted by private individuals and corporations.

It is private enterprise, then, which does most of the initial planning that leads to landscape transformation on a large scale. Nevertheless, it is incumbent upon planning bureaucracies to consider all sides of the picture, and to pay particular attention to the protests of the largely powerless citizens who feel themselves endangered by the proposals of powerful private enterprise.

The history of planning in the case of Howdendyke appears to fall into two phases. The planners of Howden Rural District Council seem to have agreed with district and county politicians that Howdendyke should be the site of future industrial growth. In the late 1960s and early 1970s the Chief Planning Officer's advice to Council regarding HS & L's initial developments included a warning that such operations would be a major departure from the County Development Plan. On the other hand, noted the planner, the area was within the newly-designated 24-acre industrial zone, and would not, in his opinion, prejudice county policy or unduly affect the amenities of the area.

With hindsight, one can readily claim this as the planners' first major error, for this first HS & L development (the downstream site) was the thin end of the wedge which led to the prying out of half of Howdendyke's population and the radical lowering of environmental quality, or amenity, within Kilpin parish. But the error is more fundamental, and should have been considered at the time. For although the HS & L facility was designated 'light industrial' with all the restrictions this implies, HS & L has never engaged in any significant form of industry in the sense of materials processing or manufacturing. HS & L, from the beginning, has been chiefly a cargo importer, warehouser, and distributor, a function readily performed by established ports and, according to the County Development Plan of 1960, supposedly restricted to such ports.

Subsequent support by planners for HS & L's further development merely compounded the initial error. By 1972, when Howden Rural District Council was having second thoughts and had questioned a proposed overhead conveyor on visual amenity grounds, their chief planner tended to agree with HS & L that because visual amenity in the area had already been severely reduced by HS & L installations, there was no good reason to refuse further ugly installations.

Once a decision had been made to contravene the County Plan, it seems, the logical procedure was to continue to contravene the plan. By the late 1970s Howdendyke was regarded by planners as a 'planning anomaly'. In 1979 the Director of Planning for Humberside County Council felt that Howdendyke was widely recognised as a 'special case' to which, presumably, normal planning guidelines did not apply.

A change of attitude on the part of local planners appears to have emerged with the local government reorganisation of 1974, when Howdendyke came under the aegis of Boothferry Borough Council, though the Planning Department remained in Howden. After 1974 Boothferry Planning appears to have decided to adhere more strongly to the County Plan's recommendation that cargo handling operations should occur only at major ports. Since 1974 Boothferry Planning Department has successfully prevented the loss of a further field, north of HS & L's downstream site, to further warehousing. Indeed, the planners have designated this and adjacent fields as an area where industry is to be resisted (Figure 21). Planning successes also include the prevention of non-river-related industry developing on the upstream (Ferry Farm) site and of the conversion of Ouse Chemical Works into warehousing. All these actions follow the rubric of the Structure Plan which reiterates the earlier county plan's guideline that cargo handling should be restricted to existing ports but permits river-related manufacturing industry at places such as Howdendyke.

Boothferry Planning must also be commended for resisting, although unsuccessfully, the conversion of the upstream glucose factory site into a cargo handling area and the building of HS & L's Wharf No. 2. It appears, therefore, that whereas the Planning Department under the Howden Rural District Council regime was happy to accommodate HS & L, its counterpart under the aegis of Boothferry Borough has tried manfully to follow county planning guidelines, only to be countermanded and frustrated, in some instances, by political decisions.

It can be claimed, however, that this change of heart on the part of the planners came too late to save Howdendyke. By seemingly encouraging the growth of HS & L in its early stages, local planners clearly endorsed the first step toward the subsequent annihilation of Howdendyke as a community.

Planners, however, are not omniscient, and cannot compel Council to follow their advice. Boothferry Planning can readily be indicted on other grounds. First, the Chief Planning Officer has taken an active stance in favour of industrial development at Howdendyke, admittedly in accordance with the political decision of 1968 to designate the area an industrial zone. But this support of industrial development has come at the expense of Boothferry Planning's active participation in the loss of half the housing in the village of Howdendyke. The Planning Department has been wholly supportive of the Hargreaves policy of destroying housing on the 'factory side' of the village. Except for the obvious lack of communication in the Spivey fiasco (Chapter 9), Boothferry Health & Housing appears to have complied with the Hargreaves/Boothferry Planning policy of destroying at least half of residential Howdendyke.

Residents affected by major planning proposals in the Howdendyke area have frequently complained of lack of information. Sometimes no notice of intent is displayed on or near the site. The plans submitted by private enterprise and endorsed by the planners may have no indication that housing is included in the plan area. Notification of planning applications may reach local newspapers at a late date, so that many residents are belatedly surprised and have insufficient time to respond. Members of Kilpin Parish Council complain that letters of inquiry or complaint sometimes receive no reply.

More generally, Boothferry Planning can be questioned for its general failure to listen to or respond to resident fears and anxieties. Howdendyke is arguably the only place in Boothferry Borough to be undergoing such radical change. It is located in the parish having the greatest population decline in Boothferry during the intercensal period 1971–81. Yet Boothferry Planning Department appears to have made little or no effort to provide information to concerned residents of the parish, either in the form of a Local Plan, information leaflets, public meetings, or consultation with more than the few of the most vociferous, frequent protestors of radical change.

Much of the time Boothferry Planning Department appears to have acted in good faith, according to its guidelines and assumptions. The planners, however, rarely seem to question their assumptions and thus, to the inhabitants of villages affected by 'planning blight', appear to be inflexible, remote bureaucrats bent on imposing their neatly-planned landscapes of the mind upon the perhaps untidy but real, living landscape.

The politicians

According to Karl Popper, the art of politics is the minimization of avoidable suffering. And despite appearances to the contrary, one of the chief roles of politicians in a democracy is to safeguard the interests of their constituents. This goal of service, of course, is sometimes lost sight of as individual politicians pursue personal policies of self-aggrandizement, power enhancement, and even pecuniary gain.

Boothferry Borough Council consists of thirty-five elected politicians who operate in a continuing political climate of high unemployment and the competing claims of urban and rural sectors. The chief concern of the Council must be to promote employment expansion in Boothferry; the problem concerns how this goal might be accomplished in an equitable and non-destructive manner. Faced with the persuasive arguments of corporate managers, it is little wonder that the politicians of Boothferry Council should follow their natural inclinations to increase employment, even if, as in the case of HS & L's Wharf No. 2, the number of new jobs created was estimated to be as low as four.

Characteristic problems of Boothferry Council appear to include strong sub-regional loyalties, and a more or less permanent conflict between rural and urban representatives, which only partially coincides with a split between those who favour Conservative versus Labour party policies in general. While the former regularly promote industrial growth and deplore regulation, the latter are particularly protective of organized labour, especially the dock and associated workers of the port of Goole. A less well-remarked aspect of Boothferry councillors is their general lack of awareness of the context of their decisions. While one must applaud the preponderance of 'grass-roots' participation in Council politics, one can only deplore the rather low level of debate on planning issues consequent upon a general ignorance of economic planning theory (e.g. regarding the possible results of the further decline of Goole as a regional centre) and the lessons learned from the literature of social planning (e.g. regarding the adverse effects of 'planning blight' upon individuals and communities such as Howdendyke).

Another characteristic of the voting majority on Boothferry Council is its tendency to reject the advice of its Chief Planning Officer. This has been particularly apparent since Boothferry Planning began to follow county guidelines more closely from the late 1970s. This tendency to override planning opinion, whether emanating from Boothferry Planning or even the Director of Planning for the county, has not gone unnoticed by the public. During the Howdendyke planning controversies of the early 1980s a number of letters to the editor of the local newspaper addressed this issue.

The decision to allow TR Chemicals and HS & L to convert the glucose factory site to a cargo handling facility, noted one correspondent:

> is yet another example of the Council's total lack of cohesion in which they waste their planning department's time and efforts in producing a comprehensive and logical plan, which is open for discussion by all interested parties, approved by the councillors, but then incredibly kicked into touch, with everyone making remarks about the planners, who, being public servants, are unable to defend themselves. (*Howdenshire Gazette*, 16 October 1981)

Although incorrect in detail, the above accusation that Boothferry Council overrode their planning department's advice in this instance is sound.

On the approval of HS & L's Wharf No. 2 other correspondents publicly suggested that:

> This Council seems hell-bent on going against their professional planning department … These councillors have completely ignored the advice and opinions of their own planning officers, the Humberside County Council planning officers, the Humberside Structure Plan [and many other agencies, whose] advice has been treated with the utmost contempt … What is the point of having a planning department when these councillors ignore it? Why have a structure plan if these councillors ignore it? … These same councillors were part of a joint team which set up the Humberside Structure Plan [at great cost]. Do they now consider this a great waste of time and money? (*Howdenshire Gazette*, 11 November 1983)

One of the chief proponents of employment expansion, deregulation, and the overriding of planning advice regarding Howdendyke has been Councillor Bill Bray. If Councillor Bray's remarks seem to have been singled out for quotation and comment in the preceding chapters, it is because this politician represents the ward in which Howdendyke is located. One would, therefore, expect that

Councillor Bray would have the interests of Howdendyke residents at heart, and would work with both them and Kilpin Parish Council for the amelioration of their lot.

On the contrary, Councillor Bray has been at the forefront of the movement to develop Howdendyke as a major employment source. Resident in the largely unspoiled village of Laxton, he is on record as being in favour of the prevention of industrial nuisance in the village of Kilpin, but takes an opposite stand on Howdendyke. Newspaper reports of Council debates on the Howdendyke issue demonstrate that Mr Bray has been unceasingly and outstandingly vociferous in favour of Howdendyke's development. During his term of office as Mayor of Boothferry in 1984, Mr Bray visited 'as many privately-owned industries as possible ... in an attempt to encourage local industries and employment prospects' (*Howdenshire Gazette*, 6 July 1984). In particular, he visited all the installations at Howdendyke, returning with rosy accounts of growing employment opportunities, which were to be belied within the year by BritAg's announcement that half of its workforce of fifty-four were to be fired 'to make the firm more competitive'.

Boothferry Council's majority, who are the ultimate decision-takers and thus bear the ultimate responsibility for the death of Howdendyke, appear to have been manipulated by the dubious expansion promises of private enterprise. This is also true to some extent of Boothferry Planning, which used Hargreaves' promises of long-term expansion as a rationale for supporting the demolition of the 'factory side' of residential Howdendyke. I am thus inclined to agree with an outside observer who remarked that Howdendyke is a classic case of 'planning blight', where 'existing buildings have been sacrificed to nebulous long-term intentions'.

Lack of public consultation

Two characteristics are common to the attitudes of private enterprise, planners, and politicians with regard to the fate of Howdendyke. The first is a certain deafness and lack of compassion on the part of all these authorities. Not one of these actors has apparently displayed, in public at least, much sensitivity towards the plight of Howdendyke residents.

Lack of sensitivity is coupled with the continuous and massive failure of these authorities to listen to the complaints of Howdendykers, register their problems, or consider their desires. Here Boothferry Council and its Planning Department must bear the brunt of the criticism, for they have clearly failed to accommodate or even take a concerned interest in the wishes of their Howdendyke constituents. That the most profound change began in Howdendyke in 1968 is most ironic, for that year saw massive demonstrations throughout the Western world in favour of greater participation in decision-taking by several groups who had formerly been merely the 'planned-for'.

The Howdendyke case, of course, is only one of many which have resulted in the wishes of residents being ignored in favour of outside interests or even the rigid application of planning guidelines. During the early 1980s both Boothferry Council and Boothferry Planning have been roundly criticized by a wide spectrum of local citizens and citizen groups. Many parish councils, including Kilpin, have voiced feelings of powerlessness in the face of a Borough Council which disregards their wishes, ignores their appeals, often fails to consult, and frequently refuses to compromise.

To take only a few examples: whereas the inhabitants of Foggathorpe, a tiny non-selected settlement, appealed for more housing to prevent their hamlet dying entirely, the residents of North Cave, a selected settlement in danger of losing its identity through massive, rapid growth, fought long and hard, but in vain, to have their village 'deselected'. Lack of consideration for nearby residents was also evidenced in Council's granting of retrospective planning permission to a rather noxious waste-processing factory in Howden, despite the fact that the factory had been operating for some time without having applied for planning permission (*Howdenshire Gazette*, 6 May 1983). And in the rather more trivial case of the siting of a home for the mentally handicapped in a residential area, the inevitable newspaper headline announced: 'Boothferry criticised for lack of consultation' (*Howdenshire Gazette*, 29 April 1983).

Failure to consult with those affected by change is clearly the most constant and pervasive aspect of the policies pursued by both Boothferry Planning and Boothferry Council. The duty of an elected Borough Council is to follow a coherent policy. Such a policy may be laid down in a Local Plan (as for Goole/Hook), the formulation and emendation of which necessarily involves debate between planners and the public. No Local Plan for Howdendyke has ever been mooted. Boothferry authorities have unilaterally imposed their policy on the villagers of Howdendyke while permitting only the very minimum of debate.

Such action is clearly inequitable. It is not, however, illegal, and thus there appear to be no grounds for accusations of maladministration. Nevertheless, this is a legal opinion, and legal opinions deal with law rather than with justice. Boothferry Council must therefore be censured for their heartlessness, crude wielding of power, wilful disregard of public opinion, probable ignorance of planning issues, and cavalier attitude towards the democratic principle of public participation in the planning process.

The following resolution of the Council of Europe's Venice Symposium on Environment (1979) points out exactly where Boothferry Council and its planners have failed to meet modern standards of planning administration and ethics:

PARTICIPATION: Every planning project that directly affects the public's living conditions should be the subject of consultation between as many as possible of the inhabitants concerned, representatives of the local authorities and professionals ... This should be achieved by supplying information to those concerned and arousing their interest, then by the formulation and comparison of opinions with a view to working out plans that will meet with the approval of a democratic majority of the population.

No comment required!

Neither Boothferry Council nor its Planning Department can claim ignorance of the ethic of public participation. Indeed, when the Structure Plan of 1979 was being formulated, Humberside County Council spent £24,350 on a public participation exercise, sending out thousands of leaflets, posters, and publicity materials. But managing public participation is a difficult art, and attempts must be made to break through public indifference. For instance, at one stage 334,000 leaflets were mailed, one to each postal address in Humberside; the response rate was under 4 percent.

Members of the public are usually unable to perceive the importance of the general guidelines embodied in a Structure Plan; they are generally unable to see just how any specific principle might affect them or their particular neighbourhood. The difficulties of consulting a whole county, however, are significantly reduced when the concern is with only a single small village of sixty or so households. If such a village is to be deliberately annihilated, its houses demolished, its people relocated elsewhere and industry built on the site, then natural justice demands that the village inhabitants should at least be informed of the existence of such a policy, if not fully consulted.

The Hargreaves/Boothferry Planning policy to reduce the community by half was not directly communicated to the villagers, nor even to their representatives, Kilpin Parish Council. And although the Humberside Structure Plan preamble emphasizes, in several places, the need to promote public participation in the planning process, planners and politicians alike seem to have taken greater heed of the statement that 'the [Humber] estuary is ripe for development'.

Never, in their long drawn out process of destroying Howdendyke, have Boothferry authorities seen fit to ask the opinions of Howdendyke residents about the future of their community. Boothferry's hatchet job on Howdendyke makes a mockery of public participation principles. The failure of both planners and politicians is basically a failure of ethics. There is clearly a long way to go before general statements of ethical principle can be reconciled with planning-on-the-ground.

Deconstructing a village

In light of the above discussion, the optimum set of conditions for annihilating a village appear to be the following:

(1) Control of land, employment, and housing by distant, profit-oriented corporations with no interest in the village except as an industrial site.

(2) A largely working-class population, poorly-educated, with little knowledge of how the planning process works, or of how to become involved in it in an effective manner. Successful community defence against the planning juggernaut is invariably led by middle-class people, often newcomers to the community (Cybriwsky 1978); such people cannot settle in Howdendyke because current planning policies prevent in-migration.

(3) A population mainly consisting of tenants (had more Howdendykers purchased their homes in 1967, resistance may have been more effective) previously dependent upon a paternalist system, and which has therefore developed no strong tradition of dissent, initiative, communal organization, or leadership.

(4) A planning department which in crucial cases has ignored guidelines and has always been unwilling or unable to engage in the public participation process.

(5) Politicians who, given high unemployment, feel able to disregard planning advice and sacrifice a village in favour of promises of increased employment.

The attitudes of local politicians have been the most crucial. While one is unable to assess the hidden agendas of Boothferry politicians, certain letters to the editor may be revealing, although it may be an extremist who castigates 'the cant and humbug of the secret dynasty that leads Boothferry Borough Council', their 'secret meetings with local businessmen', and their government 'by the few, for the few, of the many' (*Howdenshire Gazette*, 13 February 1986).

There appears to be no effective counterweight to the planner-politician-private enterprise complex. Resistance, ill-organized, ill-informed, and largely powerless, has little effect. And very few residents, or even politicians, appear to have grasped the whole picture. A major characteristic of Howdendyke's demise is that the village has been, and is being, destroyed on a piecemeal basis. Small sections are eliminated as HS & L and related industries' growth policies require. The tempo of change is slow and almost wholly decided by private enterprise. Lack of a local plan, and Boothferry Council's insistence on an application-by-application approach rather than an overall vision, has exacerbated this process.

As Greater London Council's chief development planner remarked of the Conservative government's green belt policy, 'It's like defending a castle ... against folk who are not attacking with a battering ram but are knocking out a few stones here and there – you think it's not worth bothering with the boiling oil, and the next thing you know the whole fortress has collapsed' (the *Guardian*, 28 August 1983). While public opinion may readily be aroused by a single massive assault, continuous sapping is much more difficult to detect and combat with any degree of effectiveness.

In summary, two theories may be propounded to explain Howdendyke's demise. Each is an extreme case, and the truth, as usual, probably lies in between.

(1) Catastrophe theory: as normally understood, catastrophe theory suggests that a seemingly random but time-related concatenation of events may act to significantly alter previously stable situations. According to catastrophe theory, we would be asked to suppose that the actions of Hargreaves, Humberside Sea & Land, and other Howdendyke industries, bear little or no relation to each other, but were conceived and carried out separately. We would also accept that no communication, except what was duly reported in the press, occurred between private enterprise, planners, and politicians. On the other hand, the death of Howdendyke appears to be occurring precisely because the policies of private enterprise, politicians, and planners have dovetailed so well.

(2) Conspiracy theory: which suggests that many events and historical processes occur because of covert collaboration on the part of power elites. Naturally, there is no overt evidence of conspiracy, but there is much indirect evidence of the development of very similar policies, quite simultaneously, by two or more corporations, the Planning Department, and the Health & Housing Department. It is clear that some degree of collaboration has occurred between Hargreaves and HS & L in the creation of new wharves, between Hargreaves and Boothferry Planning in the case of their joint policy to eliminate at least half the village, and between BritAg, HS & L, and both authorities in the case of the demolition of the Club in favour of a lorry park. It is fair to note that a number of interviewees suggested considerable policy collaboration between interested actors, yet I am convinced that conspiracy theory, the notion of 'huge prearranged and harmful designs' (Vacca 1971, 153), is too naive an explanation of what appears to have been less a premeditatively willed plan to destroy Howdendyke than the cumulative effect of a series of rather ad hoc responses to opportunity.

Ironically, the village is being murdered to no purpose. The chief reasons for the politicians' agreement to the demolition of half of Howdendyke village were the assurances of Hargreaves, made in the late 1970s, that their fertilizer plant had a long-term future and might possibly expand. Yet as early as 1982 Hargreaves applied for planning permission to convert the factory into yet another cargo-handling facility. This was, very properly, refused, and by late 1985 the company had made over half its workers redundant. Thus Howdendyke, half-destroyed in the name of increasing employment, may in the future generate fewer jobs.

Questions of justice

I could end this chapter with a list of largely unanswerable questions: why did Howden Rural District Council petition the county to have Howdendyke agricultural land re-zoned as industrial?; why did planners of the late 1960s support HS & L's development?; why did they partially reverse this position in the late 1970s?; how much collaboration has occurred between private enterprise, planners, and politicians?; has Howdendyke been deliberately *undeveloped*, as Frank (1969) suggests has occurred in the Third World? And, in a more positive vein: why was no Local Plan ever developed for Howdendyke?; why did politicians and/or planners not hold public meetings in Howdendyke's Jubilee Hall to explain their positions and solicit input from residents?; why has neither Hargreaves nor HS & L ever provided the residents of Howdendyke with some form of public apologia for their developments?; why could the village not be evacuated in one major operation, rather than dying the death of one thousand cuts?; and so on. The interviews of 1986 did not resolve these problems.

What is most clear is the rather trite conclusion that individuals, communities and places exist at the whim of corporate, bureaucratic, and political power elites and that, should these groups so decide, places and communities can be eliminated and individuals forced to relocate. At base we are dealing with the age-old issues of power, conflict and control, which have been the subject of so many modern novels and critical essays.

Natural justice suggests that the people inhabiting an area should be fully consulted whenever new developments are proposed. According to the planner Keith Jeremiah, 'it is of the utmost importance that local people should feel that they have a real share in creating and influencing their future surroundings' (1949, quoted in Martin 1955, 21). Martin thinks that this is the only way 'a sane and healthy planning authority would operate' (p. 21) 'in a free society' (p. 22), which naturally leads to Segal's (1973, 192) general conclusion that 'Law and order, or national survival, seems less and less adequate an excuse for the ravages of the social and natural environment; the subjugation of the person to profit.... More and more ... citizens must ... ask for whose good the state really operates.' In terms of the exercise of power, whether by Boothferry Council or at any other level, Hilaire Belloc's barbed lines seem still to express the attitudes of decision-takers:

> Now be quite calm and good, obey the laws,
> Remember your low station, do not fight
> Against the goad, because, you know, it pricks
> Whenever the uncleanly demos kicks ...
>
> It's fearfully illogical in you
> To fight with economic force and fate.

> Moreover, I have got the upper hand
> And mean to keep it, do you understand?

Let me conclude by indicating, once again, a general context for the annihilation of Howdendyke. Modernized societies, in their urge to 'grow', commonly sacrifice the needs of the few for the supposed needs of the many. The local is sacrificed to the regional, the regional to the national interest. The architects of change deal inevitably with the public good; they rarely deal with people as individuals or small groups. Hence, in the name of the public interest the valued environments (Gold and Burgess 1980) of small groups are irretrievably altered and homogenized 'blandscapes' or even 'deathscapes' (Porteous 1987) are substituted. No modern society has yet solved the problem of creating jobs without deleteriously affecting lives and landscapes. And it seems that, in Britain at least, the only way in which people can become involved in decisions is to engage in confrontation, which is usually too late. This should not be so.

Yet this unhealthy situation – powerful politicians, private enterprise and planners vs. unempowered citizens – remains the norm. Major examples can be cited from all modern societies; I quote only the more articulate.

Berman's (1982) experience of the destruction of his home in the Bronx led him to develop a lengthy discussion of the deleterious effects of nineteenth and twentieth century planned change, particularly with regard to the imposition of such change on unwilling residents by planners and corporations. Significantly for the fate of Howdendyke, Berman gave his book the title, Marxian but with shades of Jeremiah's Lamentations, of *All That is Solid Melts into Air.*

Edward Abbey's (Balian 1985) experiences in the United States and Australia led to his considered opinion that 'The central conflict of the 20th century [is] the efforts of individuals, families, and communities to preserve their freedom and integrity against the overwhelming power of the modern techno-industrial … superstate, here in America, in Europe, Asia, Africa, everywhere.' Abbey is not optimistic, and neither is Berger (1984) in his consideration of the effectiveness of personal or communal protest against the wielding of power by elite groups:

> During the eighteenth and nineteenth centuries most direct protests against social injustice were reasoned arguments written in the belief that, given time, people would come to see reason, and that, finally, history was on the side of reason. Today this is by no means clear. The outcome is by no means guaranteed. The suffering of the present … is unlikely to be redeemed by a future of universal happiness. And evil is a constant, ineradicable reality.

These rather radical spokesmen apparently agree with the conservative Paul Johnson who, in *Enemies of Society*, concludes that 'Violence, shortage amid plenty, tyranny and the cruelty it breeds, the gross stupidities of the powerful, the indifference of the well-to-do, the divisions of the intelligent and well-meaning, the apathy of the wretched multitude – these things will be with us to the end of the race' (1977, 255). These are deeply pessimistic conclusions. I cannot improve upon them, nor refute them. If industrial 'capitalist systems produce the ravages that they do because they are what they are' (Segal 1973, 148) then I can as yet only recommend Walt Whitman's dictum, 'Obey little; Resist much.'

All is not yet for the best in the best of all possible worlds. In these terms, Howdendyke is the world in microcosm.

Update: 1987

Local newspaper reports (*Howdenshire Gazette*, 1, 29 January, 26 February 1987) indicate, with no irony, that the Rural Voice in Humberside's annual conference will focus upon the theme: 'Conservation with Change: Development with Preservation?' Meanwhile, Boothferry Council has approved further 'industrial' expansion at Howdendyke as well as the construction of a 'nuclear bunker' beneath its Council chamber! Further, a Secrets File report has apparently named the Council as a 'bad practice' council for its offences against open government ...

Appendix

Dante punished schismatics by dismembering them in hell to exact a physical punishment worthy of their ideological crime ... Let us value connections.

Stephen Jay Gould

There are places I remember all my life
Though some have changed ...
... not for better ...
J. Lennon, P. McCartney

12

A much longer, more general introduction

> The hazard of the specialist system is that it produces
> specialists – people who are elaborately and expensively
> trained *to do one thing.*
>
> Wendell Berry

Those who have read the whole book before this second introduction will know that the volume comprises three related parts. Part I traces the history of the village of Howdendyke from medieval times to the early twentieth century. Part II, relying less on archives than on memories, presents a picture of the village in the period c.1930–1960. The third part investigates the processes which are currently working towards the destruction of the village.

The three parts clearly have quite different intellectual underpinnings. The background of the first is in history, particularly local history, and in historical geography. Part III is grounded in planning critique and community studies. The intervening section, based on both the author's autobiographical recollections and the collective autobiographies of interviewees and correspondents, serves to weld the outer sections together. Indeed, autobiography, biography, and personal feeling, not solely my own, are the stuff of Chapter 5 (Part I) and Chapter 10 (Part III). The stories of the Andertons, Mells, and other families form narrative threads which interweave much of the book and give it more unity than might at first appear.

This introduction provides the intellectual framework for the book. It begins by specifying three philosophical positions which come together in this work, continues by outlining the substantive disciplinary areas which, woven together, create an interdiscipline which we might term, with apologies to the French *Annales* school of historians, 'total community studies', and concludes by briefly explaining the methods used.

Philosophical background

This work attempts to meld at least three separate philosophical positions. The first, the traditional, detached, positivist approach common to the sciences, social sciences, and some of the humanities, needs no explanation. In Part I, in historical terms, it chiefly involves the historical method, the sceptical and comparative reading of available archival material, and the quantitative methodology of historical demography. The two other positions, which for convenience may be termed 'humanistic' and 'radical', require more explication. In more technical terms, this book attempts also to combine the three models of science which Habermas (1974) identifies as: *empirical-analytic* (a study of phenomena in a positivist mode); *historical-hermeneutic* (a study of meanings and interpretations); and *critical* (an attempt to uncover the real explanations and encourage people to seek to create a better world). Johnston (1985) terms the combination of these approaches a 'realist' goal.

Humanistic geography

Humanistic geography has a long history, with many roots (Buttimer 1971, Gregory 1981). Largely suppressed in the early post-war period by the power of the theoretico-quantitative revolution, it lurked underground to flower in the 1970s (Ley and Samuels 1978). During this last, programmatic period, humanistic geographers roundly criticized the prevailing positivism for suppressing subjectivity, overlooking intentionality, and emphasizing human passivity (Ley 1980). The theoretical constructs associated with positivistic modes of research were also criticized for their avoidance of any discussion of experiential relationships with environment. Tuan (1977, 1978) felt that mainstream geography severely neglected the 'internal' aspects of human consciousness, the sensations and perceptions which contribute to experience and by which man makes sense of his environment.

Humanistic geography, nevertheless, has links with behavioral geography, and many humanistic geographers began as behavioral geographers. The approach is characterized by extreme philosophic diversity; among humanistic geographers we find idealists, phenomenologists, existentialists, pragmatists, and even some who flirt with modified positive and radical ideologies. Humanistic geographers do not exist as such; rather, certain geographers adopt one or more humanistic approaches to the understanding of specific issues. The approach has been strongly criticized for its failure to generalize, its subjectivism, its inexplicable or unstated methodological procedures, and its neglect of social, political, economic or environmental (i.e. structural) context (Daniels 1985, Sayer 1979). Humanistic geographers may counter these arguments by stressing that their approach is complementary to alternative approaches, and by stressing multioperationality. The cry of the 1970s that the approach preached much but practised little can no longer be countenanced.

Of the many general themes explored by humanistic geographers, two are of most interest to this study. The first is the conceptualization of place, in opposition to the positivist's almost exclusive concern with space. 'Space becomes place when man selects a "position" from the vast extent of the world, occupies it, and "takes a stand"' (Graber 1976, 4). Place varies in size, but is always a 'small world' of its own rather than merely a 'spatial location' (Tuan 1974, 245). It implies both 'a location and an integration of nature and culture' (Walmsley and Lewis 1984, 160). Places are therefore unique.

They are also the locales 'where we experience the meaningful events of an existence' (Norberg-Schulz in Relph 1976, 42). As Relph (Entrikin 1976, 615) notes, 'Places are fundamental expressions of man's involvement in the world, and thus give meaning to space ... Places are indeed foundations of man's existence, providing not only the context of all human activity, but also security and identity for individuals and groups.' The ultimate places are, of course, one's home (Porteous 1976) and one's body (Porteous 1986). People and place are so intricately interwoven that, as Ley (1977, 508) puts it: 'a man *is* his place'. All this justification of what is obvious to the ordinary citizen would not have been necessary except for the dead hand of positivist orthodoxy which ruled geography well into the 1970s. It is noteworthy that a number of disciplines, including architecture, planning, and psychology, are following humanistic geography's lead in the exploration of the meaning of place (Canter 1977, Sime 1986).

With place, humanist geographers have also investigated the notion of 'sense of place'. Sense of place studies are concerned with the individual's involvement and attachment to places, although a sense of place does not necessarily have to be positive or involve topophilia (Eyles 1985, Porteous 1976, Tuan 1974). Although time itself does not guarantee a sense of place, 'to know a place requires long residence and deep involvement: experience takes time' (Tuan 1975, 164). As the environmental artist Gussow remarks (1971, 27–8):

> The catalyst that converts any physical location [or] environment ... into a place, is the process of experiencing deeply. A place is a piece of the whole environment that has been claimed by feelings. Viewed simply as a life-support system, the earth is an environment. Viewed as a resource that sustains our humanity, the earth is a collection of places. We never speak, for example, of an environment we have known, and recall. We are homesick for places, we are reminded of places, it is the sounds and smells and sights of places which haunt us and against which we often measure our present ... All of us have our loved places; all of us have laid claim to parts of the earth; and all of us, whether we know it or not, are in some measure the products of our sense of place.

This could hardly be expressed better, or more lyrically. Most appropriately for the argument of this book, Gussow was acting as an expert witness in a court case brought by citizens against a public utility whose plans were a threat to their sense of place.

Place, of course, can be experienced from the inside, which may lead to the development of a sense of place, or from the outside, as a stranger, a visitor, a tourist, a corporate or bureaucratic planner, or an expert. Relph (1976) provides a detailed typology of the insider-outsider dichotomy. It is enough to note here that whereas unselfconscious insiders authentically know a place, but often cannot articulate their understanding, expert outsiders are trained to write about places they have visited, but will rarely come to know and understand in a deeply meaningful way. The *inpert* (Abrams 1971, Porteous 1977) is perhaps in the best position, for he is by definition a self-conscious, articulate insider who often has 'outsider' contacts or skills. This is my own position with regard to Howdendyke.

It is the inpert who best understands how sense of place develops through time. This notion has been ignored by humanistic geographers (Cosgrove 1978) not only because they tend to see places as static (Tuan 1977) but also, as Daniels (1985) suggests, because they have neglected the narrative mode of exposition. In Daniels' words (1985, 154) 'Narrative is an essentially retrospective mode of understanding but it is not confined to studying the dead nor is it necessarily scholarly ... A historically minded scholar might make sense of his own life [in this way].' Narrative, much of it from an insider point of view (Part II, Chapter 10), and some of it from my own, is the basis of this study of Howdendyke. Moreover, in studying the village as a unique place, I have not neglected to relate its events to external politico-economic structures. Indeed, this is the chief aim of Parts I and III.

My philosophical stance then, is broadly humanistic. In its goal of trying to understand and describe Howdendyke and its meaning for both insiders and outsiders, it is essentially phenomenological. In its concern with events, intentions, and identity in a specific locality, and with bearing witness to suffering, it is existential. It is also radical.

Radical geography and history

One telling criticism of humanistic geographers is the paradoxical one that they tend to be too detached, too impersonal, too uninvolved. In this sense they may resemble positivists, and indeed humanistic geography has been seen as a means of generating hypotheses which may then be tested by positivists (Tuan 1976). Taking a different tack, Cosgrove (1978) recommends that the phenomenological method be combined with a radical structuralist approach in order to avoid falling into the trap of an idealism which explores human behaviour independent of the social, economic, and political context in which it occurs. Gregory (1978), in recommending the adoption of a critical theory approach, concurs, and sees geography as one component of a critical social science which is concerned with structural, reflexive, and committed explanation.

Humanistic approaches can readily be accommodated to a radical geography which is not heavily ideological in tone. Unfortunately, much radical geography is densely Marxist. It tends also to be overwhelmingly urban in subject matter. Like humanistic geography, the radical approach flowered in the 1970s as yet another reaction to the dull orthodoxy imposed by positivism and its offspring, behavioural and applied geography (Peet 1985). Again like humanism, radical geographers appear in many guises, ranging from liberals through socialists to Marxists and anarchists. The common thread is a belief that current social, political, and economic structures are related, are inequitable, and should be transformed. The mode of transformation, and the ultimate goal of such change, naturally vary according to political persuasion.

Radical geography, of course, is matched by similar movements in disciplines such as sociology and history. The development of a social history with a concern for the daily lives of ordinary people, often using the techniques of oral history, has wrought remarkable changes in the latter discipline, and is perhaps more relevant here than is radical geography (Chaplin 1976). Taking an explicitly socialist stance, the History Workshop movement has sought to develop a 'people's history' which may be written either by professionals or by ordinary people themselves.

People's history seeks to avoid the bureaucratism which stifles much trade union and labour history (Samuel 1975), and it attempts to create histories of forgotten groups such as women and children. Whereas humanistic geography emphasizes place, albeit as an amalgam of people and locale, or person-in-place, and radical geography remains heavily theoretical: 'The main thrust of people's history in recent years has been towards the recovery of subjective experience. One might note, in oral history, the overwhelming interest in reconstituting the small details of everyday life; in local history, the shift from "places" to "faces" ...' (Samuel 1981, viii). People's history is not always at ease with Marxism; indeed, it seems to take a populist stance and has been appropriated by the Right as well as by non-Marxist socialists. People's history is 'history from below'.

I feel more at home with people's history than with the heavily ideological Marxism which now appears to dominate radical geography. All the more so, as we shall see later, in that whereas radical geography deals largely with impersonal structures, and people's geography has hardly yet developed (Eliot Hurst 1985) in people's history 'the autobiographical mode is in the ascendancy' (Worpole 1981).

Radical notions inform many areas of life besides geography and history. Berger (1972, 1984) propounds a radical art history. Novelists, biographers, and autobiographers espouse radical causes (Joubert 1986). Theologians increasingly take the part of the oppressed, and in 1986 even a traditionalist pope felt able to endorse liberation theology. The public participation movement in planning has become established, and a quarterly newsletter, *Constructive Citizen*

Participation, dealing with the involvement of the public in environmental, planning, economic, and municipal government policies is edited in the university town in which I work. A vast planning critique literature is summarized later in this chapter, stemming in part from Jewkes' observation as early as 1948 in his *New Ordeal by Planning* that 'At the root of our troubles lies the fallacy that the best way of ordering ... affairs is to place the responsibility for all crucial decisions in the hands of the state' (1948, xi).

Journalists and popular writers often take the same tack. Postman (1982) traces the origins of 'they', the faceless organizations that increasingly control our lives, while Vizinczey (1986, 73) notes, in a discussion of Melville's *Billy Budd*, that literature generally lies about power, implying that 'authority does not illtreat its subjects out of indifference, venality, incompetence or callousness, but *for the common good*. However arbitrary and cruel it may seem in its actions, it is always benign at heart.' He goes on to assert: 'What disabling misconceptions about human nature and society are inspired by such lies!'

For Vizinczey, 'power is glamorized or it is unseen. And even when it is perceived to be harmful, it is impersonal' (1986, 73). It is, therefore, very difficult to deal with on the part of the ordinary citizen. Hence much journalism and radical social science are involved less in changing the world directly than in recounting the stories of the victims of 'them'. The 'I am a camera' technique, for example, permits us to experience the political pathology of militarist Argentina through the words of the kidnapped, the tortured, and their relatives (Simpson and Bennett 1986).

Perhaps the most valuable service that radical social science can perform is to facilitate the ordinary citizen's telling of his own story in his own words. Although E. B. White once told us that 'the whole duty of a writer is to please and satisfy himself', a radical social scientist would also wish to heed Edward Abbey's echoing of George Orwell in his uncompromising cry that 'it is the writer's duty to hate injustice, to defy the powerful, and to speak for the voiceless' (McNamee 1985, 25). This is the stance I take in this book.

Contextual background

Some of the disciplines which combine to form what I have termed 'total community studies' are historical geography, local history, community studies (mainly in sociology, and urban/rural planning), rural geography, and an emergent field which might be termed 'geoautobiography'. There are many others, including architecture, anthropology, political science, and psychology. Because the story of Howdendyke does not pretend to be a 'total community study' (it lacks sociological depth, it does not consider architecture, etc.) only those disciplinary subfields which relate directly to this study will be emphasized.

Historical geography

During the last decade historical geography has enjoyed, or suffered, an interesting but ultimately exhausting plethora of introspective self-analysis. In part this mood was stimulated by the development of positivist locational analysis in the 1950s and 1960s, for in their extremist throes location analysts were wont to ignore time or treat it in a very cavalier fashion (Prince 1980). In short, the leading edge of geography in the sixties looked down upon historical geography as a merely ideographic enterprise, solely concerned with recording the characteristics of unique features. And, according to Butlin's (1982) review, most British historical geographers continued throughout the 1970s to operate in the conventional mode, concentrating on general processes in rural areas, ignoring the role of individuals in landscape change, and only slowly taking advantage of readily-available quantitative techniques.

Changes in British historical geography began to emerge only after 1975 with sundry bugle calls and exchanges of insults. Until that time, a few practitioners had sought to 'spatialize' their subfield, and in the early 1970s historical geography became more quantitative, behavioural, and even applied, thus re-entering the orthodox geographical mainstream. Mills (1972), Prince (1978) and Baker (1978), among others, have attempted to chart this new philosophical and methodological landscape.

Perhaps because of this growth of what Gregory (1974) has called 'numerate dilettantism', few historical geographers have sought to examine critically their own philosophies and practices (Baker 1979, Clark 1977, Harris 1978). Yet after the mid-1970s a few theorists began to explore the terrain generally known as humanistic geography, and the role of ideology in historical interpretation was aired (Gregory 1978).

This is not the place to discuss the positivist vs. humanist debate. Rather, I take the obvious pragmatic and multimodal approach which has been summarized by Baker (1979, 500–01) as:

> the need to colonize and cultivate the potentially fertile middle ground between the sanitized and sterile historical geography of the logical positivist and the logically self-destructive but emotionally self-indulgent geography of the phenomenologist ... The tasks of understanding and experiencing the past will no doubt continue to be disaggregated, according to the pride of its sources and the prejudices of its students. But any total historical geography *must* logically combine these two approaches.

The problem with such sensible advice is that few take it, preferring to deepen traditional ruts or plough narrow new ones. As Butlin (1982) remarks, 'as far as the bulk of published work is concerned there is not a great amount of evidence that the new ideas have penetrated very far'.

This book attempts to fill this substantive gap by combining the traditional 'objective' goal of seeking knowledge of the landscape with the 'subjective' one of experiencing it. The ultimate goal is a meld of knowledge and experience which we might call understanding. And while Guelke's (1974, 1976) idealist goal of understanding via re-thinking the thoughts of dead people may be used for history in depth, part of this volume is based on the ultimate in phenomenology, my personal recollections of my past experiences. I do not think this has been attempted before in historical geography, although it is not unknown in history (Cobb 1975).

My approach also, I believe, attempts to fulfil Gregory's (1978) demand to go beyond the phenomenological position to the structuralist view of attempting to relate the life-worlds of the individual and the group to the social, economic, and political structures which constrain and define them. And Gregory's demand for commitment is certainly answered in Part III, which may perhaps be criticized as overly populist.

Those themes in traditionalist and humanistic historical geography which are most marked in this book are: a very traditionalist concern with the ideographic study of a single settlement; an emphasis on sense of place, of the character of places which are always in flux, always 'emergent and becoming' (Lukerman 1964); a related concentration on change (Prince 1978) and even decay (Porteous 1977), with a strong emphasis on turning points; a genetic approach, which concerns the nature of the 'generating processes' (Baker 1976, Olsson 1969) by which change is brought about; and a methodological eclecticism ranging from traditionalist modes through personal impressions (Prince 1978) to reconstructions of the past in the words of, not imaginary historical personages (Ross 1970), but my childhood self.

Overall the approach is one which Prince (1978, 33), I think erroneously, calls 'behavioural', and which 'goes beyond imaginatively reconstructing past environments. It focusses on the personalities, deeds and thoughts of men and women who lived in past times. It follows Alexander Pope's precept that "The proper study of Mankind is Man".' But my work goes well beyond even this attempt towards a 'total' historical geography. For, as I have always done in the past (Porteous 1977, 1981), I eschew the historical geography of static cross-sections or synchronism, being concerned largely with diachronic studies of places in the course of change, which cannot be halted except, temporarily and expediently, at the 'present'. Hence I am concerned not only with the experiences of people 'who lived in past times' but also of people presently living. As T. S. Eliot reminded us long ago, the present is the past of some future. For me then, historical geography involves both the past and the future.

Further, one of the recent trends in historical geography which I applaud most is the growth of an interdisciplinary approach. Yet the chief barrier to fall is only that between history and historical geography (Baker 1979, Prince

217

1978). Few historical geographers have considered that a more 'total' approach might require the insights and emphases of other disciplines. It is to some of these I now turn.

Local history

Local history is still not quite respectable in academe, despite the great growth surge of social history in the last two decades. Many academics consider the writing of local history an amateur concern, their energies being devoted to weightier matters. The success of the History Workshop movement certainly indicates that a great deal of amateur historical talent lies latent and should be tapped (Samuel 1981). History Workshop also embraces the radical philosophical approach noted earlier, for it emphasizes that local history should ideally be written by those experiencing it.

Whereas historical geography is very much an established arcane academic subfield, local history is a lusty infant with a large amateur following. Despite the several footholds which the field has in academe, and the considerable overlap in both sources and methods with historical geography, local history thrives best in small regional or community-level societies. It is at its most authentic when, as in the present volume, it is written by a 'native son'. Compared with geography, its popularity is assured in an age of rapid change, the more so 'because people appear to be more interested in narratives than in static pictures, in events that unfold in time rather than in objects deployed in space' (Tuan 1973, 216).

Local history is an exercise in geopiety. According to one of its chief exponents 'The business of the local historian ... is to re-enact in his own mind, and to portray for his readers, the Origin, Growth, Decline, and Fall of a Local Community' (Finberg 1967, 10). Finberg went on to note that an inter-disciplinary approach, including archaeology and geography, is essential, that the discipline is essentially a humane one, and that both mature scholarship and a wide background of general culture are required of practitioners 'in its higher reaches'. Would that early historical geographers had had the vision of a Finberg!

One of Finberg's major emphases was on the importance of ordinary individuals and groups in identifiable settings, a signal failing in both historical geography and in history, where until recently we learned mostly about national figures or vast agglomerations known as villeins or Puritans or whatever. In contrast,

> Local history brings us nearer to the common run of [people] that any other branch of historical study ... It studies them as social beings, as members of a ... community; but by seeking them at their home address it enables us to see them as flesh and blood, and not just as pawns on the national chessboard ... Local

history brings us face to face with the Englishman at home … (Finberg 1967, 13–15).

The approach may be radical or nostalgic, quantitative or celebratory; what matters is that the lives of ordinary people in ordinary landscapes (Meinig, 1979) are deemed important.

Local historians have had to battle those who regard the field as merely providing illustrative material for national or regional history (Skipp 1967). For a number of years in the 1960s the *Amateur Historian*, now the *Local Historian*, carried a debate chiefly sustained by the regional historian Marshall who decried local history for its lack of structure or theme, its emphasis on gathering data on bounded units such as parishes, which are not natural landscape entities, its apparent concern for artifacts rather than human beings, its lack of underlying problems or concepts, and the excesses practised in its name by amateurs.

This debate continued desultorily into the late 1970s when, despite the development of local history emphases at a number of institutions, Marshall (1978) was still advocating the rather geographical concept of regional history as superior to 'parish-type history', which he condemned as an unworthwhile exercise leading to 'antiquarianism and narrowness of view'. This debate would have been greatly improved had the combatants considered the concept of place, a commonplace for humanistic geographers, as their field of care. For places exist at many scales, from the room within a house to regions and nations, and are not necessary bounded by political or legal boundaries, but by human conceptualization.

Some of Marshall's strictures are, however, relevant. He notes that the study of local political units such as parishes produces 'dull dead lawyer's history'. His answer was regional-scale study; mine is to study the small place, as recognized by its inhabitants, at the sub-parish level. Local history and geography, above all, deal with the ordinary lives of people in their habitual activity spaces. Until recently such activity spaces were often very local indeed.

Marshall also notes the tendency of local historians to avoid the complexities of history later than the mid-nineteenth century. In view of the release of 1881 census manuscript returns, this complaint now seems odd, but it is certainly true of some of the classics of local history, such as Hoskins' *Midland Peasant* (1965) and Ravensdale's *Liable to Floods* (1974). More importantly, local histories hardly ever consider very recent history, and almost never deal with the far-reaching effects of post-war planning controls on local lives and landscapes. It is the rare local historian who continues his history to the present day or attempts an anthropological role by going to live in the village he is studying. Here Steel's (1979) *Lincolnshire Village* stands out.

Local history may be approached philosophically and methodologically in many ways. Oral history may be the major technique (Blythe 1970, Bragg 1976), or the traditional methods of archives and field archaeology may be employed. A village's history, unsatisfactorily revealed by archival or other data, may be conjectured and fictionalized (Girling, 1983), or one may take Ralph Whitlock's (1985) recollective stance to generate 'local history as it happens'. 'Total' historians attempt to portray the villager 'in the round' rather than as economic man or political animal (Le Roy Ladurie 1975, Spufford 1973).

I personally enjoy the local history approach because, despite world-wide wanderings as a geographer, I have a deep feeling for the local. I appreciate both the gentle essay on the virtues of parochialism which prefaces Gilbert White's *Natural History of Selborne* (1978) and William Blake's debatable and paradoxical dictum that 'to generalize is to be an idiot'. And as a geographer who continues to turn his hand to a wide variety of themes, in order to keep out of the grip of the narrow rut that awaits all experts, I greatly appreciate Finberg's (1967, 44) remark that local history 'is – and long may it remain! – the last refuge of the non-specialist'. Next century, perhaps, the currently ridiculous barriers between related disciplines will have gone. Local history is a catalyst in the casting down of such barriers. It also bridges, to some extent, the gap between professional and amateur, and this can only be applauded.

Community studies

Given the existence of almost one hundred definitions of 'community', I refuse to add another; we all have an intuitive, intersubjectively-derived conceptualization of the term. Like local history, community studies are necessarily particularistic. The tradition of particularistic research in individual communities is still strong in sociology and anthropology. The case-study approach in geography, however, has been suppressed in recent decades by the development of a theoretico-quantitative orthodoxy which has yet to be overcome by radical and humanistic geographers.

A similar trend in history has had a less suppressive effect. Historical studies of village communities have a lengthy pedigree, and the common theme of 'the vanishing village way of life' had become well-established by the end of the nineteenth century (Jefferies 1890). Bourne's (1912) title, *Change in the Village*, is surprisingly modern. Most of the recent work in rural history has been rather generalist, however (Horn 1980, Mingay 1977, Samuel 1975).

One of these general themes most relevant to the story of Howdendyke is that of paternalism. Historical studies of village communities have laid stress on the distinction between 'open' and 'closed' villages, the second type chiefly distinguished by the overwhelming control of land, housing, and employment by a single owner. Ralph Whitlock aptly summarizes the distinction as one between 'church' (traditional, paternalist, deferential, strongly class-structured, often an agricultural estate) and 'chapel' (small owners and tradesmen with independent views) villages. An extreme version of the 'closed' settlement would be the planned estate village or the company town (Porteous 1970).

Mills (1980), in an extensive study of the open/closed dichotomy, devotes some attention to closed industrial villages, although much more work in this area has been done by geographers, especially on company towns (Lewis 1979, Porteous 1970, 1972, 1973a, 1973b, 1975, 1978, 1981). General studies of paternalism make a distinction between the *noblesse oblige* of rural landowners and the self-interested concern of captains of industry (Roberts 1979). None of these studies, however, gives much attention to either the rural industrialist or, especially, to the process by which an open village can be transformed, by such a rural industrialist, into a closed one. Nor, except in obvious cases such as the interior coal-mining areas of the Northumberland-Durham Coalfield, has much attention been paid to the demise of village communities. This book attempts to deal with all these issues.

In sharp contrast, sociological and anthropological community studies tend to emphasize the present at the expense of the past. Indeed, anthropological studies are often 'historyless' (Bell and Newby 1971), while the methodological problems of sociological studies have led such work to be characterized as 'the poor sociologist's substitute for the novel' (Glass, quoted in Bell and Newby 1971, 13). Distinct differences between American, British, and European modes are apparent (Bell and newby 1971, Frankenberg 1966, Minar and Greer 1969), but the common themes of socio-anthropological studies generally include family, kinship, ceremonies, neighbouring, associations, social class, work, and links with the outside world. The emphasis is upon the multiplex relationships between and within groups, rather than on the individual.

Early studies were criticized for being innumerate, neglecting even the manipulation of historical census data which is the stuff of historical demography. Methodological variation, from anthropological observation to sociological surveys, prevented inter-study comparison. To the horror of mainstream geographers undergoing the quantitative-theoretical revolution of the sixties, most community studies remained resoundingly idiographic. At this time also, the rather premature and shallow notion of the 'global village' led at least one American planner to declare the death of the notion of community (Webber 1963, 1964).

Happily, community studies have weathered these criticisms well. Those which have adopted the methods of historical demography and local history have aided comparability, and the use of statistical data derived from surveys has become common. Indeed, as with the convergence of historical geography with both history and local history, so are community studies witnessing the pragmatic co-operation of related disciplines in the development of a kind of 'total community study'. One of the more recent, an investigation of Elmdon, Essex, through the period 1861–1964, involved the collaboration of anthropologists, sociologists, historians and geographers, the final account being synthesized, naturally, by a geographer (Robin 1980).

This same book illustrates another trend in community studies, that of an emphasis upon the contrast between continuity and change. These issues lie at the heart of all history, and are certainly the chief themes of modern historical geography (Prince 1978). It is also refreshing to find recent community studies involving themselves in the problems of rural planning. *New Society's* (29 October 1964) question, 'what's happening to the village?' was largely concerned with planning issues. The question was partly answered by a detailed study of Ringmer, Sussex, through the period 1871–1971 (Ambrose 1974). Certainly not historyless, admirably local yet set in the context of national and regional trends, fully grounded in theory, yet written in a sympathetic, committed manner, this book represents an attempt to describe village change in an interdisciplinary manner. Above all, like a local historian, Ambrose writes in a style understandable by the educated layman, and hopes that this perhaps mythical person will read his book.

This is an excellent model, although to follow it fully in my book would have been to create something rather unwieldy, given my wish to emphasize both the long mercantile history and the details of the planning process with regard to Howdendyke. I am most impressed by Ambrose's attention to issues of planning, and it is to these I now turn, in the context of rural geography.

Rural geography and planning

Rural geography has a very broad scope, involving *inter alia* studies of agriculture, mining, industry, service provision, housing, transportation and a host of other geographical themes (Cloke 1980, Clout 1972, Grigg 1978, Lewis 1979, Roberts 1977). When geographers deal with the nature of rural settlements and their problems, it is often quite difficult to distinguish their work from that of rural sociologists (Bowles 1981) or planners (Hodge and Qadeer 1983). Even those whose work has a more literary and historical bent tend also to deal with recent village history in terms of geographical themes and planning problems (Martin 1955).

Clout's series of reports on rural settlement geography in *Progress in Human Geography* (1977, 1979, 1980) provides a broad context for this study. Rural geography suffered a distinct decline after the 1950s as geographical fashion turned towards the problems of urbanization. During the 1970s, however, the increasing urbanization of the countryside, via tourism, recreation, second homes, and the forces of residential counter-urbanization, among other influences, led to a rapid resurgence of interest in rural themes. Rural housing has become a major research issue, with some emphasis on 'tied housing' and on the growing use of 'key settlement' policies among British rural planners. Research on the latter asserts that while living conditions in 'selected settlements' ('key villages') has improved, conditions in smaller settlements have progressively worsened as services and residents have progressively withdrawn (McLaughlin 1976). Work on tied housing has generally considered only agricultural cottages, excluding the similar provision of work-related housing by rural industrialists. Both these substantive themes are of great relevance to the story of Howdendyke.

The late 1970s saw the flowering of rural geography in Britain, Europe, and North America, with an increasing emphasis on rural resource use, settlement systems, landscape change, and planning problems. Issues of poverty and rural deprivation became important, and by 1980 the romantic aura which so often colours English rural literature had been exploded by telling exposes of the plight of the poorly educated and the 'transport-poor' (Shaw 1979). Here rural geographers have benefited from a convergence with rural sociology (Newby 1978) and the field has become not only interdisciplinary but also internationalized. Of great note for this book is the work of French rural geographers, who emphasize the obvious point that 'rural dwellers experience a sense of powerlessness when confronted by urban-based planners and resource managers' (Clout 1979, Houssel 1978).

Indeed, rural geography in the 1980s has a strong flavour of social concern and even radicalism. Along with the resurgence of historical geography, still often rural-based in Britain, has emerged an applied, sometimes radical contemporary rural geography. Moseley (1980) notes the emphasis on policy evaluation in recent books such as that by Gilg (1978), outlines the growing 'geography of welfare' theme (Shaw 1979), commends the increasing convergence with planning and sociology, and recommends that increasing attention be paid to analyzing the motives and actions of those in power. In this view, for example, Cloke (1983) has again criticized key settlement policies, Moseley (1979) has dealt with the vexed problem of accessibility to services, and the investigation of rural industrialization has begun (Healey and Ilbery 1986).

The most recent text in the field (Gilg 1985), however, demonstrates how the type of problem exhibited by Howdendyke is not dealt with by rural geographers. A summary of 'factors likely to cause migration' does not include place destruction, unless 'retreat because of catastrophe' involves this (p. 68). Studies of social change ignore forced change (p. 80 ff.). The rural planning section has little to say about industrial encroachment (p. 138 ff.). On the other hand, the growing interest in planning as a means of conflict resolution has made an encouraging start on the study of conflict between power groups and value systems (Cherry 1976), an issue which lies at the heart of the Howdendyke problem.

By the early 1980s, then, rural geography and planning, as a subfield, had begun to catch up with the much more well-established field of urban geography. Cloke (1980), however, sees the chief current problems as being the need to develop conceptual frameworks, if not theory, to refine analytical tools, and to further integrate rural geography with the planning fields. The theme of interdisciplinary, problem-oriented work has been common to all the fields discussed above, as has the growing emphasis on social concern and the need to understand planning processes. To these we now turn.

Planning critique

Geography, when applied, becomes very difficult to distinguish from urban, regional, or rural planning. Just as the development of rural geography lagged behind that of its urban counterpart, however, so rural planning critique followed upon a healthy development of the approach in the urban context.

Planning critique is not a discrete discipline or a field, but an approach which is strongly interdisciplinary. It is fundamentally political, and can be traced back to the three questions posed by Webber in the 1960s in relation to planning decisions – who decides? who pays? who benefits? (Moseley 1980). Planning critique is an approach suitable for historians, geographers, and sociologists as well as architects and planners themselves. Its practitioners may take a liberal or a radical stance, but they will tend to agree that the powerless have been studied to death while the less accessible power elites have gone largely scot-free. The fundamental issue is one of power – who has the power to do what to whom? We are therefore urged to change our ways and to study 'the actions of the powerful rather than the powerless, the propertied rather than the propertyless, and the wealthy ... rather than the landless and ... poor' (Newby, Bell, Rose and Saunders 1978, Rose, Saunders, Newby and Bell 1979). Similarly, Grey (1975) called for a re-direction of urban geography away from sterile models to a study of those elite groups who manage urban space.

Planning critique has a long history (Porteous 1977). Man is essentially a planning animal, and planners are highly goal-oriented. Yet those who plan and design layouts and structures which other people occupy clearly have the potential for enormous and lasting influence upon the lives of these occupants. The power of the planner over the behaviour and well-being of others is great, and all the more insidious in the recent era of the 'evangelistic bureaucrat' (Davies 1972).

The planned environment reflects the largely untested assumptions about human behaviour held by the planner. 'Planners are not doctors; they do not deal with individuals' (Bolan 1971). Indeed, the planner's client today is likely to be a specific but rather impersonal group which might be labelled 'government' or 'planning commission'. The *user-client*, he who actually inhabits the planned environment, has very little input into the decision-taking which results in the formulation of the goals which are to be achieved by the plan.

Although he is planning with the good of the public in mind, the planner is more aware of social, economic, and political constraints, that is, the issues relevant to the powerful, than of the desires of the powerless. The social distance between planner and the planned-for is further widened by administrative distance (Lipman 1974); the planned-for have little effect on the planner's will. Yet the most restrictive constraints under which the planner must work are not those imposed by others but those imposed by himself. Elsewhere (Porteous 1977) I have summarized a vast literature on the ideologies held by planners. Those ideological constructs most relevant to the story of Howdendyke include:

(1) *The search for order.* Orderliness is an urban middle-class preoccupation. The urban bourgeoise is offended by untidy farms, Indian reservations, and 'wasted space', and he prefers to pack away the deviant, disorderly, and dependent into institutions (Rothman 1971), an ethos only partly broken down by the emergence in the 1970s of the concept of community care. Orderliness is also related to a tendency to define situations in terms of arbitrarily designated criteria sets – a 'slum' may be defined by residential density data, rather than social criteria. Perin (1974) suggests that professionals merely share in the ordinary human need to reduce anxiety by generating order. She adds, however, that those who go about their business of creating order should continually ask themselves '*whose* chaos are we taming?'

(2) *Elitism.* Many of the assumptions and assertions of planners are bound up with an overall belief that the planner knows best. This attitude has been carried to the point where viable communities have been deliberately disrupted in an attempt to redesign human relationships and generate 'social happiness' (Shankland, Cox and Associates 1966). Deliberate disruption as a policy is typified by the statement of a major British bureaucratic planner that slums should be demolished and their inhabitants relocated 'even though the people seem to be satisfied with their miserable environment and seem to enjoy ... social life in their own locality' (Burns 1963).

The evangelistic bureaucrat who 'knows best' and has a 'broader view' than those he is planning for is a dangerous animal (Berman 1982, Davies 1972). If constraints are imposed upon him, he will more likely bend to the desires of the powerful rather than to those of the voiceless.

Planning critique, then, attempts to articulate the desires and feelings of the powerless. Its form may vary from detached policy analysis to committed involvement; it may even lead to advocacy (Spiegel 1968) or to guerrilla architecture (Goodman 1972). The general aim, however, is always to look critically at the common policy of planning *for* people, while advocating planning *with* or even *by* people (Porteous 1977). Planning critique may also involve a strong autobigraphical element; Berman (1982, 295) remembers: 'standing above the construction site for the Cross-Bronx Expressway, weeping for my neighborhood'.

Indeed, some of the earliest and most powerful examples of modern planning critique emerged from the urban renewal phase which American cities underwent in the 1950s and 1960s. Defined as a slum by planners – 'why, that's the worst slum in the city. It has 275 dwelling units to the acre' (Jacobs 1961, 10) – and in the way of magnificent renewal projects, the West End of Boston was targeted for destruction in the late 1950s. A team of anthropologists, sociologists and social planners studied the area in depth (Fried 1963, Fried and Gleicher 1961, Gans 1962, Hartman 1966, Ryan 1963) and found it to be a healthy, viable community of 10,000 people. Its destruction by planners and bureaucrats led to what has been called 'the pathology of forced relocation', involving grief, physical illness, nausea, general sadness, and prolonged depression. Similar effects have been reported from a variety of countries, and the relocation of forced migrants in public housing has also led to considerable distress, not to speak of financial loss for individuals and city alike (Porteous 1977). In South Africa, much of the non-white population has been defined as surplus to (white) requirements and is being brutally relocated to so-called homelands (Platzky and Walker 1985).

Rural planning critique is less well developed, and, unlike its urban counterpart, has not involved many professional planners, its chief practitioners being geographers and sociologists. The work of Moseley (1979) on accessibility and of Cloke (1979) on key settlement policies has already been noted in the context of rural geography. Newby (1980) documents social change in rural England and asks if England really does remain a green and pleasant land, and if so, for whom?

Perhaps the most useful trend in recent rural geography has been precisely this growing interest in how planning policies affect rural communities (Cloke 1980). Clout (1977) noted a groundswell of opinion against current techniques for planning villages, and key settlement policy is increasingly regarded as detrimental to the future viability of small villages where growth is discouraged (Ash 1976, Hancock 1976, McLaughlin 1976). Cloke (1980) calls for further policy analysis, including 'a careful study of how decisions are made both within and outside the political planning process'. Moseley (1978) asks researchers to 'lay bare the realities of decision-making by powerful agencies'.

These calls are opportune, for they are moving towards a realisation, not common in urban planning critique until recently, that simplistic 'planner-bashing' is not enough. The chief forces behind change in rural, as well as urban areas, are the driving thrust of private corporations and the related decisions taken by politicians. For planners give only advice, and their important day to day work involves the evaluation of proposals which emanate from private enterprise and which will later be decided upon by politicians (Ambrose 1974).

These urgent calls for the investigation of power elites, including planners, are answered in this case-study of the demise of Howdendyke. The more specific context of Howdendyke's story, that of the planned destruction of places, follows.

Place annihilation

Planning studies include a significant amount of research on the planned relocation of residents or even of whole communities. Most emphasis has been placed on the relocation of agriculturalists or the elimination of urban neighbourhoods. There is overwhelming evidence that grandiose modern planning projects, from Third World 'resettlement' schemes to the Vancouver World Fair of 1986 (Porteous 1986) have deleterious effects on impacted social groups. Change almost invariably means loss (Marris 1974). Marris specifically includes slum clearance and other planning-related issues along with mourning and bereavement in his general study. Yet his emphasis on the response to loss means that he largely ignores 'the political and economic causes of loss'. In my study this emphasis is reversed, although some degree of balance has been aimed for.

Place destruction occurs at all times and in many regions. It may be due to natural causes, as with the destruction of whole towns by volcanic eruption. Or it may occur because of deliberate human agency. The destroyed unit may vary in size from a house, a neighbourhood (Boston's West End), or a city ('*delenda est Carthago*') through the loss of integrity of provinces and counties (the loss of Rutland and other entities during British political reorganization in 1974) to whole countries (Poland and the Baltic states) and empires (as after 1918).

The most spectacular efforts at 'place annihilation' (Hewitt 1983) may be the least effective; Dresden, Hamburg, Hiroshima and Nagasaki have risen from the ashes, an astounding manifestation of place loyalty (Porteous 1985). Physical deconstruction, using crowbars, bulldozers, explosives, and fire can be effective, as with many cases of cities laid waste by Babylonians, Assyrians, and Romans to the American destruction of the Japanese-Micronesian town of Koror, in Palau, towards the end of World War II. Perhaps the most effective method is drowning, as innumerable valley villages now below the surface of reservoirs bear witness.

The destruction of places by modern bureaucratic and political fiat is more common than might be supposed. Elsewhere I have chronicled the efforts of left-wing Chilean governments to rid their land of American-built company towns, hated symbols of economic dependence (Porteous 1972, 1973, 1974). In the United States small towns have commonly been relocated because of resource-extraction demands; a recent case involves a decision by the U.S. Army Corps of Engineers that the best location for a second power-house at the Bonneville Dam on the Columbia River would be the site of the town of Bonneville itself (Comstock and Fox 1982). George Mackay Brown's *Greenvoe*

(1972) chronicles in compelling detail, albeit in novelistic form, the destruction of a Scottish island community when external authorities decide that the island is the best location for a military installation. The inhabitants of numerous islands in the Pacific and Indian oceans – notably those of Bikini, Eniwetak, Kwajalein, Banaba, and Diego Garcia – have been removed wholesale to less viable environments and reduced to misery and penury because of the political, economic, and military 'needs' of Britain and the United States.

Company towns, or, as they are known euphemistically, single-industry settlements, are particularly vulnerable to destruction due to resource depletion or changes in market forces. As there are approximately 700 such towns in Canada, the problem has been addressed most frequently in that country. Bowles' *Little Communities and Big Industries* (1982) draws some attention to the issue of community death, including a study of the arbitrary closing and re-opening of the town of Elliot Lake with changes in the world uranium market. Another book by the same author (Bowles 1981) raises the questions of possible, probable, and plausible futures for company towns in terms of social impact assessment methodology.

Bradbury and St Martin (1983) have investigated the 'winding-down' process in relation to the town of Schefferville, Quebec, whose iron mine was closed down in 1982. Their analysis points to the parallel processes of decreasing company involvement (withdrawal from public service provision and from municipal affairs; disinvestment) and community winding down (emigration, instability, rumours, social dislocation). Of most interest for the research on Howdendyke are the authors' assessment that:

(1) Corporations, especially conglomerates, feel no compunction in opening or closing plant (and thus destroying or reviving the raison d'etre of a one-industry town) for 'a variety of reasons directly related to the nature of centralized management and control' (Bluestone and Harrison, 1980). Effectively, this means that although decisions taken on an international or national basis have profound repercussions at the local level, these effects are of little account in the corporate world view.

(2) The prevailing atmosphere among the inhabitants of declining or dying one-industry communities is one of rumour, uncertainty, and anxiety. This is often due to failure of communication on the part of the company, which merely emphasizes 'residents' feelings of neglect, as well as their feelings of impotence in the face of changing circumstances resulting from changes in the company's structure [and] the absence of local participation in decision-making' (Bradbury and St.-Martin 1983, 142).

The chief difference between this case and that of Howdendyke is that the latter is being destroyed not by contracting but by expanding industry.

Within Britain, studies of place destruction have tended towards the historical, with an emphasis on the annihilation of early modern villages in favour of sheep pasture and parkland. The study of historic deserted villages has become an academic growth industry since the development of extensive and accurate aerial photography (Allison 1970). Contemporary studies of place annihilation more commonly concentrate on Third World locales (Sutton 1977). Military coercion is infrequently studied by geographers, but has clearly led to the destruction of places through both bombing and the resettlement of millions of peasants in 'resettlement areas', from Afghanistan and Algeria (Sutton 1978, Sutton and Lawless 1978), to Vietnam and Zimbabwe. Places have been destroyed or fundamentally reshaped by military policy throughout the Arab-inhabited areas of Israel (Brawer 1978, Harris 1978). I have witnessed the loss of place experienced by Israeli Bedouin concomitant upon increasing military demands in the Negev subsequent to the Israeli withdrawal from Sinai. Coercive political and economic policy underlay the 'villagization' policy in Tanzania (Hirst 1978).

Surprisingly, it was not until 1976 that any significant attempt was made to generate a comprehensive theory of place destruction (Gallaher and Padfield 1980). The 'dying community' seminars held at the School of American Research in Santa Fe, New Mexico, in the 1970s brought together anthropologists, archaeologists, sociologists, psychiatrists, and members of departments of English and Social Work. Although little theory emerged, several insights are important for the Howdendyke study.

First, the emphasis on the small community; little settlements are clearly more vulnerable than cities. Second, the affirmation that community death is perhaps less common than community persistence in the midst of decay. Third, that the metaphor of death can be appropriately applied to communities; although sociologists and economists may debate this issue, 'few archaeologists or historians will have any reservations on this score' (Adams 1980, 23). Fourth, we may profitably distinguish between communities which die a more lingering 'natural' death and those which are 'killed' by 'the violence of man or nature' (Adams 1980, 23). Fifth, the two most interesting and pertinent questions are: why communities die; and how they die. These questions form the stuff of Part III of the Howdendyke study.

More specifically, Gallaher provides context for the case-study of Schefferville, reported above, as well as for Howdendyke, by confirming the dependence of small communities on external authority. Addressing himself to the deaths of communities which come about as a by-product of corporate policy change, he asserts that 'The basis for such decisions ... is not the desire to destroy a community ... but rather relates more to company production, profits, or changes in technology. Thus, decisions made in distant boardrooms, involving variables not addressing human needs per se, have the incidental effect of destroying a human community' (Gallaher 1980, 93–4). Dependence on external authority, further, often breeds a 'culture of dependence' (Porteous

1976, 1980) which encourages co-optation of community inhabitants and discourages protest or reaction.

This emphasis on local powerlessness is confirmed by Padfield, who affirms that:

> Clearly, *local* applies to the boundaries of small communities' political power and not to the boundaries of the political ties enjoyed by the industries which dominate them. The effective environment of industry ... has grown continually larger, while the effective environment of the local community ... has grown smaller. Clues to the mystery of the small community's demise are not to be found locally, but in far away places, like the central headquarters for multinational corporations, and regulatory agencies (Padfield 1980, 173).

Levin suggests that one's geographic sense of community relates to the area over which one feels a sense of control. In small communities dominated by big industries, especially those in which the company controls much of the housing and public services, the individual controls very little. 'And when the sense of control is missing it diminishes the sense of community' (Levin 1980, 258).

Significantly, the 'dying community' seminar series involved no geographers. Little effort was made, therefore, to investigate the effects of normal planning decisions on the life of small communities. Nor have planners themselves paid much attention to this issue. Indeed, the dying community receives less attention in frontier Canada and Australia than future-oriented 'boom town' studies (Gilmore and Duff 1975). Clearly, the boom end of the 'boom and bust cycle' in frontier zones is deemed more exciting and lucrative. In these terms Howdendyke is enjoying the worst of both worlds, being in an industrial 'boom' while simultaneously undergoing a residential 'bust' phase.

The growth of scholarly concern for those whose lives are disrupted by either growth or decay renders it imperative that planners and academics alike both provide data on, and interpretations of, such ongoing processes. Too often, despite the growth of social impact assessment, the reactions of the impacted population are neglected (Goodman 1972, Gilg 1978). This book seeks to remedy some of these areas of neglect.

Strangely, no attempt has been made to develop a term to encompass the notion of place annihilation. I suggest topocide, despite its hybrid etymology, because the wholly-Greek (topothanasia) or wholly-Latin (lococide) alternatives are less likely to be understood. Indeed, one Latin alternative, urbicide, would be an atrocious pun in American English. Topocide is most likely to affect those whose place is being destroyed, and hence involves geoautobiography.

Geoautobiography

Howdendyke is undergoing the process of place annihilation. I feel all the more strongly about this because the village was my childhood home. Although I have not lived there since 1965 (aged twenty-one), I have made frequent visits. Hence my study will inevitably be coloured by personal feeling and opinion.

Herein lies the importance of geoautobiography. Partial accounts of change may be given by those responsible for such change. Impartial accounts, as far as such detachment is possible, are given by experts. But the term 'expert' derives from the Latin verb 'to experience' and the modern expert, though generally experienced in a particular specialism, almost never has any lived experience of the locale on which he is called upon to pronounce judgement. Hence, ungrammatically, I choose to emphasize the *ex*-pert as an outsider with little knowledge of what it is like to live in the situation at which he peers. In contrast, the *inpert* is defined by such lived experience (Abrams 1971, Porteous 1977).

We are back, of course, to the insider/outsider dichotomy beloved of humanistic geographers. Recently, however, some attempt has been made to meld the two approaches. Jackson (1980) calls for geographers to distinguish between 'folk' and 'academic' definitions of a situation; Buttimer (1974) wishes to understand social space as an interplay of insider and outsider. Giddens (1976) calls for a 'double hermeneutic' approach which grasps the actors' frames of reference and then interprets these within new frames of meaning according to the expert's technical conceptualizations. Geertz (1973), less formally, asks for 'thick description'.

My approach to this problem is inherent in my own personal nature. I am a scholar, attuned to the prevailing 'expert' mode of detachment. In relation to Howdendyke, I am also an 'inpert', or at least a former inpert, and can therefore take an insider's point of view. I am at once on the inside looking out and on the outside looking in.

Clearly, however, only an insider or former insider can write an authentic geoautobiography.

Biography and autobiography

According to the German philosopher Dilthey (Thompson 1978, 45) 'autobiography is the highest and most constructive form in which the understanding of life confronts us'. Human beings have an insatiable desire to know about the lives of others, eclipsing by far their wish to learn about the past (history) or other places (geography). Biography occupies considerable space in airport bookstores, and autobiography is usually included with it. The greatest sellers are those books which penetrate the lives of the rich, famous, or notorious. A single issue of the *Manchester Guardian Weekly* (20 December 1981) contains biographical or autobiographical accounts of, *inter alia*, Sakharov, Simenon, Scargill, Sillitoe, Jaruzelski, and Cobb.

Self-portraits may be thinly disguised, as in Margaret Penn's novel trilogy

(1980), or may, indeed, reveal very little (White 1981). They may take the form of a novel (Grusa 1983), a surrealistic picaresque 'semiautobiography' (Bunuel 1983), a series of newspaper articles (Ralph Whitlock, in *The Guardian* during the early 1980s), or even a film, most notably Fellini's *Amarcord*. There is often great emphasis on childhood (Read 1946, Coe 1984), tempered by accounts of exotic forays in later life (Lewis 1985). Motives include the desire to recreate a lost ambience (Bates 1969), strong nostalgia, the need for self-therapy, and, in Laurie Lee's (1977, 49) words, 'Autobiography can be the laying to rest of ghosts as well as an ordering of the mind. But for me it is also a celebration of living and an attempt to hoard its sensations …' Milne (1976) wrote his autobiography 'to please himself', but more commonly there is also a more public posture, that of witness to events. Like Walt Whitman (Trilling 1956), many autobiographists want to flesh out the declaration that: 'I am the man. I suffered. I was there.'

Autobiographies vary in content but generally cover in detail the questions asked by Margaret Cole in *Growing up into Revolution* (1949): 'When I think about the life of any human being there are always three questions to which I want to know the answers. First, who and of what kind were his family … secondly what was his social class or group … and thirdly what was his physical home?' Individual personality, family and social context, and geographical locale are the stuff of autobiography. Few autobiographers, however, emphasize the latter. Yet, as Barker, reviewing one of Richard Cobb's accounts of 'the geography of my childhood' (Cobb 1975) remarks, 'to write about a place is also to write about the people in it. And about yourself.' Geoautobiography then, while emphasizing the humanistic geographer's concern with place, will not neglect either the individual or his significant others.

Towards the autobiography of ordinary people

Ordinary people shrink from autobiographical confession; they feel they are not 'important enough', and they also feel that such expression would be conceited. Yet, as Tacitus (1948, 51) noted 2000 years ago: 'Famous men from time immemorial had their life stories told … Men even felt that to tell their own life's story showed self-confidence rather than conceit …' The breakthrough toward 'ordinary autobiography', as with the growth of interest in the history of ordinary people in ordinary landscapes, came in the 1960s. In history, the 'structures of everyday life' were emphasized (Braudel 1981) and in geography and planning there developed a growing interest in 'planning and everyday urban life' (Porteous 1977) and 'ordinary landscapes' (Meinig 1979). The development of social history, and especially of labour history (Hunt 1980) after 1960 confronted the underdevelopment of detailed scholarship, especially at the local level, which dealt with the lives of working-class people.

With the growth of the History Workshop movement, explicitly socialist in inspiration, 'people's history' was developed; 'History Workshop mobilised the people for history and history for the people' (Samuel 1981). Ordinary people were encouraged to write of their ordinary lives in ordinary places. Encouragement was clearly needed, for working-class British people had long become self-effacing unpersons. They were unpersons, first, to the rich and famous – Vita Sackville-West found a charwoman cleaning her front steps, and 'stepped over the dreary slut' (Fairlie 1981) – and, second, to themselves. The oral history movement, pioneered by Paul Thompson in Britain, Studs Terkel in the United States, and Barry Broadfoot in Canada, has also had considerable effect in improving the confidence of ordinary people (Banks 1980, Morrison and Zabusky 1980).

Results naturally vary. But one may derive both instruction and delight from accounts such as Winifred Renshaw's *An Ordinary Life: Memories of a Balby Childhood* (1984), an account of early twentieth century working class life in a village near Doncaster, Yorkshire. As noted before in relation to unordinary people, the reconstruction of one's childhood is a major thrust in autobiography (Rooke and Schnell 1982). This may be of great importance if, as Postman (1982) suggests, childhood is about to disappear.

Family history

Recent reviews of contemporary historical writing include a number of new specialties such as labour history, women's history, urban history, and family history (Kammen 1980). Family history, often called 'the history of the family' to distinguish it from amateur work, varies from broad perspectives on the development of the modern family (Shorter 1975, Stone 1977) to the heavily quantitative analyses of parish registers common to both the French and British schools of historical demography. Such work denies Popper's dismissive comment that history is unable to produce laws or generalizations (Popper 1957).

For Cobb (1976, 8), however, history is largely concerned with 'the wealth and variety of human motivations'; this he expresses, *inter alia*, by means of personal family history with a strong sense of place. Local history may also be written from a personal family viewpoint; one of the best examples is Ashby's *Joseph Ashby of Tysoe 1859–1919: a study of English Village Life* (1961). In this book Ashby makes a very personal study of her father based on his own reminiscences, her own recollections, and those of others. There is a strong emphasis on the village setting from the insider's, or inpert, point of view.

Famous families, of course, have always written family histories (Acland 1981), which may attract reviews by equally well-known historians (Briggs 1982). Family sagas are the stuff of romantic novels and television series. As with autobiography, however, the family histories of ordinary people were uncommon until the 1960s. Amateur family history is strongly related to genealogy and surname studies, all of which have become exceedingly popular among the general public on several continents, aided and abetted by Haley's partly fictitious *Roots*. So many family history societies have been formed in Britain that a Federation of Family History Societies has been formed to keep track of them, in much the same way that the *Journal of One-Name Studies* attempts to record the activities of surname societies. Numerous guides for amateur researchers and writers are available (Dixon and Flack 1977).

Genealogy, surname studies and family history, like the local history to which they are closely allied, have also penetrated academe. The University of Leicester has a research fellowship in surname studies, and geographers have also made contributions in this field (Porteous 1982). Despite being looked upon with contempt by many academics, genealogy has been used to make fascinating contributions to migration studies, place loyalty, and agrarian history (Porteous 1982, Richards and Robin 1975). Family history in general has been encouraged by the History Workshop (Newens 1981).

Geographers have not ventured into this area. The only significant contribution is by Cragg (1982) whose beautifully evocative piece, complete with her own poems, she calls 'a family geography'. Cragg (1982, 48) confesses that, like most family historians, her work is motivated by nostalgia for a landscape lost, but for her 'nostalgia has become a key to determining what I valued in that landscape and what responses prompted my emotional and imaginative growth'. As with autobiography, there is also a deeper, life-enhancing, survivalist motivation among family historians, articulated clearly by the psychiatrist Carl Whitaker (Humphreys 1981, 6): 'The family should ... have a three or four generation psychic picture of itself and know family stories back three or four generations, giving a sense of family history as a unit. This type of family picture of the past probably helps a family envision its future.'

Geoautobiography

In a world increasingly dominated by large corporations, huge agencies, and the State, and in which a person is measured by his power, money, or achievement, any consideration of the individual as having intrinsic value is decidedly at a discount. Jacques Ellul (1981) sees 'everywhere today ... the negation of the individual, of the person'. In such a world, the excessive emphasis on social individualism paradoxically results in individuals lacking individuality. The search for individuality may very properly involve the writing of autobiography in an attempt to answer the age-old questions 'who am I?' and 'how did I become who I am?' Both questions involve place.

Autobiography has a very long history; the most important work prior to St Augustine's *Confessions* was by the Eastern Orthodox Churchman Gregory Nazianzen whose 'Song of Himself' upstaged Walt Whitman by a millenium and a half. It began to flower in the eighteenth century and is now a very popular form of expression. During the nineteenth century a few working class autobiographies began to appear; in the present century they are at last becoming common.

A theory of autobiography is being developed (Abbs 1974, Weintraub 1978), and the nature, origins, and content of the form are under investigation. Autobiography is a very necessary affirmation of the self, but Weintraub (p. xiii) warns of the dangers of solipsism and uncreative egocentrism, the Greek notion of 'idiocy'. He notes (p. 12) that there are:

> dangers in fascination with individuality, since it can so easily be bastardized into egocentric addiction to arbitrary whim, into a mindless glorification of 'doing one's own thing' ... Yet we are captivated by an uncanny sense that each one of us constitutes one irreplaceable human form, and we perceive a noble life task in the cultivation of our individuality, our eneffable self.

That cultivation, of course, may result in autobiographical writing.

Geoautobiography is autobiography with a strong sense of place. Many childhood autobiographies have this (Coe 1984), as do the accounts of those confined to small islands (Edwards 1981) or tied to the land (Kitchen 1963).

Strangely, geographers are not geoautobiographers. The notion of 'environmental autobiography' is more common among architects (Cooper Marcus 1979). Geographers may use autobiographies as data sources, as in my study of smellscape (Porteous 1985), or they may seek to discover how certain persons become geographers by means of recollection (Buttimer 1983).

Humanistic geographers have considered autobiography, like so many other themes, in a very abstract way. Tuan (1982) traces the progressive awareness of self from the Middle Ages onward, concluding that 'subjectivism grows with the conviction that reality is what we make of it' and 'subjectivism is the hallmark of the modern age'. Tuan also notes (p. 164) that modern man considers 'that the authentic self is located in one's past – in unselfconscious childhood'. Samuels (1979), in contrast, speaks of the unrelenting modern 'battle against the individual', and the need to bring back 'the I' to counter this 'war against the self'. Jackson and Smith (1984) fault the idealist approach for its excessive concern with individualism and its failure to consider the individual in context.

Duncan (1985) counters this by developing a methodology which gives 'primacy to the individual'. Samuels (1979) speaks of the need to deal with 'authored landscapes' by investigating those individuals who did the authoring. Johnston (1985) points to the 'realist' approach, which involves 'the interpretation of the situation by the individual capitalists, in their local contexts'. But all of this is not autobiography, but 'place biography', which, in Samuels' words, asks about 'the *who* behind the image or facts of landscape'. I have used this biographical approach in both the historical and the planning sections of this book.

Few geographers have considered the self from either a generalist or a biographical point of view. Fewer still have used the autobiographies of others, and hardly any have developed their own autobiographies. One might expect something more of humanistic geographers. Yet one can read through their work and gather their opinions without ever discovering a single fact about their own lives. Buttimer (1980) is one of the few exceptions. Unlike physicists and biologists, anthropologists and historians, geographers preserve an air of serene detachment from their subjects and refuse to expose themselves to their colleagues' scrutiny *as* subjects. This, I think, betrays either lack of self-confidence or excessive modesty, lack of confidence in the discipline, and a voluntary subjection to extreme notions of detachment. I reject this timidity; this book, then, is possibly the first real attempt at geoautobiography made by a geographer.

Methodology

This study of Howdendyke attempts to combine positivist, humanistic, and radical philosophical positions, while also pursuing an interdisciplinary path among the fields of historical geography, local history, community studies, planning critique, and geoautobiography. Given this rich variety of approaches, it is inevitable that a multioperational methodology will be espoused. Methodological discussion will be brief and will focus chiefly on traditionalist vs. humanistic methods in relation to the three different parts of the work.

Part I: historical

Historical methods include the critical examination and interpretation of archival material, the statistical manipulation of data derived principally from manuscript census returns of 1841–81, and fieldwork observation. Together these methods provide a rich source for reconstruction of the historical Howdendyke. The very wide variety of sources used is illustrated in Table 41.

The nature of sources 1–7 is self-explanatory. The material was available in a variety of repositories, all of which are mentioned in the Preface. Items 16–20 will be discussed in relation to Parts II and III. Other items require a word of explanation.

Supplementing fieldwork, and lacking other sources, the chief means of piecing together the history of Howdendyke during the eighteenth and nineteenth centuries has been through the use of title deeds (2, 3, 8, 9). Deeds offer details of owners, prices, mortgages, occupiers, function, building materials, previous and adjacent owners and occupiers etc. for each building or lot. Four sources were used, all of which provide data which overlap considerably: individual property owners; a large collection held by Hargreaves/BritAg; those deeds recorded, chiefly as copyholds, in the Howden

Manor Court rolls; and the very time-consuming East Riding Deeds Registry. Besides deeds, other company records (10) from 1909 were made available by Hargreaves/BritAg Ltd.

The shipping registers (11) of the ports of Hull (1804–1985) and Goole (1828–1985) contain rich information on all ships registered in those ports. *Inter alia*, ship details include tonnage, other physical details, type of vessel, owner, owner's residence and occupation, master, year built, where built, and by whom built. The material available in the archives of the Church Commissioners (12) and of the Bishop of Durham (13) overlaps considerably. It consists largely of account books relating to the upkeep of waterside facilities from the fifteenth to the twentieth centuries. The family archives made available by the directors of George Anderton & Sons Ltd. of Cleckheaton (14) permitted investigation of the background of Howdendyke's most prominent entrepreneur.

Item 15 relates to detailed census manuscript returns, which were available for 1841, 1851, 1861, 1871, and 1881. These permit the identification of individuals and families, and the analysis of age, sex, occupational, industrial, and social class structures, as well as migration paths. The period 1841–81

Table 41. Archival and other historical sources

———————————— discontinuous coverage
————————————— continuous coverage

	1760	1850	1985
1 Maps and plans	———————————————————		
2 Variety of minor sources	———————————————————		
3 Manor rolls (copyholds)	————————————————		
4 Directories		————————————	
5 Local newspapers			————————————
6 Census		—————————————————	
7 Existing building fabric	———————————————————		
8 Title deeds	———————————————————		
9 Deeds registry	———————————————————		
10 Company records			————————————
11 Shipping registers		—————————————————	
12 Church Commissioners	————————————————		
13 Bishop of Durham	————————————————		
14 G. H. Anderton Ltd.		———————	
15 Ms. census returns		—————————	
16 Useful electoral records			————————————
17 Social reconstruction			———————
18 Parish council			————————————
19 Planning offices			————————
20 Oral history			———————————

conveniently includes census years before (1841–51), during (1861) and after (1871–81) the establishment in 1857 of the factory which radically transformed Howdendyke's way of life. Data were coded according to accepted principles of historical demography and were computer-analyzed using SPSS (Armstrong 1966, Lawton 1978). This, with its corresponding 1951–81 'social reconstruction' (17), forms the most quantitative section of the book.

Part II: the living village

The central part of the book ranges widely between the extremes of quantitative and qualitative methods. A statistical view of Howdendyke's demography 1951–81 was provided by the technique of 'social reconstruction' (Edwards 1964, 1971). Briefly, 'social reconstruction' involves the generation of a modern data set which corresponds with that available in the 1841–81 census returns (15). The simple S.R. form asks for details of name, age, sex, birthplace, occupation etc. for each member of every household. Some basic data, mainly adults' names and addresses, were available from electoral registers (16). The bulk of the information, however, was completed, by mail, by two village 'gatekeepers'. It was checked in the field with a long-term resident and found to be almost wholly accurate. A complete demographic series for 1951, 1961, 1971, 1981 emerged (data are unavailable from the census at this level). These data were comparable with 1841–81 returns, and like them, neatly spanned the onset of recent change, which began in the late 1960s.

In sharp contrast, most of Part II is based on very qualitative methods, especially oral history, personal recollection, and participant observation. So much has been written on oral history that no explanation is required (Evans 1970, 1976, Langlois 1976, Roberts 1979, Thompson 1978, Vansina 1964). Oral history interviews were held with all available residents or former residents sixty years of age or older, providing details of the nature of village life during the 1930–1960s period, and reactions to the village's decline after 1968. Anonymity was assured. The chief problem in eliciting historical material was that interviewees regarded me as an 'insider', often mis-estimated my age, and assumed that 'I knew all about it already'. Hence personal recollection has been relied on to supplement oral history data.

Participant observation is a well-known technique in anthropology and sociology (Bastin 1985, Bogdan and Taylor 1975, Lofland and Lofland 1984, Smith and Manning 1982). It is an ethnographic approach little practiced in geography (Smith 1984). Sociological literature emphasizes the problem of 'getting in' to a social setting and recommends entry via 'gatekeepers' (Bell and Newby 1971). This was unnecessary in my case as I am well-known as a former resident of the village, a position which reduced the value of oral history interviews, as noted above, but permitted excellent rapport during depth interviews.

Part III: planning

Information on planning proposals was obtained by detailed search of local parish council minutes (18), the use of planning reports in current local newspapers (5), and extensive examination of planning applications and reports in the files of Boothferry Borough Council Planning Department. These were supplemented by short interviews with representatives of private enterprise, planners, politicians, and public health and housing officials.

The point of view of residents and former residents was obtained through depth interviews (Jones 1985a, Jones 1985b). No rapport problems were experienced here; all respondents but one had known me since childhood. Indeed, so eager were interviewees to air their views of the contemporary state of Howdendyke that little time was left for the elicitation of oral history material.

An experiment in consultation

One of the major faults common to the three groups identified as power elites in the case of Howdendyke's destruction was their lamentable failure to consult with the population impacted upon by industrial growth. In contrast, one of the chief ethical imperatives of qualitative social research in the reflexive mode is the need to give those involved in one's research as 'subjects' or 'respondents' the right to comment upon and criticize one's interpretations.

In order to facilitate this process of researcher-respondent consultation, I followed the following sequence of steps. I wish I could state that this experiment was conceived, as a whole, from the beginnings of the research in 1980. It is more honest to say that the process, though sequentially logical, grew ad hoc during the research process (which began as historical geography, passed through a stage of geoautobiography, and ended chiefly as a planning critique – which, not incidentally, is the sequential format of this book).

The consultation process followed the following stages:

(1) Historical research began in 1980 and my general interest was made known to Howdendykers and other interested parties. In 1981 a former resident of the village (Correspondent A), upset by newspaper reports of the Hargeaves/Boothferry Planning policy, which had recently emerged (Chapter 9), sent me a number of newspaper cuttings and asked if I could do anything to defend the village. Accordingly, I corresponded (unsuccessfully) with Sir Paul Bryan, the Tory MP for the area, and wrote an article (Item No. 1, below) which was printed, retitled, in two consecutive issues of the *Howdenshire Gazette* and other newspapers of the *Goole Times* series.

Item No. 1   An article originally entitled 'Planned to Death: the case of Howdendyke', retitled and printed in the *Howdenshire Gazette* 10, 17 July 1981, in two parts with the following editorial comment:

(a) 'A village doomed to die'

The future of Howdendyke has been said by Kilpin Parish Council to be one of three courses of action: to get rid of industry, to get rid of people, or to develop both to make a viable village. In this article, specially written for this newspaper, Professor J. DOUGLAS PORTEOUS, of the University of Victoria in Canada – a resident of Howdendyke for more than 20 years – examines the reasons for the village's decline and asks what chance the people most involved – those who live in Howdendyke – have had to express their opinions.

(b) 'A plea to the planners'

Last week, in an article specially written for this newspaper, Professor J. DOUGLAS PORTEOUS of the University of Victoria in Canada – a former resident of Howdendyke – examined the reasons for the village's decline. In the concluding part of his article Professor Porteous makes a strong plea for the village's residents to be consulted by the planners before Howdendyke either dies or is dismembered.

The response, unfortunately, was nil. Neither the newspaper editor nor myself received any correspondence pertaining to the article. On visiting Howdendyke, however, a number of residents indicated that they felt encouraged by my interpretation of the issue. I visited Howdendyke in 1980, 1982, 1983, 1984, 1985, and 1986, performing most of the interviews with residents and various representatives of authority groups in the first three years.

(2) During 1985 I was asked by a different correspondent (B), not a resident of Howdendyke but closely involved, to again make some kind of stand on the issue. At that time I was writing chapters 8–11 of this book. The first draft of a shortened version, in the form of a report (Item No. 2, below) was sent, requesting comments, to the following eleven persons: Correspondents A and B; the Howdendyke managers of HS & L and BritAg; the Chief Planning Officer and the director of Health and Housing of Boothferry Borough; Boothferry Borough Councillors Bray and Park; the interview respondents identified in the text as Joe Apthorpe and Mavis Westoby; and Councillor Bob Lewis of Howden Town Council; all of whom were quoted or referred to in the text.

Item No. 2 A draft article, perhaps too provocatively entitled 'How to Murder a Village', later revised and published as Porteous (1988).

Response to this work was mixed. Not one of the politicians replied, nor did the director of Health & Housing. The replies from BritAg, HS & L, and the Chief Planning Officer were very brief acknowledgements of receipt, and none made comments. In contrast, three of the four respondents/correspondents replied immediately, commending the report and offering comments. I am very pleased to quote from 'Mavis Westoby's' response. Mavis commends:

the way you have been able to explain the feelings which we *all* have regarding the unfeeling and uninterested way we have been treated ... 'they' call it progress and creating jobs but it is so wicked to have everything cut and dried for themselves and ... we are not given an opportunity to state our feelings ... I wonder to myself, how, if the positions were reversed, would they feel? ... I agree in every context of the word [that] they have murdered our village ....

It is such comments which make the difficult work of committed qualitative research worthwhile.

(3) Brief letters reiterating my request for commentary on Item 2 or an explication of their position regarding Howdendyke's future were sent in June 1986 to BritAg, HS & L, and Boothferry Planning. No replies were received.

(4) As many of the 11 persons identified in section 2 (above) as were willing and available were interviewed (in most cases, re-interviewed) in July 1986. Interviews were conducted with all the chief participants, namely, directors of BritAg and HS & L, the Chief Planning Officer, the director of Health and Housing, and Boothferry Borough's mayor, Councillor Bob Park. Councillor Bray refused to be interviewed. No significant changes in attitude occurred, but considerable information was forthcoming from companies, politicians, and bureaucrats on their views of the Howdendyke situation. These were incorporated throughout Part III and especially in a revised version of Chapter 10.

Bias

I expect to be accused of bias not only by those who, I suggest, are destroying Howdendyke, but also by the academic fraternity. Humanist geographers should always state their biasses, so I plead guilty.

My biasses tend to be in favour of the planned-for (Porteous 1971) and this position has been strongly reinforced by my experiences in this research. I naturally feel some distress that one of the most central focusses of meaning, for me, on the face of the earth, is being erased (compare Berman 1982). And I feel with some passion that ordinary people deserve, at least, an opportunity to tell their own stories.

Like anyone else, I would dearly like to believe that all is for the best in the best of all possible worlds. But neither private enterprise, nor politicians, nor planners have provided me with sufficient data to support such a belief. By their fruits, then, ye shall know them.

References

Abbs, P. (1974) *Autobiography in education*. London: Heinemann.

Abrams, C. (1971) *The language of cities*. New York: Equinox.

Acland, A. (1981) *A Devon family: the story of the Aclands*. Chichester: Phillimore.

Adams, W. Y. (1980) 'The dead community: perspectives from the past', pp. 23–54 in Gallagher, A. and Padfield, H. (eds.).

Allison, K. J. (1970) *Deserted villages*. London: Macmillan.

Ambrose, P. (1974) *The quiet revolution: social change in a Sussex village 1871–1971*. London: Chatto & Windus/Sussex University Press.

Anonymous (1886) 'Assessment roll of the poll-tax for Howdenshire, 1379' *Yorkshire Archaeological Journal* 9, 129–62.

Armstrong, W. (1966) 'Social structure from the early census returns' in Wrigley E. A. (ed.) *English historical demography*. London: Weidenfeld.

Ash, M. (1976) 'Time for change in rural settlement policy' *Town and Country Planning* 44, 528–31.

Ashby, M. K. (1961) *Joseph Ashby of Tysoe 1859–1919: a study of English village life*. Cambridge: Cambridge University Press.

Baker, A. R. H. (1976) 'The limits of inference in historical geography', pp. 169–82 in Osborne, B. S. (ed.) *The settlement of Canada*. Kingston, Ontario: Queen's University Press.

Baker, A. R. H. (1978) 'Historical geography: understanding and experiencing the past' *Progress in Human Geography* 2, 495–504.

Baker, A. R. H. (1979) 'Historical geography: a new beginning?' *Progress in Human Geography* 3, 560–70.

Balian, C. (1985) 'The Carson Productions interview', pp. 58–61 in Hepworth, J. and McNamee, G. (eds.) *Resist much, obey little: some notes on Edward Abbey*. Salt Lake City: Dream Garden Press.

Banks, A. (ed.) (1980) *First-person America*. New York: Knopf.

Bastin, R. (1985) 'Participant observation in social analysis' pp. 92–100 in Walker, R. (ed.).

Bates, H. E. (1969) *The vanished world*. London: Michael Joseph.

Bell, C. and Newby, H. (1971) *Community Studies: an introduction to the sociology of the local community*. London: Allen and Unwin.

Beresford, M. (1955) 'The lost villages of Yorkshire' *Yorkshire Archaeological Journal* 38, 44–70.

Beresford, M. and Hurst, J. G. (eds.) (1971) *Deserted medieval villages*. London: Lutterworth.

Berger, J. (1972) *Ways of seeing*. London: Penguin.

Berger, J. (1984) *And our faces, my heart, brief as photos*. New York: Pantheon.

Berman, M. (1982) *All that is solid melts into air: the experience of modernity*. New York: Simon and Schuster.

Bertrand, A. L. (1980) 'Ethnic and social class minorities in the dying small community', pp. 187–206 in Gallaher, A. and Padfield, H. (eds.).

Bluestone, B. and Harrison, B. (1980) *Capital and communities: the causes and consequences of private disinvestment*. Washington D.C.: The Progressive Alliance.

Blythe, R. (1970) *Akenfield: portrait of an English village*. New York: Delta.

Bogdan, R. and Taylor, S. J. (1975) *Introduction to qualitative research methods: a phenomenological approach to the social sciences*. New York: Wiley.

Bolan, R. S. (1971) 'The social relations of the planner' *Journal of the American Institute of Planners* 33, 386–96.

Bourne, G. (1912) *Change in the village*. London: Duckworth.

Bowles, R. T. (1981) *Social impact assessment in small communities*. Toronto: Butterworths.

Bowles, R. T. (1982) *Little communities and big industries*. Toronto: Butterworths.

Bradbury, J. H. and St Martin, I. (1983) 'Winding down in a Quebec mining town: a case study of Schefferville' *Canadian Geographer* 27, 128–144.

Bragg, M. (1976) *Speak for England*. New York: Knopf.

Braudel, F. (1981) *The structures of everyday life: the limits of the possible* (Civilization and capitalism, vol. 1). New York: Harper & Row.

Brawer, M. (1978) 'The impact of boundaries on patterns of rural settlement: the case of Samaria, Israel' *Geographical Journal* 2, 539–47.

Briggs, A. (1982) 'A family's fortune' *Manchester Guardian Weekly* 10 January.

Brown, G. M. (1972) *Greenvoe*. London: Hogarth Press.

Bunuel, L. (1983) *My last sigh*. New York: Knopf.

Burgess, A. (1978) *1985*. London: Penguin.

Burns, W. (1963) *New towns for old*. London: Leonard Hill.

Butlin, R. A. (1982) 'Developments in historical geography in Britain in the 1970s', pp. 10–16 in Baker, A. R. H. and Billinge, M. (eds.) *Period and place*. Cambridge: Cambridge University Press.

Buttimer, A. (1971) *Society and milieu in the French geographic tradition*. Chicago: Rand McNally.

Buttimer, A. (1974) *Values in geography*. Washington D. C.: Association of American Geographers.

Buttimer, A. (1980) 'Home, reach, and sense of place' in Buttimer, A. and Seamon, D. (eds.) *The human experience of space and place*. London: Croom Helm.

Buttimer, A. (1983) *Creativity and context*. Lund, Sweden: University of Lund Studies in Geography.

Canter, D. (1977) *The psychology of place*. London: Architectural Press.

Chaplin, R. (1976) 'Ordinary men' *Local Historian* 12, 131–35.

Cherry, G. (ed.) (1976) *Rural planning problems*. London: Leonard Hill.

Clark, A. H. (1977) 'The whole is greater than the sum of the parts: a humanistic element in human geography' in Deskins, D. R., Kish, G., Nystuen, J. D., and Olsson, G. (eds.) *Geographic humanism, analysis and social action*. Ann Arbor: University of Michigan Press.

Clarke, T. (1850) *History of the church, parish, and manor of Howden*. Howden, East Yorkshire: Pratt.

Cloke, P. J. (1979) *Key settlements in rural areas*. London: Methuen.

Cloke, P. J. (1980) 'New emphases for applied rural geography' *Progress in Human Geography* 4, 181–217.

Cloke, P. J. (1983) *An introduction to rural settlement planning*. London: Methuen.

Clout, H. D. (1972) *Rural geography: an introductory survey*. Oxford: Pergamon.

Clout, H. D. (1977) 'Rural settlements' *Progress in Human Geography* 1, 475–80.

Clout, H. D. (1979) 'Rural settlements' *Progress in Human Geography* 3, 417–24.

Clout, H. D. (1980) 'Rural settlements' *Progress in Human Geography* 4, 392–98.

Cobb, R. (1975) *A sense of place*. London: Duckworth.

Cobb, R. (1976) *Tour de France*. London: Duckworth.

Coe, R. N. (1984) *When the grass was taller: autobiography and the experience of childhood*. New Haven: Yale University Press.

Cole, M. (1949) *Growing up into revolution*. London: Longmans.

Comstock, D. E. and Fox, R. (1982) *Participatory research as critical theory: the North Bonneville, USA, experience*. Paper presented at 10th World Congress of Sociology, Mexico City, August.

References

Cooper Marcus, C. (1979) *Environmental autobiography*. Berkeley, Calif.: University of California Institute of Urban and Regional Development Working Paper No. 301.

Cosgrove, D. (1978) 'Place, landscape and the dialectics of cultural geography' *Canadian Geographer* 22, 66–72.

Cragg, B. (1982) 'Wild Daniel's farm: a family geography' *Landscape* 26, 41–48.

Cybriwsky, R. (1978) 'Social aspects of neighborhood changes' *Annals of the Association of American Geographers* 68, 17–33.

Daniels, S. (1985) 'Arguments for a humanistic geography', pp. 143–58 in Johnston, R. J. (ed.).

Darby, H. C. (1962) 'The northern counties', pp. 419–453 in Darby, H. C. and Maxwell, I. S. (eds.) *The Domesday geography of northern England*. Cambridge: Cambridge University Press.

Davies, J. G. (1972) *The evangelistic bureaucrat*. London: Tavistock.

Dennis, R. J. (1980) 'More thoughts on Victorian cities' *Area* 12, 313–17.

Dixon, J. T. and Flack, D. D. (1977) *Preserving your past: a painless guide to writing your autobiography and family history*. Garden City, N.Y.: Doubleday.

Duckham, B. (1967) *The Yorkshire Ouse*. Newton Abbott: David and Charles.

Dugdale, W. (2nd. ed., 1772) *The history of imbanking and drayning*. London: privately published.

Duncan, J. S. (1985) 'Individual action and political power', pp. 174–89 in Johnston, R. J. (ed.).

Edwards, A. (1964) *The settlement factors in the rural problems of north-east England*. Unpublished PhD Thesis, University of Durham.

Edwards, A. (1971) 'The viability of lower size order settlements in rural areas: the case of Northeast England' *Sociologia Ruralis* 11, 247–76.

Edwards, G. B. (1981) *The book of Ebenezer Le Page*. London: Hamish Hamilton.

Eliot Hurst, M. (1985) 'Geography has neither existence nor future', pp. 59–91 in Johnston, R. J. (ed.).

Ellul, J. (1981) 'Socialism yes … an interview' *Manchester Guardian Weekly* 15 November.

Entrikin, J. N. (1976) 'Contemporary humanism in geography' *Annals, Association of American Geographers* 66, 615–32.

Evans, G. E. (1970) *Where beards wag all: the relevance of the oral tradition*. London: Faber.

Evans, G. E. (1976) *From mouths of men*. London: Faber.

Eyles, J. (1985) *Senses of place*. Warrington: Silverbrook Press.

Eyles, J. and Smith, D. M. (1988) *Qualitative methods in human geography*, in press.

Fairlie, H. (1981) 'The rich what gets the pleasure?' *Manchester Guardian Weekly* 15 February.

Farrar, W. (1914) *Early Yorkshire charters*. Edinburgh: Ballantyne, Hamon.

Faull, M. L. (1974) 'Roman and Anglian settlement patterns in Yorkshire' *Northern History* 9, 1–25.

Finberg, H. P. R. (1967) 'The local historian and his theme', pp. 1–24, and 'Local history', pp. 25–44 in Finberg, H. P. R. and Skipp, V. H. T. (eds.) *Local history: objective and pursuit*. Newton Abbott: David and Charles.

Frank, A. G. (1969) *Capitalism and underdevelopment in Latin America*. New York: Monthly Review Press.

Frankenberg, R. (1966) *Communities in Britain*. London: Penguin.

Fried, M. (1963) 'Grieving for a lost home', pp. 151–71 in Duhl, L. J. (ed.) *The urban condition*. New York: Simon & Schuster.

Fried, M. and Gleicher, P. (1961) 'Some sources of residential satisfaction in an urban slum' *Journal of the American Institute of Planners* 33, 164–66.

Gallaher, A. (1980) 'Dependence on external authority and the decline of community', pp. 85–108 in Gallaher, A. and Padfield, H. (eds.).

Gallaher, A. and Padfield, H. (eds.) (1980) *The dying community*. Albuquerque: University of New Mexico Press.

Gans, H. J. (1962) *The urban villagers*. New York: Free Press.

Gaunt, G. D. (1975) 'The artificial nature of the River Don north of Thorne, Yorkshire' *Yorkshire Archaeological Journal* 47, 15–21.

References

Gaunt, G. D. (1980) personal communication.

Geertz, C. (1973) *The interpretation of culture*. New York: Basic Books.

Giddens, A. (1976) *New rules for sociological method*. London: Hutchinson.

Gilg, A. W. (1978) *Countryside planning*. Newton Abbott: David and Charles.

Gilmore, J. S. and Duff, M. K. (1975) *Boom town growth management*. Boulder, Colo.: Westview Press.

Girling, R. (1983) *Ielfstan's place*. London: Hamlyn Paperbacks.

Gold, J. R. and Burgess, J. (eds.) (1980) *Valued environments*. London: Allen and Unwin.

Goodman, R. (1972) *After the planners*. London: Pelican.

Gosling, R. (1980) *Personal copy*. London: Faber.

Graber, L. (1976) *Wilderness as sacred space*. Washington D.C.: Association of American Geographers.

Gregory, D. (1974) 'New towns for old: historical geography at the I.B.G.' *Historical Geography Newsletter* 4, 26–28.

Gregory, D. (1978) *Ideology, science and human geography*. London: Hutchinson.

Gregory, D. (1981) 'Human agency and human geography' *Transactions, Institute of British Geographers* NS 6, 1–18.

Grey, F. (1975) 'Non-explanation in urban geography' *Area* 7, 228–35.

Grusa, J. (1983) *The questionnaire*. New York: Random.

Guelke, L. (1974) 'An idealist alternative in human geography' *Annals of the Association of American Geographers* 64, 193–202.

Guelke, L. (1976) 'The philosophy of idealism' *Annals of the Association of American Geographers* 66, 168–9.

Gussow, A. (1971) *A sense of place*. San Francisco: Friends of the Earth.

Habermas, J. (1974) *Theory and practice*. London: Heinemann.

Hancock, J. C. (1976) 'Planning in rural settlements' *Town and Country Planning* 44, 520–23.

Harris, C. (1978) 'The historical mind and the practice of geography' in Ley, D. and Samuels, M. S. (eds.).

Harris, W. W. (1978) 'War and settlement change: the Golan Heights and the Jordan Rift 1967–77' *Transactions, Institute of British Geographers* NS 3, 309–30.

Harrison, H. (1903) *The history of the Anderton family*. Handwritten ms. in possession of George Anderton and Sons Ltd., Cleckheaton, Yorkshire.

Healey, M. and Ilbery, B. (1986) *The industrialization of the countryside*. Norwich: Geo Books.

Hewitt, K. (1983) 'Place annihilation: area bombing and the fate of urban places' *Annals of the Association of American Geographers* 73, 257–84.

Hirst, M. (1978) 'Recent villagization in Tanzania' *Geography* 63, 122–25.

Hodge, G. and Qadeer, M. A. (1983) *Towns and villages in Canada: the importance of being unimportant*. Toronto: Butterworths.

Horn, P. (1980) *The rural world 1780–1850: social change in the English countryside*. London: Hutchinson.

Hoskins, W. G. (1965) *The Midland peasant: the economic and social history of a Leicestershire village*. London: Macmillan.

Houssel, J. P. (1978) 'Amenagement officiel et devenir du milieu rural en France' *Revue de Geographie de Lyon* 53, 283–93.

Humphreys, T. (1981) 'Marriage, politics must mix' *The Ring* (University of Victoria, B.C.) 16 January.

Hunt, E. D. (1980) *British labour history*. London: Weidenfeld and Nicholson.

Hutchinson, W. (1891) 'Howdenshire: its rise and extension' *Yorkshire Archaeological Journal* 11, 361–71.

Jackson, P. (1980) *Ethnic groups and boundaries*. Oxford: Oxford University School of Geography Research Paper No. 26.

Jackson, P. and Smith, S. J. (1984) *Exploring social geography*. London: Allen and Unwin.

Jacobs, J. (1961) *The death and life of great American cities*. New York: Vintage.

References

Jefferies, R. (1890) *Hodge and his masters*. London: Smith, Elder.

Jensen, G. F. (1972) *Scandinavian settlement names in Yorkshire*. Copenhagen: Akademisk Forlag.

Jewkes, J. (1948) *The new ordeal by planning*. London: Macmillan.

Johnson, P. (1977) *Enemies of society*. London: Weidenfeld and Nicholson.

Johnson, R. J. (ed.) (1985) *The Future of Geography*. London: Methuen.

Jones, S. (1985a) 'Depth interviewing', pp. 45–55 in Walker, R. (ed.).

Jones, S. (1985b) 'The analysis of depth interviews', pp. 56–70 in Walker, R. (ed.).

Joubert, E. (1986) *Poppie Nongena*. New York: Norton.

Kammen, M. (ed.) (1980) *The past before us: contemporary historical writing in the United States*. Ithaca, N.Y.: Cornell University Press.

Kitchen, F. (1963) *Brother to the ox*. London: Dent.

Kubler-Ross, E. (1969) *On death and dying*. New York: Macmillan.

Langlois, W. J. (ed.) (1976) *A guide to aural history research*. Victoria, B. C.: Provincial Archives.

Lawton, R. (ed.) (1978) *The census and social structure*. London: Cass.

Le Patourel, H. E. J. (1973) *The moated sites of Yorkshire*. London: the Society for Medieval Archaeology Monograph 5.

Le Roy Ladurie, E. (1975) *Montaillou*. Paris: Gallimard.

Lee, L. (1977) *I can't stay long*. London: Penguin.

Levin, H. (1980) 'The struggle for community can create community', pp. 257–77 in Gallaher, A. and Padfield, H. (eds.).

Lewis, G. J. (1979) *Rural communities: a social geography*. Newton Abbott: David and Charles.

Lewis, N. (1985) *Jackdaw cake: an autobiography*. London: Hamish Hamilton.

Ley, D. (1977) 'Social geography and the taken-for-granted world' *Transactions, Institute of British Geographers* NS 2, 498–512.

Ley, D. (1980) *Geography without man: a humanistic critique*. Oxford: University of Oxford Department of Geography.

Ley, D. and Samuels, M. S. (eds.) (1978) *Humanistic geography*. Chicago: Maaroufa.

Lipman, A. (1971) 'Professional ideology: "community" and "total"' *Architectural Research and Teaching* 1, 39–49.

Lofland, J. and Lofland, L. H. (1984) *Analyzing social settings: a guide to qualitative observation and analysis*. Belmont, Calif.: Wadsworth.

Loughlin, N. and Miller, K. R. (1979) *A survey of archaeological sites in Humberside*. Hull: Humberside Joint Archaeological Committee.

Lukermann, F. (1964) 'Geography as a formal intellectual discipline and the way in which it contributes to human knowledge' *Canadian Geographer* 8, 167–72.

Marris, P. (1974) *Loss and change*. New York: Pantheon.

Marshall, J. D. (1978) 'Local or regional history' *Local Historian* 13, 3–11.

Martin, E. W. (1955) *The secret people: English village life after 1750*. London: The Country Book Club.

Maxwell, I. S. (1962) 'Yorkshire: the West Riding', pp. 1–84, and 'Yorkshire: East Riding' pp. 164–232 in Darby, H. C. and Maxwell, I. S. (eds.) *The Domesday geography of Northern England*. Cambridge: Cambridge University Press.

McLaughlin, B. P. (1976) 'Rural settlement planning: a new approach' *Town and Country Planning*, 44, 156–60.

McNamee, G. (1985) 'Scarlet "A" on a field of black', pp. 23–32 in Hepworth, J. R. and McNamee, G. (eds.) *Resist much, obey little: some notes on Edward Abbey*. Salt Lake City: Dream Garden Press.

Meinig, D. (ed.) (1979) *The interpretation of ordinary landscapes*. New York: Oxford University Press.

Mills, D. (1972) 'Has historical geography changed?' in Mills, D. (ed.) *Political, Historical and Regional Geography*. Bletchley: Open University Press.

Mills, D. (1980) *Lord and peasant in nineteenth century Britain*. London: Croom Helm.

References

Milne, C. (1976) *The enchanted places*. London: Penguin.

Minar, D. W. and Greer, S. (1969) *The concept of community: readings with interpretations*. Chicago: Aldine.

Mingay, G. E. (ed.) (1977) *Rural life in Victorian England*. London: Heinemann.

Morrison, J. and Zabusky, C. F. (1980) *American mosaic: the immigrant experience in the words of those who lived it*. New York: Dutton.

Moseley, M. J. (ed.) (1978) *Social issues in rural Norfolk*. Norwich: University of East Anglia Centre of East Anglian Studies.

Moseley, M. J. (1979) *Accessibility: the rural challenge*. London: Methuen.

Moseley, M. J. (1980) 'Rural geography: from liberal to radical?' *Progress in Human Geography* 4, 460–63.

Neave, D. (1979) *Howden: a town trail*. Beverley: Council for the Protection of Rural England.

Newby, H. (1978) *Changes and continuity in the rural world*. Chichester: Wiley.

Newby, H. (1980) *Green and pleasant land?: social change in rural England*. London: Penguin.

Newby, H., Bell, C., Rose, D., and Saunders, P. (1978) *Property, paternalism, and power*. London: Hutchinson.

Newens, S. (1981) 'Family history societies' *History Workshop: a journal of socialist historians* 11, 154–59.

Olsson, G. (1969) 'Inference problems in locational analysis' *Northwestern University Studies in Geography* 17, 14–34.

Opie, P. and Opie, I. (1956) *The lore and language of school children*. Oxford: Oxford University Press.

Orwell, G. (1949) *1984*. London: Secker and Warburg.

Padfield, H. (1980) 'The expendable rural community and the denial of powerlessness', pp. 159–86 in Gallaher, A. and Padfield, H. (eds.).

Palmer, J. (1966) 'Landforms, drainage, and settlement in the Vale of York', pp. 91–121 in Eyre, S. R. and Jones, G. R. J. (eds.) *Geography as human ecology*. New York: St. Martin's Press.

Peel, F. (1893) *Spen Valley past and present*. Heckmondwike, Yorks: privately published.

Peet, R. (1985) 'An introduction to Marxist geography' *Journal of Geography* 84, 5–10.

Penn, M. (1980) *Manchester fourteen miles*. London: Caliban Books.

Perin, C. (1974) 'The social order of environmental design', pp. 31–42 in Lang, J., Burnett, C., Moleski, W., and Vachon, D. (eds.) *Designing for human behavior*. Stroudsburg, Pa.: Dowden, Hutchinson, and Ross.

Platzky, L. and Walker, C. (1985) *The Surplus People: forced removals in South Africa*. Johannesburg: Ravan Press.

Popper, K. (1957) *The poverty of historicism*. London: Routledge and Kegan Paul.

Porteous, J. D. (1969) *The company town of Goole*. Hull: University of Hull Press.

Porteous, J. D. (1970) 'The nature of the company town' *Transactions, Institute of British Geographers* 51, 127–42.

Porteous, J. D. (1971) 'Design with people' *Environment and Behavior* 3, 155–78.

Porteous, J. D. (1972) 'Urban transplantation in Chile' *Geographical Review* 62, 455–78.

Porteous, J. D. (1973a) 'The corporation as frontier developer: American enterprise in the Atacama desert', pp. 79–88 in Leigh, R. (ed.) *Malaspina Papers*. Vancouver: B.C. Geographical Series.

Porteous, J. D. (1973b) 'The company state: a Chilean case-study' *Canadian Geographer* 17, 113–26.

Porteous, J. D. (1974) 'Social class in Atacama company towns' *Annals of the Association of American Geographers* 64, 409–17.

Porteous, J. D. (1975) 'Quality of life in British Columbia company towns' *Contact* 7, 26–37.

Porteous, J. D. (1976) 'Home: the territorial core' *Geographical Review* 66, 383–90.

Porteous, J. D. (1977a) *Environment & Behavior: planning and everyday urban life*. Reading, Mass.: Addison-Wesley.

Porteous, J. D. (1977b) *Canal ports: the urban achievement of the Canal Age*. London: Academic Press.

References

Porteous, J. D. (1980) 'Richard Portas' pp. 214–15 in Porteous, B. (ed.) *The Porteous story*. Montreal: Porteous Associates.

Porteous, J. D. (1981) *The modernization of Easter Island*. Victoria B.C.: Western Geographical Series.

Porteous, J. D. (1982) 'Surname geography: a study of the Mell family name c. 1538–1980' *Transactions, Institute of British Geographers* NS 7, 395–418.

Porteous, J. D. (1985a) 'Place loyalty' *Local Historian* 16, 343–45.

Porteous, J. D. (1985b) 'Smellscape' *Progress in Human Geography* 9, 356–78.

Porteous, J. D. (1986) 'Bodyscape: the body-landscape metaphor' *Canadian Geographer* 30, 2–12.

Porteous, J. D. (1987) 'Intimate sensing' *Area* 18, 250–1.

Porteous, J. D. (1988) 'Topocide', in Eyles J. and Smith, D. M. (eds.), in press.

Porteous, J. D. (1987) 'Deathscape' *Canadian Geographer*, 31, 34–43.

Porteous, J. D. (in press) 'Locating a surname' *Local Historian*.

Postman, N. (1982) *The disappearance of childhood*. New York: Delacorte Press.

Prince, H. C. (1978) 'Time and historical geography' pp. 17–37 in Carlstein, T., Parkes, D., and Thrift, N. (eds.) *Making sense of time*. London: Arnold.

Radley, J. and Simms, C. (1970) *Yorkshire flooding*. York: Sessions.

Ravensdale, J. R. (1974) *Liable to floods: village landscape on the edge of the Fens AD 450–1850*. Cambridge: Cambridge University Press.

Read, H. (1946) *Annals of innocence and experience*. London: Faber.

Relph, E. (1976) *Place and placelessness*. London: Pion.

Renshaw, W. M. (1984) *An ordinary life: memories of a Balby childhood*. Doncaster: Doncaster Library.

Richards, A. and Robin, J. (1975) *Some Elmdon families*. Elmdon: privately published.

Roberts, B. K. (1977) *Rural settlement in Britain*. Folkestone: Dawson.

Roberts, D. (1979) *Paternalism in early Victorian England*. New Brunswick, N.J.: Rutgers University Press.

Roberts, E. (1979) 'Oral history and the local historian' *Local Historian* 13, 408–16.

Robin, J. (1980) *Elmdon: continuity and change in a north-west Essex village 1861–1964*. Cambridge: Cambridge University Press.

Rooke, P. T. and Schnell, R. L. (1982) *Studies in childhood history: a Canadian perspective*. Calgary: Detslig.

Rose, D., Saunders, P., Newby, H., and Bell, C. (1979) 'The economic and political basis of rural deprivation: a case-study' in Shaw, J. M. (ed.).

Ross, E. (1970) *Beyond the river and the bay: some observations on the state of the Canadian Northwest in 1811*. Toronto: University of Toronto Press.

Rothman, D. J. (1971) *The discovery of the asylum*. Boston: Little, Brown.

Ryan, E. (1963) 'Personal identity in an urban slum', pp. 135–50 in Duhl, L. J. (ed.) *The urban condition*. New York: Simon & Schuster.

Saltmarshe, P. (n.d) *History of the township and family of Saltmarshe*. York: privately published.

Saltmarshe, P. (1920a) 'The river banks of Howdenshire' *Transactions, East Riding Antiquarian Society* 23, 1–15.

Saltmarshe, P. (1920b) 'Ancient drainage in Howdenshire' *Transactions, East Riding Antiquarian Society* 23, 16–27.

Saltmarshe, P. (1928) 'Ancient land tenures in Howdenshire' *Transactions, East Riding Antiquarian Society* 26, 137–48.

Saltmarshe, P. (1932) 'Local history from the Howdenshire Poll Tax Roll' *Transactions, East Riding Antiquarian Society* 27, 81–97.

Samuel, R. (ed.) (1975) *Village life and labour*. London: Routledge and Kegan Paul.

Samuel, R. (ed.) (1981) *People's history and socialist theory*. London: Routledge and Kegan Paul.

Samuels, M. (1979) 'The biography of landscape', pp. 51–88 in Meinig, D. (ed.).

Sayer, A. (1979) 'Epistemology and conceptions of people and nature in geography' *Geoforum* 10, 19–43.

References

Segal, R. (1973) *Whose Jerusalem?* London: Cape.

Shankland, Cox, and Associates (1966) *Expansion of Ipswich*. London: H.M.S.O.

Shaw, J. M. (ed.) (1979) *Rural deprivation and planning*. Norwich: Geo Books.

Sheppard, J. (1966) *The draining of the marshlands of South Holderness and the Vale of York*. York: East Yorkshire Local History Series, No. 20.

Shorter, E. (1975) *The making of the modern family*. New York: Basic Books.

Sime, J. D. (1986) 'Creating places or designing spaces?' *Journal of Environmental Psychology* 6, 49–63.

Simpson, J. and Bennett, J. (1986) *The disappeared and the mothers of the plaza*. New York: St. Martins Press.

Skipp, V. H. T. (1967) 'The place of teamwork in local history', pp. 87–102, and 'The use of local history in the schools', pp. 103–127 in Finberg, H. P. R. and Skipp, V. H. T. (eds.) *Local history: objective and pursuit*. Newton Abbott: David and Charles.

Smith, A. H. (1937) *The place-names of the East Riding of Yorkshire*. Cambridge: Cambridge University Press (English Place-Name Society Vol. 14).

Smith, R. B. and Manning, P. K. (eds.) (1982) *Qualitative methods*. Cambridge, Mass.: Ballinger.

Smith, S. J. (1984) 'Practicing humanistic geography' *Annals, Association of American Geographers* 74, 353–74.

Spiegel, H. B. C. (1968) *Neighborhood power and control: implications for urban planning*. New York: Columbia University Institute of Urban Environment.

Spufford, M. (1973) 'The total history of village communities' *Local Historian* 10, 398–401.

Steel, D. I. A. (1979) *A Lincolnshire village: the parish of Corby Glen in its historical context*. London: Longman.

Stone, L. (1977) *The family, sex, and marriage in England 1500–1800*. London: Weidenfeld and Nicolson.

Sutton, K. (1977) 'Population resettlement – traumatic upheavals and the Algerian experience' *Journal of Modern African Studies* 15, 279–300.

Sutton, K. (1978) 'A note on the use of preparatory census documentation in the study of rural settlement in Algeria' *Peuples Meditèrranèens* 5, 137–46.

Sutton, K. and Lawless, R. I. (1978) 'Population regrouping in Algeria: traumatic change and the rural settlement pattern' *Transactions of the Institute of British Geographers* NS 3, 331–50.

Tacitus (1948) *On Britain and Germany*. London: Penguin.

Trilling, L. (1956) *A gathering of fugitives*. Boston: Beacon Press.

Thompson, F. (1954) *Lark Rise to Candleford*. London: Oxford University Press.

Thompson, F. M. L. (1963) *English landed society in the nineteenth century*. London: Routledge and Kegan Paul.

Thompson, P. (1978) *The voice of the past*. Oxford: Oxford University Press.

Tuan, Y-F (1974a) *Topophilia*. Englewood Cliffs, N.J.: Prentice-Hall.

Tuan, Y-F (1974b) 'Space and place: a humanistic perspective' *Progress in Geography* 6, 211–52.

Tuan, Y-F (1975) 'Place: an experiential perspective' *Geographical Review* 65, 151–65.

Tuan, Y-F (1976) 'Humanistic geography' *Annals of the Association of American Geographers* 66, 266–76.

Tuan, Y-F (1977) *Space and place: the perspective of experience*. Minneapolis: University of Minnesota Press.

Tuan, Y-F (1978) 'Landscape's affective domain: raw emotion to intellectual delight' *Landscape Architecture* 77, 132–34.

Tuan, Y-F (1982) *Segmented worlds and self: group life and individual consciousness*. Minneapolis: University of Minnesota Press.

Vacca, R. (1971) *The coming dark age*. Garden City, N.Y.: Doubleday.

Vansina, J. (1964) *Oral tradition: a study in historical methodology*. London: Routledge and Kegan Paul.

Vizinczey, S. (1986) 'Engineers of a sham: how literature lies about power' *Harper's Magazine* 272, 69–73.

References

Walker, R. (ed.) (1985) *Applied qualitative research*. London: Gower.

Walmseley, D. J. and Lewis, G. J. (1984) *Human geography: behavioural approaches*. New York: Longman.

Webber, M. M. (1963) 'Order in diversity: community without propinquity' pp. 23–54 in Wingo, L. (ed.) *Cities and Space*. Baltimore: Johns Hopkins Press.

Webber, M. M. (1964) 'The urban place and the non-place urban realm' pp. 79–153 in Webber, M. M. (ed.) *Explorations into urban structure*. Philadelphia: University of Pennsylvania Press.

Weintraub, K. J. (1978) *The value of the individual*. Chicago: University of Chicago Press.

White, G. (1978) *The natural history of Selborne*. London: Dent.

White, P. (1981) *Flaws in the glass: a self-portrait*. London: Cape.

Whitlock, R. (1985) 'Local history as it happens' *Manchester Guardian Weekly* 15 September.

Williams, W. M. (1956) *The sociology of an English village: Gosforth*. London: Routledge and Kegan Paul.

Worpole, K. (1981) 'A ghostly pavement: the political implications of local working-class history', pp. 22–32 in Samuel, R. (ed.) (1981).

Index

138431

LINKED